THE SEQUENCE TO

ALIGNED WEALTH

THE SEQUENCE TO ALIGNED WEALTH

Think Wealth, Speak Money, Be Rich, and Build Wealth from the Inside Out

CHRISTINA OSTROSKI

THE SEQUENCE TO ALIGNED WEALTH
Think Wealth, Speak Money, Be Rich, and Build Wealth from the Inside Out

2025 Christina Ostroski
Copyright © 2025 CHRISTINA OSTROSKI

All rights reserved. No part of this book may be reproduced, scanned, or distributed in any printed or electronic form without permission. No portion of this book may be used in any alternative manner whatsoever without express written consent from the publisher/author.

The author in this book has made every effort to ensure the accuracy of the information they have provided at the time of publication. The author does not assume and hereby disclaims any liability to any party for loss, damage, or disruption caused by errors or omissions, whether such errors or omissions were from accident, negligence, or any other cause. This book is not intended as legal, financial, or therapeutic advice. Always consult a qualified professional. This book is not a replacement for medical advice from a registered physician.

The publisher is not responsible for websites, social media, or other content that is not owned by the publisher.

ISBN Paperback: 978-1-7774334-2-0
ISBN E-book: 978-1-7774334-4-4
ISBN Hardcover: 978-1-7774334-3-7

www.christinaostroski.com

Christina OSTROSKI

Dedication

To Phoenix, Tatum, and Raya,

You've been with me through every messy chapter, every pivot, every book I had to buy, every 'this course is the one,' and chasing the next best thing.

You watched me grow, fall apart, rebuild, cry on the kitchen floor, and laugh through the chaos.

From overdue bills, the wild ideas, and the late nights writing this very book when I should've been sleeping.

Never once did you ask me to be perfect. You just let me be me, and that gave me the guts to become who I am today.

All three of you are the realest part of this journey, the why behind every decision I've made.

This book holds the wealth lessons you pushed me to learn. Pieces of you live on each page.

Thank you for being my greatest teachers, my mirrors, my loudest cheerleaders — even when you didn't know it. You reflected my truth back to me — the good, the bad, the ugly — sugarcoating none of it.

You showed me *me*.

Love,
Mom

CONTENTS

Introduction 1

W - Within 9

   Chapter 1: 13
   CHA-CHING! That's the sound of you not being broke anymore. 13

   Chapter 2:
   Money Is Made Up Anyways 19

   Chapter 3:
   The Five Types Of Wealth 35

   Chapter 4:
   Stop Cheating On Your Money 45

   Chapter 5:
   Money, Often Seen As A Mirage, A Mere Reflection Of Something Deeper 57

   Chapter 6:
   Swipe Right For Wealth 65

   Chapter 7:
   Wealth From Within 73

   Chapter 8:
   The #1 Cause For Success Or Failure In Your Life, Drum Roll Please ...81

E - Elicit 93

   Chapter 9: 97
   Calibrate Your Compass: True North Or Bust 97

   Chapter 10:
   The Gamble: More Than Just Loose Change 111

   Chapter 11:
   The Great Goal Heist - Busting Goals Like You Own The Joint 119

   Chapter 12:
   Conjuring Cash With The Seven-Step Sorcery System 123

Chapter 13:
Blurring The Lines Between Spending Reality Vs Spending Fantasy .139

Chapter 14:
Habits - The Automatic Actions For The Financially Fierce 146

Chapter 15:
Rituals - The Intentional Actions For The Financially Fierce 157

A - Attract **165**

Chapter 16: 169
Imagination: Understand The Power 169

Chapter 17:
Map It. See It. Practice It Daily 182

Chapter 18:
The Treasure Hunt Is Back On 189

Chapter 19:
Divine Desires 198

Chapter 20:
Turning Doubts Into Fuel 208

Chapter 21:
Momentum 215

Chapter 22:
Gratitude Seals The Deal 218

Chapter 23:
The Frequency Of Money 226

Chapter 24:
Social Currency 234

Chapter 25:
Direct Impact 239

L - Language **247**

Chapter 26: 251
Limiting Beliefs: The Lies Keeping You Stuck 251

Chapter 27:
Rewire Your Wallet 258

Chapter 28:
The Brick Road 264

Chapter 29:
Scripted Spells 272

Chapter 30:
Money Incantations 275

Chapter 31:
Life Is A Game And There Are Rules…Or Should I Say 12 Laws To Be Exact 279

T - Thought-Catching **293**

Chapter 32: 297
Rewriting Reality: Dodging Mental Mayhem 297

Chapter 33:
Money Meter 307
Spot Your Setpoint

Chapter 34:
Mindshift Magic 319

Chapter 35:
The Daily Thought Audit; Your 5-Minute Wealth Rewire 327

H - Heal **333**

Chapter 36: 337
Your Relationship With Money - Purging Your Poverty Mindset 337

Chapter 37:
The Five Emotional Debts: Why Your Wallet Bleeds Dry 348

Chapter 38:
Mind Your Money, Honey 356

The Unfolding **365**

Chapter 39: 367
Past, Present, Future 367

Chapter 40:
Letter From Your Future Self 372

Chapter 41:
Final Message 374

Your Exclusive Wealth Bonuses **377**

Bibliography **379**

These pages carry my story, but they're here to unlock yours.

— *Christina Ostroski*

INTRODUCTION

EVER FEEL LIKE you're on a never-ending quest for Willy Wonka's golden ticket to wealth? You've devoured self-help books searching for answers, and you're not alone. The difference? This book cuts through the recycled advice and shows you how to stop chasing wealth and start living like you already have it.

Now, I bet you're wondering what being wealthy really means. Is it just a number in your bank account, or does it really reach beyond money?

You've read the books, meditated, journaled, pulled cards, danced around fires, scrolled social media, and even howled at the moon. And yet, you're still waiting for something to click, but nothing seems to be happening. Why is that? That's exactly what I'm going to show you here.

This book explains why, despite reading a million personal development books, listened to podcasts, watched YouTube, and scrolled Pinterest, your life still hasn't taken off. You're not wildly wealthy...yet.

At its core, *The Sequence to Aligned Wealth* is not just another money book. It's a guide to help you understand and align with wealth on a deeper level, not just in your finances, but in every part of your life.

This is the book that will make the other self-help books you read jealous.

This one will click for you.

Maybe you've heard some of this before. Maybe you've even tried some of the things I'll be sharing. That's fine. Take what resonates and leave the rest behind. This will cut through the noise, so you actually get it. I wrote this to give you what you need to become wealthy.

The real shift starts with how you think about money and your relationship with it.

Once you see it, you can't unsee it. You can change how you think, how you feel, and how you act around money.

Most self-improvement books go into detail about exercises and routines we 'must' adopt if we want to succeed. They suggest that if we don't, we will fail in life. That's bullshit! I don't intend to send you off on a wild goose chase, searching for the next best thing or chasing the pot of gold at the end of the rainbow. There is a method to my madness.

I'm sharing in these pages, tools, techniques, exercises, and knowledge that people pay big bucks for and don't want to share for free.

I challenge you to read the book once, take notes, and then read it again, allowing the ideas to sink in.

All methods or rituals in any book could work, but the most important thing is to find what works for you, and then run with it. Whatever you have tried already isn't working, but it's not too late to fix that. They say someone can see a therapist for 15 years and then, just one day, something clicks. Did it click because of everything done in the 15 years, or was it that something clicked that "one day", that one sentence? Is that when it clicked for them?

One might call it luck or synchronicity, but I believe our paths crossed for a reason. Something told you that this was your next step, and you took massive action by purchasing this book. Fist pumps all around.

I am so proud of you for finding yourself in a book like this. You are 100% ready to bring in the wealth you desire. Alright, enough's enough. You've been misled for far too long and it's time for someone to tell you the truth about wealth.

There's no cure-all or secret formula, so stop believing everything you read on the internet. And if you expect miracles from quick-fix promises, that's like hoping your double-double shows up in under three minutes at the Timmie's or Starbucks drive-thru. Yep, I'm Canadian—had to sneak Tim Hortons in here somewhere.

Wealth and the subconscious fascinate me. Reprogramming my mind around self-concept, money, and abundance has been a wild ride, but if I've learned anything, it's this: attracting wealth

Introduction

can actually be easy. You already have everything you need. My job is to remind you of that.

Most people only see money as currency and miss the deeper meaning. Wealth is more than money—it's an energy exchange that reflects the value you give. Your income mirrors your impact, and there's no cap on either. Wealth grows with aligned action and creativity.

Don't worry if you're feeling uncertain about where you stand—I've got you. That's exactly why you're here. You grabbed this book because you're looking for real solutions. You're tired of the financial struggles and ready for a change. I've been there too, as you'll soon read. The good news? We can turn it around—together.

In today's world, we're overwhelmed with promises of instant wealth, fitness, and youth, all for a few easy payments of $19.99. It's everywhere, isn't it? We've lost touch with the simple, powerful principles that lead to success and real wealth.

I refuse to stand idle while these misleading messages steer people off course. I wrote this book to rise above the noise and guide you back to basics.

In my early days, I had a naïve relationship with money. I didn't think I had issues with it; I thought money had issues with me.

When I got pregnant at 18, my boyfriend and I made the tough call for him to move away for better financial opportunities. During that time, I moved back in with my parents. Money became a constant source of tension, tearing us apart before we even hit our twenties.

Our dream was financial freedom for our family, but cycles of separation and money struggles dragged on for over a decade. We moved back and forth across the country, chasing stability while raising our kids. Constant money arguments convinced me that financial security always came at a cost. Later, I realized you can have it all. Back then, lack clouded my view, and I believed wealth meant hard work and having lots of money.

My money story used to be all about this idea that you could either have love or money, but not both. Earning money always seemed like a constant struggle. There were constant fights about how to spend it, or even worse, when there wasn't enough. This repeated for years, leaving me feeling poor.

It took consistent work to change my mindset about money. I used to believe love meant sacrifice, and money always came with struggle. Over time, I learned that having lots of money doesn't automatically mean you're wealthy.

Of course, I have upgraded my money story, and a lot of what I did is in these pages for your benefit, too.

I wanted to create this book so you wouldn't have to spend six figures like I did trying to figure it all out. (Talk about a pricey learning curve, right?)

I took the leap and wrote this book because I believe in the inherent capacity for wealth within each of us. We are all born worthy of wealth, but it's up to us to claim it. We all deserve abundance, yet sometimes a little push is all it takes to rediscover it.

Not every method is a one-size-fits-all approach. Nope. It's about discovering what resonates with you, what gets your juices flowing, and letting go of the rest. Create your own blend by sampling a bit of this and a splash of that.

The bottom line? It's your journey, so set your own rules.

BEFORE YOU ENTER

Let's explore the captivating world of beliefs for a hot second. These little powerhouses shape everything — from our thoughts and behaviours to our presence in the world. While many of them are ingrained early on, they're not set in stone. We can rewrite those scripts, change the narrative, and create a new story filled with empowerment and abundance. Sure, it takes some effort and a sprinkle of determination, but believe me, it's worth every bit.

As you read these chapters, remember that wealth isn't just about money. By the end of this book, you'll have the tools, insights, and mindset to create aligned wealth on your own terms.

I aim to show you something unbelievable, yet true. I've witnessed this change over and over. Money shouldn't be a source of stress, and it doesn't have to stay a mystery. It's not sinister, and it doesn't control your destiny. You can build a healthy relationship with it, and I can't wait to share my strategies.

In the past, I struggled with feeling inadequate—wondering if I had the smarts, the skills, or the worth to attract wealth or even write this book. Maybe you've felt that too. If you have, I wrote this book for you.

Right now, at this moment, we're the youngest we'll ever be. And the beliefs we hold deep in our subconscious are shaping everything. That's where the real shift happens. Thoughts create beliefs. Beliefs create reality.

True wealth goes far beyond money. It means possessing abundance in mind, body, and soul. It's about building an inner richness that shines outward, creating both magic and money.

Ask yourself right now, are you a match for wealth at this very moment?

If you don't have wealth, then what defines you?

That question lingers because you might struggle financially, feeling the sting of past setbacks that have shaken your self-belief and left you feeling defeated.

Money shouldn't define you or determine your identity. It doesn't change who you are, it just amplifies who you already are. Money is a tool. It's not bigger than you. What you're capable of goes far beyond money, so stop putting it on a pedestal. You have power over it. Wealth is accessible with or without it. Your mind is an extraordinary tool, and it already believes you're wealthy, and if you want it, you're meant for it.

Many times, what you believe about money coexists with your identity, your self-image, and what you're subscribing to daily.

Money is taboo to some, but not to others. Many adults want more financial freedom and wealth. Without the right aligned money mindset, it's harder to build that momentum.

There is nothing outside of you that is required to increase your wealth. Everything needed lies inside you right now; you may have forgotten, but it is there. This book helps you remember that.

You've been searching and scrolling, but nothing happens. Why is that? I'm here to fix that. Get ready to watch those other books gathering dust on your nightstand turn green with envy and break out into a sweat.

I'll unveil the wealth formula that's been shaping our lives, for better or worse. By using this sequence to your advantage, you can transform your reality in ways you've never imagined. You've heard the saying "you can achieve anything you set your mind to," but the key is knowing how.

"The Sequence to Aligned Wealth" serves as your comprehensive guide, teaching you how to master wealth from the inside out. Once you do, there's no limit to what you can accomplish.

THE SEQUENCE

Your subconscious mind handles over 95% of your reality, meaning your mindset handles 95% of your success. Holy shit, Christina, right to the point, huh? I sure am! Without incorporating positive ways of thinking into your life, your reality will not align with what you want. Money mindset is true magic!

If you don't believe you'll be wealthy, abundant, or successful, it won't matter how much you do or how hard you work. Without faith in your future wealth, it stays out of reach.

In the Sequence to Aligned Wealth, each letter breaks down a key part of your journey to financial abundance

SEQUENCE TO ALIGNED WEALTH
ROADMAP

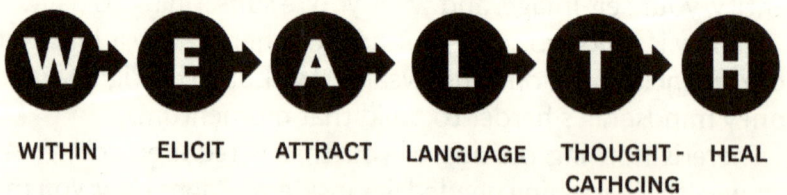

WITHIN   ELICIT   ATTRACT   LANGUAGE   THOUGHT-   HEAL
                                           CATHCING

W — Within: the version of you who's stepped into their wealthiest self. It's the fullest understanding and expression of who you are as a limitless, magical being — your highest self. This version has everything you want. At the core of aligned wealth is your self-concept and inner abundance. This section guides you through self-discovery, unlocking your potential, and building a mindset of prosperity and wealth from within.

E — Elicit: bring out the emotions and energy for your goals, one step at a time, and embody that feeling. Trust your feelings and energy. This is where you meet yourself. Uncover the hidden beliefs and behaviours that can sabotage your financial success. This part will reveal the patterns that block wealth, helping you break free and embrace abundance.

A — Attract: this is where your thoughts, feelings, and actions align with what you want to receive. Where your desires and how feelings line up. This is where alignment pulls wealth your way. In this section, you'll learn how alignment works, how to strengthen it, and how to stay in the energy that draws prosperity to you naturally.

L- Language: - The words we use shape the way we see ourselves and our wealth. In this section, you'll explore the power of "I am" statements and discover how they influence your identity and financial reality. You'll learn to spot limiting phrases, shift them into empowering ones, and create a story that builds confidence, prosperity, and abundance.

T — Thought Catching: the practice of noticing the thoughts that run your life on autopilot. In this section, you'll learn how to recognize the patterns that sabotage your success, interrupt the stories that hold you back, and replace them with thoughts that create confidence, clarity, and wealth.

H — Heal: the process of releasing past hurts, guilt, shame, and money wounds that weigh you down. In this section, you'll learn how to uncover emotional debts, reframe painful money memories, and free yourself from the baggage that keeps you stuck.

Now that you understand the sequence, let's look at how your wealth consciousness actually shapes your reality. Your wealth consciousness connects to your net worth, and your net worth connects to your self-worth. As you raise your value, your income rises with it. Set a higher standard for yourself.

Remember, you already have everything inside you to create anything. Wealth goes beyond money, so keep that in mind as you move forward.

So, what needs to change to shift your bond with money?

Well, writing a new money story for one.

Growing up, authority figures lied to us about money and wealth. Teachers, bosses, police officers, and even our parents and guardians bent the truth. Society misled us completely.

That's why we've developed some ridiculous, self-limiting beliefs about money. Perhaps others taught you that money is evil, and you've lived in lifelong poverty, struggling without knowing why, or you feel guilty about your success despite your wealth.

Grab a notebook, scribble, sketch, or jot down your thoughts right here on these pages. This reading material isn't just some sacred artifact; it's your personal playground for growth and exploration.

Whether you prefer a trusty pen or a good old pencil, the choice is yours. This is your space to be yourself, get messy, and most importantly, get moving towards your dreams.

As you dive into these pages, remember that you hold the power to manifest your desires.

Take a deep breath and get ready to cast a spell to attract more money and wealth into your life faster than you can say 'abracadabra'

W
WITHIN

WEALTH STARTS FROM THE INSIDE OUT

Two roads diverged in a wood, and I—I took the one less traveled by, and that has made all the difference.
-Robert Frost

LET'S GET ONE thing straight right out of the gate—this isn't about chasing paper for the sake of flashing it. Wealth, in the way we're about to talk about it, is a whole damn vibe. It's the energy you carry. It's the frequency you tune into when you walk into a room and your presence alone feels like a paycheck.

This section? It's about claiming all forms of wealth. Yes, the money, but also the wealth of time, freedom, health, love, peace, creative flow, deep breaths, and the guts to ask for what you want.

I'm not here to give you some "boss babe" hustle culture lecture. I'm here to remind you of your magic. The kind that doesn't just attract abundance, it creates it. On purpose. With clarity and fierce focus.

Before we dive into the rituals, journal prompts, mindset shifts, and steps that get you paid and powerful, know this:

You don't chase wealth; you calibrate to it.
You don't hustle for worth; you embody it.
You don't seek approval; you own it.

Let's step into your wealth era, your way, with sass, substance, and soul.

Now, the beginning of it all: the Fusion Reaction. The Fusion

Reaction is your daily energy shift — the way each choice, thought, or habit either fuels your growth or drains your power. Think of it as the chain reaction inside your mind that builds momentum toward wealth or keeps you stuck.

Every tiny decision nudges your life's direction. The fusion reaction isn't just about recognizing these choices; it's about making ones that amplify your life.

Think of your brain as a magical pot that absorbs whatever you throw in. Dump in negativity: doom scrolling news, toxic talk shows, pessimistic chit-chat, rage-fueled reality TV, Debbie Downer gossip — and you're sipping on a self-sabotage smoothie.

And guess what brews? A concoction of muck, clouding everything you do. It's a simple formula: junk in, junk out.

Every tiny decision is a cosmic nudge shaping your life's path. This fusion reaction that we call personal growth isn't just noticing choices; it's owning them, consciously. What if you threw in power instead? What if you stirred in intentions, aligned actions, and vibes that support your goals? That's the real alchemy. That's how transformation starts. That's the Fusion Reaction at play.

CHAPTER 1
CHA-CHING! That's the sound of you not being broke anymore.

WINNING MY HOMETOWN'S tiara felt like a dream, but life had bigger lessons in store. Being a sixteen-year-old pageant queen, it was a quick flash of glamor in an otherwise normal life — thrilling but gone in a blink. That shiny crown didn't shield me from real life's money messes. It marked the start of a wild ride of financial ups and downs that taught me more about wealth than any crown ever could.

My secondary school years were a mix of boring moments, teenage drama, and weekend bush parties. I lived under my parents' roof with my two older brothers, which meant constant spies reporting where I was, what I was doing, and who I was with. Privacy? Non-existent. In my hometown, I was just Travis and Scott's little sister, so looking at a boy was off-limits. My high school dating life? Didn't exist.

Then came the out-of-towner — a heartthrob who blew into my life with equal parts excitement and chaos. Our love story was classic. Boy meets girl. Boy leaves town. Girl throws a hissy fit and longs for him. It proves distance makes the heart grow fonder, or at least makes for juicy locked-up diary entries.

Our visits were like those rare paydays that come once in a blue moon, worth the wait and juicier than the gossip in the girls' locker room. Honestly, it wasn't just a high school romance; it was an epic saga of childish love. Proving that even on a shoestring budget at home, you can still live out a grand, passionate affair.

As I reminisce about my time in high school, I can't help but think about him. While I was still navigating the halls of our high school, he had already tossed his cap in the air and was out in the real world making moves. It felt like we were living in parallel universes. I was stuck in the familiar routine of classes and homework. He was in another town, clocking in at work, making bank, carving his path into adulthood.

It was surreal. We were once so intertwined, but now on separate paths, each of us heading into uncharted territory.

When I was just a little teeny bopper, I was clueless about bills or managing finances. My very first gig was at the local Dairy Queen, beside my high school. I worked Friday and Saturday nights back when a banana split cost just $1.99 plus tax, bringing it to a grand total of $2.13. Believe me, I was unaware of the magic happening in the background. With my trusty cash register by my side, I punched in the numbers without a notion of the realm of taxes, calculations, money, and wealth. Ah, ignorance truly was bliss!

Soon, graduation caps swirled in the air and adulthood beckoned. Like most high school grads, I made a life-altering decision.

At 18, I said goodbye to my childhood home and tossed college aside. I was prepared to move in with the out-of-towner heartthrob, in a city that felt as exhilarating as making a first credit card purchase without worrying about reaching the limit. It was a leap into the unknown, leaving my familiar hometown, friends, and family for a shared future with the boy I met in high school.

Navigating the Financial Maze

All moved in, ready to start our happily ever after. Bam. Reality smacked me in the face like a bag of hammers. I had to start adulting fast. Bills? Clueless. My first big-city job was in a crowded call center during the day. At night, I moonlighted as a waitress in a dive bar so shady even the cockroaches needed ID.

I wasn't exactly the legal working age for a bar, but desperate times called for desperate measures. When life gives you lemons, sometimes you just make a cocktail, grab the salt, and take the shot!

But hey, you do what you gotta do, right?

Money felt like this slippery object I was always trying to catch. I had no clue about its significance or how to deal with it. It's like every dollar I made was this big question mark, and I just spent it without really thinking. I was in the dark about adult "stuff". Just stumbling through life, trying to figure it all out. I wish they had taught this when I went to high school.

Let me paint you a picture of A Day in the Life of a graduated teen and those frosty January mornings in Northern Ontario. My boyfriend and I shared one vehicle. It was a 1988 Neon Lime Green Chevy half-ton. He started work earlier than I, so he won the who gets to drive to work toss-up daily.

Picture me, bundled up like an overstuffed burrito, braving the biting cold and trudging through snow for an hour just to get to work. The air was so bitterly cold it felt as if I was getting acupuncture from Mother Nature herself, all for the grand prize of earning minimum wage.

Downtown, where I worked, was a whirlwind of honking cars and people rushing everywhere. In all that chaos, it's easy to chase wealth and success without seeing the truth. Plenty of people who seemed to have it all. Fancy suits, flashy cars, were barely holding it together behind closed doors. They were drowning in debt and losing sleep over money. Wild, right? You never really know what someone's fighting behind the scenes.

As soon as I moved in with him, the excitement bubbled up. I was playing house for real! Suddenly, I was in the adult world with thrilling tasks like paying bills, buying groceries, and fueling our clunker of a truck. We even paid $350 a month to rent our little two-bedroom home. Fast forward to when I'm writing this book, and that same rent has ballooned to a jaw-dropping $4,350 a month. Yep, you read that right. Talk about inflation. But like everything else in life, things change.

I'd trek an hour downtown through knee-deep snow just to sell credit cards. People yelled at me for interrupting Sunday football or Friends on Thursdays. No pause button back then! All for $4.75 an hour. Worth it? Nope. Money was this elusive thing I was chasing, without understanding its value or how to handle it.

There I was, pounding the pavement downtown, feeling like I was in the middle of some crazy hustle. Between working at the call center and picking up shifts at the dive bar, I was pulling double duty just to make ends meet. Money was always on my mind. Thinking about money was my new hobby I didn't ask for, always playing 'Where's Waldo?' with the next paycheck. Forever playing hide and seek, but it seemed like Waldo was winning.

I was unaware that, while I was busting my butt trying to make a living, fate had some tricks up its sleeve. It would shake things up in ways I didn't see coming. Life threw me a curveball so sneaky that even as a teenager, it caught me off guard.

Just dipping my toes into adulthood, and bam! It appeared the universe decided I needed a fast-track course in 'Surprise 101'.

Unexpected Turns and New Beginnings

As I held the pregnancy test in my trembling hands, it was like grasping onto the very essence of my future. Waiting to see either one line or two. The fear of becoming a statistic loomed over me. I'm going to be a pregnant, broke-ass teenager.

Christina: "Daryll, you better sit down for this one."

Daryll: "Why? What's up? Did the cat do something again?"

Christina: "No, it's not the cat. Look at this." (Shows him the test) "I'm pregnant. Seriously, I was just getting good at keeping our plants alive!"

Daryll: "Pregnant? I can barely cook mac and cheese without burning it!"

Christina: "What are we going to do? This is major."

Daryll: "Okay, okay... You kept that houseplant alive for a month, right? We can totally do this."

Christina: "A baby is not a houseplant, Daryll!"

Daryll: "Right, right. But we'll figure it out. People do this all the time."

Christina: "This is crazy. I was just worried about Y2K, and now we're having a baby?"

Daryll: "I know, right? Thought I'd be changing tires for a while, not diapers."

And there I was, just weeks later, back at my parents' place while he moved across the country alone to a different province. Fear and uncertainty about the future consumed me.

Money wasn't just for bills anymore; it was for providing for a future that was about to get a lot more complicated.

Daily snail mail, a long-distance relationship, impending parenthood, and financial insecurity replaced the comfort of living together quickly.

We needed cash to raise a kid. Babies don't take IOUs. As broke teens, we knew financial stability was non-negotiable. Daryll went to where the money was. Unfortunately, that meant 2,200 kilometers (about 1,367 miles) away. A 36-hour drive, solo. Quite the trek for a paycheck, but back then, you did what you had to do.

Peeing on a stick was my first real lesson in wealth and money management. Weird, right? The challenges I encountered at the beginning of adulthood showed me that money has a deeper significance than simply being a tool to an end.

It's a tool to build a stable future. It was a rocky start, but it laid the foundation for the money wisdom I share in these pages, turning fears into lessons and struggles into stepping stones toward financial empowerment.

THE NOT SO FAIRY TALE BEGINNING

At 16, I was stepping out of the world of glamor and grace as a contestant. It was 1999, a year etched in my memory, not just for the end of my reign and the tiara I won, but also for the day I met my future husband, April 1st. Our journey began with teenage love, navigating life's challenges and victories, with money shaping the twists and turns along the way.

Reflecting on those transformative years, I don't just see a journey from a pageant queen at 16 to a pregnant teen at 18. It was a saga of love, growth, and the enduring wealth that became the cornerstone of our family. Wealth isn't just about money.

17

Everyone defines it differently. For some, wealth means many things.

As a pregnant teenager, I felt like I had a giant neon sign above my head flashing "Look at me!" It was like being in a fishbowl, with everyone's eyes glued to my belly as if it were a reality TV show. And let me tell you, the commentary was brutal. People gawked, whispered, and shot me those judgmental side-eye glances that could cut through steel.

I was sure wealth was all about the money—and that's why people stared.

How old is she?
Is she still in school?
Does she have a job?
Where is the baby's father?
How will she manage financially?
How is she going to feed the baby, diaper the baby?
How will she afford to live?
She can't afford to have a baby!

Money, money, money–that's what it was all about, right? Little did I know, there's a lot more to it than cash in the bank. But hey, hindsight's 20/20.

Amid the drama, I couldn't help but find some humor in the madness. I mean, come on, the absurdity of it all was laughable. As a pregnant teenager, I received more attention than a Kardashian, yet all I desired was to fade into the background. But life doesn't always give you what you want, does it?

Despite the chaos and the haters, I held onto the belief that I was worth more than their stares and whispers. I didn't have a fat bank account. But I had something better: guts, determination, and a damn good sense of humor. Those things are priceless.

CHAPTER 2
Money Is Made Up Anyways

IN THE FORM of wealth for the moment, let's address the elephant in the room and talk about money.

Money is simply a tool we use. While it can seem like life is smoother with it, we can still function without it. Our interactions with money involve debts, spending, gifting, and receiving. But why do we desire money so much, and what causes our fears surrounding it?

Wealth, on the other hand, is an abundance of all things (mind, body, and soul). There are so many ways to touch wealth. You can be rich without being wealthy, and wealthy without being rich. Wealth is accessible with or without money. You can still feel lack, even when you have money.

We're going to learn the ability to hold the fact that being a wealthy person starts from the inside out.

Are you a match for wealth right now?

You're probably pondering that because you might not have the amount of money you want in your life. Money should not define your identity. Money is not bigger than you or me. What you're capable of is beyond money. You have absolute power over it.

You have the power. Money is just the tool — stop putting it on a pedestal. Our mind is an extraordinary tool. Believe that you are a wealthy being.

If you want it, you're meant for it.

BEHIND THE CASH CURTAIN

During the transition from teenager to adult, my relationship with money was a constant battle. I was scraping by, with every penny pinched and every decision weighed against my nonexistent savings.

It was more than just being broke; it was about feeling powerless and out of control, a far cry from the pageant stage where I once felt on top of the world. This struggle wasn't just about making ends meet; it was a profound lesson in the value of money and the importance of financial planning.

Dealing with money issues early on wasn't just my private battle—it's something a lot of us go through. It's like we're all tossed into the deep end of handling our finances with no help, figuring it out as we go.

It often feels like the missteps outnumber the wins. One step forward, two steps back. It's a path filled with worries and unknowns, where every bit of financial know-how we gain feels like a major win.

But as tough as it is, this struggle is something we all share. It helps us get a grip on what money really means in our lives.

Cultivate your wealth and the value you offer.

Think about how you perceive your own worth. What's your belief about your value? Are you valuing yourself based on a price tag or defining your worth by your income? It's time to dive deeper into how you see yourself and your financial potential. I once saw myself as just a pregnant teen with no money, accepting struggle as my reality. But I was so much more than that.

Do you know how wild our perceptions can be for money? Imagine you're holding up two Canadian bills—one's a $20, all green and crisp, and the other's a $50, rocking bold red. Both are just paper, right? But in Canada, our money looks like it partied with a rainbow—we've got blues, purples, greens, the works! People even joke, calling it "funny money" because it's so colorful.

Now, if you pause and consider holding a green one in one hand and a red one in the other, eyes shut, could you tell them apart? The red one isn't made of luxurious paper, nor does it feel heavier, right? Nor does the green or red dye cost more to produce. So, what's the actual difference? Why is the $50 valued more than the $20? Is it simply because it's red and flaunts a '50', while the green one modestly bears a '20'?

They're likely made from the same tree. It's not about the paper's sheen, the weight, or the ink. It's all about the perceived value, the numbers printed on them that dictate their value.

Imagine if suddenly, everyone's like, "Nah, red's not our jam. It's too flashy, or it gives off villain vibes." If we all started snubbing the red bill, its value could plummet, not because of its color or what it's made of, but because of our collective change of heart.

Our perception, that sneaky little thing, shapes what we believe and how we act, turning something as arbitrary as color into an entire system of value. Isn't that something? It's all in the collective handshake we've given to the idea that red equals more moolah in our world.

Isn't it wild to think about money? Like, seriously, someone up there decided, "Let's make the red bill worth more than the green one," and we all just nodded and went along with it. It's all in our heads, right?

These bills may come from the same tree, yet we've all bought into this idea that one is worth more than the other. That's the power of collective belief shaping our money system.

It's quite amusing how the color of paper can wield so much influence over our lives, isn't it?

Just like we agreed on the value of those colorful bills, we can shift our own money story. Mine changed big time, and yours can too. It's all about questioning those old tales we tell ourselves about cash and realizing that it's just paper. We give it power, we can change the story, and suddenly, what once seemed set in stone is totally up for grabs. Just like that, your view on money can take a whole new turn, showing that wealth is not just about what's in your wallet, but also what's in your mind.

We've all heard these tales, the classic, overused saying: "Money doesn't grow on trees." Heard that one before? It probably came from someone you looked up to, maybe a parent or grandparent, someone who had your ear and trust. If they drilled into you that cash was tough to earn and even tougher to keep, then that's the mindset you've been carrying around.

But it's time to question that, to ask yourself if those old sayings really hold up or if they're just hand-me-down beliefs that don't fit the life you want to live.

Understand that money is an idea. Some people high up decided that the red one is worth more than the green one, that this is worth more than that. And because we collectively took that in and said, "Okay, sounds good to us," we didn't fight against it. That's why our monetary system works the way it does. But if you actually think about it, one piece of paper isn't worth more than the other piece of paper. It probably comes from the same tree, right?

Your perspective on wealth, money, and all the stuff in the middle is often a narrative you've either inherited or continuously reinforced within yourself. Your money story can shift, just like mine did, just like countless others have. And it absolutely will if you're open to it.

Society has conditioned us over countless years to believe that a $20 bill is worth $20 and a $50 bill is worth $50.

That is the value.

That is our truth.

That is what we're taught.

That's what we're told.

But that's not the only thing we learn about money; over time, we are taught different things about money. Some are facts, some are fiction, some are totally true, and some are totally false. But what if we look beyond the physical attributes of money? What if we see it as something more than just paper and coins?

Money is literally just energy.

When we talk about 'money is energy,' it's not just a random idea—it's actually rooted in science. Everything in the universe, including money, is made up of tiny particles vibrating with energy. This is basic physics stuff. When we view money through this lens, it starts to make sense. It's not just paper or numbers—it's part of this energetic flow that connects everything in the universe. And just like how energy can be harnessed to create change, our thoughts and actions around money can shape our financial reality. So, when we talk about money as energy, we're tapping into some pretty fundamental laws of the universe (which we dive deeper into in the 'Life Is a Game and There Are Rules' chapter).

Its value doesn't come from the physical bills or coins themselves, but from our collective belief in their worth. We've agreed as a society that these pieces of paper and coins represent purchasing power. So, when people say 'money is just an idea,' they mean its value is based on our shared agreement rather than any inherent quality. It's a concept we've all bought into.

Money's just an idea, and whatever idea you're putting on that—specifically, your financial wealth, your capacity meter for money—shapes how you perceive its value and your relationship with it.

Growing up, it's like we're spoon-fed this idea that money is scarce. We're told you gotta put in the hard work, grind away those 40-hour work weeks, just to make ends meet. And if you're lucky, maybe you'll hit the jackpot or inherit a fortune.

Looking back, it's like, whoa, were we ever fed some stories! Remember, being told 'money doesn't grow on trees' or that you've gotta work yourself to the bone to see any green? It's no wonder we've got all these ingrained money beliefs rattling around in our heads. These stories reflect the broader societal narrative we've discussed, shaping how we view and interact with money.

We have to subscribe to who we want to be as this wealthy, abundant person. It's not this elusive thing we have to chase after; it's something we can consciously shape and subscribe to.

We've got the power to rewrite those old money scripts and step into our role as wealthy, abundant individuals. Throughout this book, we're going to dig deep into those ingrained money stories, unpack those limiting beliefs, and start reshaping your money mindset. Don't you agree that it's time to ditch those old narratives and start living your life with financial freedom and abundance?

A lot of times, our beliefs about money coexist with our identity and what we choose to subscribe to. Growing up, my mom was a bus driver and my dad a heavy equipment operator. So we weren't rich by any means, but we weren't poor either. As a young mother, I was nowhere near wealthy. I felt like I was just maintaining the status quo, more like fitting into a statistic than breaking free from it.

At the beginning of my journey, I had a ton of money mindset issues, which drastically held me back without even realizing it. Over time, that changed as I learned about the value of money and, more importantly, how to value myself. Understanding my worth and the true value of wealth led me to realize the profound impact I could have on sharing my knowledge and experiences.

However, there's an important point I want to emphasize: failing to share our talents, insights, and education is a disservice, not just to ourselves but also to those we could inspire and support. It's about breaking through the mental barriers that restrain us and recognizing the incredible value we bring to the table. It's a disservice because when we hesitate to step up and help someone, we miss out on golden opportunities.

By letting doubts and fears dominate, we hold ourselves back. It's high time we overcome these limitations and fully embrace our potential to contribute and make a difference.

You have that fear, that money fear, the value fear, the 'I'll never attract wealth' fear, of not valuing yourself enough—it's holding you back.

I want to help change that. Let's shake up your money story together.

Now, think about what you're making money mean in your life. Ask yourself, when you create wealth and abundance, how will it positively impact you and everyone around you, including those you may not even know? Reflecting on this can reveal the powerful positive effects of wealth, not just for you, but for others as well.

People in the world don't need a ton of money. Really, they don't. Money's awesome, sure. You can buy this, do that, learn this, or give to charity. But pause for a moment. If you see yourself as a six-figure earner, and you realize you don't actually need all that cash, who are you actually helping? When you have that money, who's benefiting directly from it? Whether it's supporting your parents, investing in your kids' future, assisting your family, or giving back to your neighbors or charities. Or perhaps it's about elevating your own knowledge, pursuing further education so you can empower and uplift others. And then, doing that, you create this ripple effect.

So the power of one, you can help one person, and then when you have this money, you can help more people, and those people help more people, and those people help more people, and vice versa, the next thing you know, it's a ripple. Understanding this broader impact is an essential part of money's true value. It's not just about the numerical figure attached to one's income, but about how effectively that money is used to foster growth, support, and positive change within the community and beyond.

By changing how you view and use money to support others, you've upleveled your identity. This isn't just about financial transactions; it's about the value you're creating and sharing. When you help one person, you set off a chain reaction. Your action might not just touch their life but could indirectly benefit hundreds or thousands more.

This ripple effect of your generosity extends far beyond what you might see or know, illustrating the profound impact you can have through your financial choices.

Right now, you might not even be aware of the impact you could have because money blocks are holding you back. These blocks can prevent you from helping someone who truly needs your support. And let's be clear, it's not all about money—absolutely not. While we're exploring the importance of money, it's crucial to remember that the real essence lies beyond just the cash. Money is a conduit for value exchange, enabling us to make a significant difference in the lives of many, often beyond our immediate circle. Therefore, while money is a vital tool, it's ultimately the value and impact we create that matter most. And interestingly, creating this impact isn't solely dependent on having money.

As we evolve into our most impactful selves, creating immense value, it's crucial to remember that the universe aligns with our clear, focused intentions, magnifying our efforts and turning our financial aspirations into reality.

In the end, we're trying to evolve into our most impactful selves, where we can provide the most value. In creating this transformation, it is not just about gaining financial gain; it is about uplifting and assisting those in need, creating an everlasting positive ripple effect.

Money is taboo for some people, but not for others. The goal of many adults is to achieve greater financial freedom and build wealth. Without the right money mindset from the start, gaining financial freedom can be difficult. If you're just starting out and feel uncertain about finances, wealth, or money, I want you to know that the universe heard you the first time. But, if you're sitting on your couch and you are just wanting more money, just chilling, meditating, praying, burning candles, or doing what you're doing, having those thoughts of wanting more money but not being specific… If you turn around and you find a penny on the floor, a dime, a nickel in your couch, the universe heard you the first time, she's going to say, holy shit, look what I just did. I gave you more money, exactly what you asked for. Cha-ching! That's the sound of you not being broke anymore. You're welcome! I just gave you more money because you asked for more money. More money is more money.

In reality, you have to be specific.

To call in wealth, finances, and money itself, you must be clear about what you are aiming for. So, if you're looking for an extra hundred dollars, ask for an extra hundred dollars. Specifically.

You're going to be walking down the street one day and find a dime on the ground. And the universe, the creator, spirit, whatever you want to call it, but for this book, I'm just going to use "universe." The universe will be like, "Oh snap, I gave you more money. My job is done. You asked for more money, and I gave you more money."

Being specific sets you on the right path and helps create the financial abundance you're seeking. This principle can also affect relationships, health, and fitness journeys. For instance, if someone says, 'I just want to lose weight,' they might only lose a pound because that's as specific as they got.

The way you phrase your goals is very important because your subconscious mind drives nearly all your daily habits and behaviors, influencing 99.6% of them, with your conscious mind making up just the remaining 0.4%

This means that how you talk to yourself matters immensely. You're the first to feel, say, and hear your own words. When you say, 'I want to lose weight,' I want to lose this, I want to lose that, and you're not specific, your brain only hears 'lose weight.'

What happens when you lose something? You kinda want it back, right? If you lose something, instinctively, you want to find it again. That's why being precise with your intentions is crucial. Be mindful of what you say to yourself. Reflect on your words. If you keep saying 'I'm broke,' you'll likely notice more bills piling up, as you're sending these negative signals to your brain. It's crucial to understand that your words shape your perception and can attract more of what you focus on.

Every time you catch yourself saying things like 'I'm broke,' 'I'm too tired,' 'I can't do this,' or 'I can't do that,' it's a signal to be mindful of your words. Instead of dwelling on what you can't do, reframe your thoughts to ask, 'What can I do instead?' This shift is powerful because your identity shapes your reality; by changing your words, you change how you see and interact with the world around you.

The way you speak to yourself and see yourself shapes your reality. Start watching what you say to yourself. Reframe what you're going to say to yourself. If you catch yourself saying, I am not enough, or I can't, or I shouldn't, or, oh my gawd, like that's not me. I can't. Change it.

What you believe your value to be fuels your momentum. Your subconscious mind picks up on these beliefs. It's like a tape playing in the background, repeating what you tell yourself because your conscious mind is just the tiny 0.004% in control. So, if you're constantly thinking, 'I am broke,' it's time to switch tracks. Reframe those thoughts. Instead of focusing on what you can't do or have, flip the script.

For example, change 'I can't be happy' to 'I am discovering new joys every day.' By reshaping your words, you'll notice a shift in your mindset. And trust me, you're going to be amazed. You'll catch yourself saying things that reflect your true value and potential, making you think, 'Wow, I should have been affirming this to myself years ago.'

The 'W' in the Sequence to Aligned Wealth stands for Within, understanding the true nature of money, how it's created and received, and grasping the mindset of a wealthy person—how they look, think, and act. My goal is to transform your perception of money completely.

The thoughts you entertain, whether negative or positive, shape your self-talk. By consistently thinking positively about money and fostering empowering beliefs, you're more likely to attract and create a reality that aligns with your subconscious desires.

If you don't fill your mind with these positive thoughts, however, your reality won't match your true aspirations. Believe me, mastering your money mindset is like unlocking real magic.

If you don't believe you are going to be successful, then it doesn't matter what you do physically, how much action, how much work you put into it; if you don't believe you are going to be wealthy, then it's that much harder to create wealth.

Money is just an idea - Money is just energy - Everything is energy.

Imagine having a super-powerful microscope, zooming in on an atom. You'd see it's actually 99.9999% empty space! So, the chair you're sitting on, or any object you've used today, is mostly just a dance of electrons and protons, all buzzing with energy. Yes, I'm diving into nerd territory for a moment, but stick with me—it's fascinating stuff!

Money Is Made Up Anyways

Everything in our reality is essentially energy. When you look at any object through a powerful microscope, you're greeted with a dance of vibrating atoms. Dive deeper into an atom, and you'll discover it's composed of 99.99999% space. Now, here's a mind-blowing fact: if you could remove all the empty space from the atoms of every human being on Earth, keeping only the solid parts, everything could be squished into a sugar cube. Yes, a tiny sugar cube!

Just think about it—every person on this planet, compacted down, would fit into such a small space when you remove all the space and keep only the subatomic particles. Isn't that wild? My hometown's symbol is actually an atom, represented by a huge metal atom sculpture right smack dab in the center of town. It's a powerful reminder that even the tiniest things hold incredible energy and potential—just like the mindset shifts that create real wealth.

This means that nearly everything is empty space, and this empty space is filled with energy. Since everything on this planet, including money, is essentially energy, you have control over it. Think of yourself as the universe in human form, wearing this 'meat suit,' commanding the energy around you. You are the boss of money, guiding its flow and direction in your life.

When diving into the finance world, you'll find fascinating statistics, like most of the money we talk about is, literally, made up. In our society, most of what we consider money is just numbers on a computer screen—like something out of 'The Matrix.' In fact, only 8% of all the world's money exists in physical form, as actual cash. That means if you consider all the money in everyone's bank accounts globally, just 8% of it is in physical cash; the remaining 92% is purely electronic, mere numbers on screens.

Think about your own money for a moment. Like me, you probably handle most of your transactions electronically.

I mainly use cash for small, everyday purchases, like a quick coffee at the drive-thru. But the bulk of my finances? All electronic. And at its core, what is electronics but another form of energy?

Why do we hold on to our beliefs about money as if they're the absolute truth, unchangeable and set in stone? These are just

29

our 'money stories'—the mix of notions and teachings about finances we've picked up from others. It's not like we emerged from the womb with firm beliefs about money. I mean, the idea of a newborn with a wealth mindset is amusing, but pretty unlikely. Our financial beliefs are learned, not built in. Maybe it's time to rethink whether they should remain unchallenged in our minds.

Creating energy and co-creating life with the universe means you're also shaping your physical reality. Nobody mentioned that in the sandbox, right? Growing up, we're told, 'money is the root of all evil,' 'money doesn't grow on trees,' or 'you need to win the lottery to get rich.' Complete myths. Unless you were that annoying kid, 'But money does grow on trees because paper comes from trees, duh.' Don't be that kid–nobody likes a smart-ass. I had a money tree once, and guess what? I killed it. It needed just one ice cube a week, and I couldn't even manage that. Talk about a financial green thumb, or lack thereof. I always thought, well, that's my luck. I guess if I didn't have bad luck, I wouldn't have any luck at all.

When you understand that money is just energy, it's neither good nor bad. One is simply exchanging value for a different kind of value. It's simply an energy exchange; money isn't evil.

So, when people say to me, 'Christina, I'm not sure if this works,' or 'what if it doesn't work?' or 'Why should I believe this?'—you know, all that doubt—it's time for a reality check. I ask them, 'Are you 100% thrilled with every aspect of your life? Is everything just lollipops and rainbows? If I handed you a magic wand, could we go bippity boppity boo and instantly turn your life into your dream scenario? Are you living that dream right now?'

Usually, the answer is a big fat 'No.' Clearly, what they're doing currently isn't working. So, I say, why not allow yourself to try something new and create the reality you've been dreaming of? What beliefs, thoughts, and feelings need to shift? Who do you need to become to manifest this new reality? Remember, there's no right or wrong answer here.

This is your permission slip to go all in!

Make It Real

Write your answers to make this exercise more impactful.
Ask Yourself:
Who in your life would be **directly impacted** if you became wealthy beyond your wildest imagination?

List the ways your financial success could change their lives:

- **Your partner:** How?
- **Your parents:** How?
- **Your siblings:** How?
- **Your extended family:** How?
- **Your friends:** How?
- **Your employees:** How?
- **Anyone else?** Who and how?

Now close your eyes and **imagine** it —

Scenarios where your wealth positively impacts the people around you.

What if...?

If you had the wealth that you desire, you could do whatever you want with it. What would happen, what would you do, and who would it impact?

Use that as your green light to create and achieve what you desire.

Money is an unlimited resource that is in constant flow around you. There are trillions of dollars floating around you. You just need to direct the money flow in your direction, while providing value, which I will go over in more detail later in the book.

I'll give you a quick example of value. Most people drink coffee in the morning—Starbucks, Dunkin Donuts, Tim Hortons, or brewed at home, maybe with a Keurig.

I mostly drink coffee at home. A box of Keurig pods costs about $10 at the grocery store. So, for $10, I get a box of coffee.

Money flows from various sources: earning it, receiving it as a gift, or even manifesting it. Sure, it might seem to appear out of thin air, like when someone wins the lottery. Yet, consistently channeling money involves exchange—a transfer of value.

I'm giving someone $10, and they're giving me this beautiful box of Keurig coffee valued at $10. I want you to understand, to know, when I went to the grocery store to get this box of coffee, did the creator of Keurig, the CEO of the company himself, need to sell this to me? Did he have to wake up out of bed and hop on a plane and fly to Canada, hop in a taxi, knock on my door, and say, Here you go, Christina, here's your Keurig Coffee?

The CEO of Keurig's time is no longer connected to money. If the CEO of Keurig had to work for every hour that he sold this drink, he wouldn't have enough hours in the day. Money is not connected to how much time you spend on it. It's connected to the exchange, the value.

Are you creating channels where money can flow to you, without you needing to spend more time because if you want to get to the point where you're making big moves, you're bringing in big money, like Keurig money, you cannot be controlling every single transaction, because eventually, you're going to tap out, you're going to have to charge $20,000 per box of coffee, or you're going to run out of time, and you're going to cap out how much money you create. Therefore, it's so important to create channels for money to flow for you.

It's about shedding old, unreal perceptions of money, because money is essentially what we believe it to be. How you perceive money will determine its role in your life. When I believed making money was hard, or that $18 an hour was the peak, that belief capped my earnings. And when I feared asking for a raise, thinking it would upset others, I never did ask. My beliefs shaped my financial reality about money. But once I released the negative emotions and misconceptions about money, viewing it simply as a medium of exchange, I realized my focus should be on providing value, not more time or effort than the day allows. This isn't about undermining fast food jobs—I've managed such places before—but it's clear the value required there differs from, say, a pilot, nurse, teacher, or police officer. Each job demands different levels of value contribution.

Money is just a tool for creating a bigger impact. This idea is super common among those with a millionaire mindset or people earning six figures a year.

They all see money as just that—a tool. It's not there to boss you around or to be used as a superpower over others.

Think of it as a hammer, a knife, or any tool you'd use in daily life. Now, if you're thinking money turns people into Mr. Greedy or Ms. Selfish, let me throw a curveball at you with the knife analogy. Random, I know, but stick with me here. When you have a knife, you've got choices, loads of them. It's the same with money. It's not the tool itself but how you choose to use it.

With a knife, you can either create a beautiful meal for your family, slicing cheese, cutting up bread, chopping vegetables, filleting a chicken, or whatever you want to create. Or you can use that knife, if you're a surgeon, to save someone's life. Or you can use that knife to cause harm. Is it the knife's fault for what happens with the knife? Or is it the person behind the knife?

It's the same thing with money. Is it money's fault for what happens with your money? As a good-hearted person, you would do good things with money, right? You want to make a mark that lasts beyond your years. So when money is in your hands, you get to use it and create a greater impact on how you deem fit for you. It's not about money itself, but how people handle it. Money is really just an opportunity enhancer and a choice giver.

Your value is something inherent. You don't have to do anything to earn your worthiness for money. By simply being yourself, you can tap into your natural stream of abundance.

I believe that you're in control of money; money's not in control of you. Just like energy's limitless, there's limitless money too. You just have to figure out how to draw it into your life, how to open up the channels of abundance and draw it in based on the vibration that you are putting out. It's something you attract rather than chase. Whether it's adding more value to the world, or more value to who you believe to be. There are going to be weeks, there are going to be months, there are going to be seasons and cycles where you couldn't be bothered in life, where you just don't want to do shit, you are flooded with self doubt; you are just flooded with how am I going to make this work, you're overwhelmed, you're stressed out, you just want to throw in the towel and give up.

I have gone through at least six of those kinds of seasons in my life, probably even the last year. And yes, I've gotten to places in my life where I've wanted to give up. For me, it's always my kids that remind me of why I started doing what I do. It's also really beneficial, naturally, to have support. You need to put yourself in an environment where you're going to succeed and have support along the way.

Seth Godin, a well-known author and marketing expert, says we're basically the sum of the 10 people we hang out with most. So, if there are go-getters and positive thinkers, that's going to rub off on you too.

As long as you do not give up on creating your dreams, creating your desires, and you know that deep down, even though you might feel like giving up today, you will not give up because you have 100% committed to yourself to making this work.

Show up for yourself no matter what.

CHAPTER 3
The Five Types Of Wealth

BEFORE WE GO any further in this book, you need to understand something clear: money alone isn't wealth. It's just one piece of it. True wealth has layers. It runs deeper. It's not just the balance in your bank account; it's the freedom in your calendar, the energy in your body, the strength of your relationships, and the peace you feel when you're alone. If you chase money but ignore everything else, you'll end up rich and still feeling broke. In this chapter, we're going to walk through the five types of wealth so you can see exactly where you're in alignment—and where you're leaking time, energy, or value without realizing it. Once you see the full picture, you'll stop treating money like the only thing that matters and start building a life that feels wealthy and looks damn good, too.

Let's be clear—this concept isn't new. The five types of wealth have been around for generations. Ancient teachings, spiritual traditions, and even modern psychology have pointed to the truth that real wealth is layered. This isn't a trend, and I didn't invent this framework. What I *created* — fully, originally, and from scratch—is the W.E.A.L.T.H. Sequence. That's mine. The method you're reading throughout this book is my proprietary framework, built from lived experience, client work, and years in this field. But these five types of wealth? They've stood the test of time. They're the foundation we're standing on before we go deeper into the W.E.A.L.T.H. work that follows.

So, what are the Five Types of Wealth? Wealth isn't just financial. There are five key areas that shape a wealthy life:

1. Financial Wealth
2. Time Wealth
3. Physical Wealth
4. Social Wealth
5. Spiritual Wealth

These aren't vague concepts. Each one directly impacts how you live, give, create, and lead. You'll see what each type really means, how it shows up in real life, and how to apply it to your own world with clear prompts, tools, and integration strategies.

Financial Wealth

This is the one everyone chases first, but let's be real. It's only part of the picture. This is the money in your account, the income flowing in, the resources that fund your life and your future. While it's not everything, it sure as hell matters. I still remember the shock of my first sale as an entrepreneur. It was two weeks before Christmas, out of nowhere, and it hit me—I could make my own money, from scratch.

Before that, I had spent over a decade in sales, running the numbers, leading as a manager, and being the go-to person in my field. I understood money. I was good at it. But building it on my own terms? That moment changed everything.

Financial wealth isn't just about reaching a number; it's about knowing you have options. It's about the freedom to say yes, the confidence to lead, and the ability to create an impact without waiting for permission. If you're reading this, ask yourself—are you building wealth, or just managing lack? Money wants to move. It wants direction. Start tracking what's coming in, what's going out, and what you want that gap to look like. *We'll walk through exactly how to do that later in the book.* Automate your savings, get honest with your spending, and stop pretending you're "bad with money." You're not. You just haven't been taught how to lead it yet.

But let's go deeper. Financial wealth is about power and possibility. It gives you leverage. It lets you walk away from what drains you and walk toward what lights you up. That kind of power isn't greedy; it's grounding. It's the power to choose—where you live, how you work, what your kids experience, who you support, and how you show up. Money gives you a voice in rooms you used to shrink in. It buys back time, energy, and peace. I see too many people limit what they ask for financially because they've been told that wanting more is selfish or excessive. It's not. Wanting overflow is not about greed. It's about being well-resourced enough to live, give, and lead fully. It's about not having to explain every dollar, or feeling guilt when you invest in yourself. It's about owning that your vision deserves to be backed by real numbers, not just good intentions.

Your relationship with money tells the world how you value yourself. So stop ghosting your finances. Stop waiting until things fall apart to pay attention. Wealth building is not luck. It's leadership. And leadership starts with responsibility.

This means checking your accounts weekly, knowing your income sources, honoring your priorities, raising your standards, and being honest about where you're bleeding money. It's time to stop playing small with your money story and start rewriting it.

Financial wealth is earned, yes—but it's also received. It's allowed. Decide you're available for it. Make space for it emotionally, mentally, and energetically. And when it comes, hold it—not sabotage it, not shrink around it, and not apologize for it. That's what financial maturity looks like.

Money doesn't create your worth. But it does expand your reach. So take the reins. Lead it. Direct it. Multiply it. Because financial wealth doesn't just fund your lifestyle—it funds your legacy.

Time Wealth

Time wealth is the wealth most people don't realize they want until they're burned out, overstretched, and constantly rushing. It's not just about having time off. It's about owning your time. It's the ability to say no without guilt, to move through your day on your own terms, to unplug without the world falling apart. Time wealth gives you space to breathe, to be, to think, and to actually live the life you're working so hard to create. For me, time wealth shows up every summer & Christmas Break. That's when I completely disconnect from the grind, go camping or head to our ranch on Manitoulin Island—the largest freshwater island in the world. Summertime means I get to float down the river, swim, roast marshmallows by the fire, stargaze, and move slowly. There's no schedule. No pressure. Just space. And every time I come back from that week, I'm recharged in a way no amount of hustle could e ver buy.

Ask yourself—if you had full control of your calendar, what would your day actually look like? Design it. Start with just one protected hour a day where you move slow, unplug, or pour into yourself without distraction. Let that hour be untouchable. Guard it like your life depends on it—because it does. Integration means you don't wait for a vacation to feel rested. You live like your time matters now. Build your life around what matters most, not just what's most urgent. That's wealth.

Let's call it what it is—most people are time-broke. They trade hours for survival, squeeze in life between meetings and errands, and then wonder why they feel disconnected and exhausted. Time debt is real, and it quietly robs people of joy.

You can't keep overbooking your calendar and expecting to feel aligned. The truth is, if your schedule is packed with things you resent, you're paying a steep price for your peace.

Time wealth means choosing presence over productivity. It means prioritizing what matters, not just what screams the loudest. It's not lazy to rest. When you protect your time, you're saying, "My energy is not for sale." And that boundary? It's powerful. If you want to start living in alignment, time is the first thing you need to reclaim. Stop letting your calendar run by default. Block off time for thinking, for dreaming, for doing nothing at all. Because in those moments of stillness, clarity speaks up. And from clarity, aligned action follows.

Time wealth also means not needing to explain why you're unavailable. It's knowing your worth without putting it on the clock. It's walking away from the guilt of saying no and stepping fully into the power of intentional yeses. If it's not aligned, it's a no. Period. There's no badge for burnout. You don't win by being the busiest. You win by being in control of your energy and choosing how it's spent. So check your calendar. Does it reflect your values—or just your obligations?

True wealth is a time that feels like yours. Don't wait for "someday." Live like your time is your most valuable currency. Because it is.

Physical Wealth

Physical wealth is your body, your health, your energy. It's the foundation everything else rests on. You can have the money, the freedom, the vision—but if you're running on fumes, it all falls apart. Physical wealth is the stamina to show up for your life fully, not just survive it. It's about treating your body like the vessel that carries your mission.

I built this one intentionally. I became a certified yoga and aerial yoga instructor, not because I wanted a cute side hustle, but because I needed a way to ground myself. Breath by breath, pose by pose, I learned how to regulate my stress, keep anxiety out of the driver's seat, and stay strong through chaos. Yoga became my anchor. It still is. It reminds me that my body isn't separate from my purpose—it's the engine behind it. When my body feels strong, I feel unstoppable. When it's exhausted, everything else crumbles.

Let's stop glamorizing burnout. Let's stop bragging about how little we sleep or how many hours we hustle. That's not wealth. That's a warning sign. Your body is not a machine. It's your home. And if you wouldn't neglect or abuse your actual house, why do it to the only one you've got to live in for life?

Physical wealth means fueling yourself like you matter. It means tuning in before your body screams for help. Are you hydrated? Are you nourishing your system with food that actually gives you energy instead of crashing you? Are you moving your body in a way that builds resilience, or are you ignoring it until it forces you to rest?

Ask yourself—how are you fueling your physical vessel? Are you burning out, or building up?

You don't need to be perfect. You don't need six-pack abs or a strict diet. You need energy, clarity, and strength to lead your life and carry your vision forward. Start by building in one non-negotiable health ritual that centers you—whether it's breathwork, movement, stretching, or sleep. Let that practice become part of your identity. Let it be the anchor you return to again and again.

Maybe it's a morning walk. Maybe it's five deep breaths before a meeting. Maybe it's choosing sleep over scrolling. Whatever it is, choose it on purpose. Choose it because you're not here to hustle yourself into exhaustion. You're here to lead with energy that lasts.

Integration isn't about pushing harder. It's about honoring the body that's carrying your dreams. Treat it like a priority, not a backup plan. Because when your physical wealth is solid, your mind is sharper, your decisions are stronger, and your impact grows. This is the wealth that allows all the others to thrive.

You can't build wealth if you're falling apart. Take care of you, now.

Social Wealth

Social wealth is your network, your reputation, your relationships—the energy you move through the world with and the people who amplify it. This isn't about being popular. It's about being powerful in connection. It's about the currency of trust, the depth of your community, and the ripple your name creates even when you're not in the room.

You build social wealth by showing up in truth, over and over again. You build it by being the real deal—not just when it benefits you, but especially when no one's watching. Hearing someone recommend my work to a friend, not because they're paid to do it or asked, but because it genuinely moved them and they wanted to share, that makes me feel socially wealthy. I feel it when a stranger messages me and says, "My friend told me I *had* to find you." That's impact. That's alignment in action. Social wealth isn't transactional. It's relational.

It's built in the small moments—when you follow through, when you support someone else expecting nothing back, when you lift someone's name in a room full of opportunity because you know they're aligned for it.

It's built when your presence carries weight because people *know* you're real.

Ask yourself—do your connections lift you or drain you? Do they reflect on where you're going, or keep pulling you back to who you used to be? Who do you trust to speak your name in a room full of opportunity? Who are you willing to do that for? Audit your circle. Be honest. Alignment isn't just about who you keep around—it's also about who you stop chasing.

The tool here isn't a gimmick. It's a decision. It's a commitment to connection that feels clean, clear, and real. Social wealth grows when you show up for your people with value, with presence, and with consistency. That includes your family, clients, your audience, your friends, your colleagues, and your community. Even when the return isn't instant. Even when the spotlight isn't on you yet.

Over time, those deposits compound. The results might not always be public, but the effect is powerful. One introduction, one shout-out, one DM can open a door that changes everything. And the more rooted you are in who you are, the stronger that social current becomes. Integration here means treating your name like a brand.

Your energy is like a signal, and your relationships are like a legacy. Social wealth isn't just social currency. Currency can be quick—likes, shares, mentions. Social wealth runs deeper. It's built over time through trust, alignment, and the integrity that keeps your name strong even when you're not in the room. Social currency is part of how you build social wealth, and I go deeper into that later in the book. But for now, just know this: social wealth is a long game. It's earned, not just traded. Speak well. Move with integrity. Be someone worth knowing—not just for what you do, but for how you do it.

Be the one they remember, for all the right reasons. That's real wealth. And no algorithm or algorithm update can ever replace it.

Spiritual Wealth

Spiritual wealth is your connection to something bigger. It's your values, your intuition, your inner compass. It's the voice inside that doesn't shout but speaks the truth. The one that cuts through the noise, the pressure, and the chaos. It's the internal knowing that doesn't need external validation. It just *knows*.

For me, spiritual wealth started with curiosity. I gravitated towards things most people dismissed—astrology, yoga, coaching. That's where the doors cracked open.

But it didn't fully land until I got certified. That's when everything shifted. I stopped questioning if I was supposed to lead and started owning that I was built for it. I didn't just want to help people—I wanted to train them, certify them, show them what was possible. And it wasn't because someone handed me a permission slip. It was because I listened to my gut. Loud and clear.

I even used to read tarot. Not because I needed a deck to tell me who I was—but because I respected energy, intention, and instinct. Most people ignore those signals. They wait for proof, for logic, for someone to agree. But your spiritual wealth doesn't play by those rules. It's not religion. It's alignment. And when you're aligned, you don't beg for clarity. You embody it.

So ask yourself: do you actually listen to your own instincts? Or do you override them with other people's opinions, doubts, or fears? Spiritual wealth shows up in how deeply you trust yourself. How often do you check in and say, "Is this really mine?" or "Is this someone else's story I'm living?" That level of honesty will shake you. But it will also set you free.

You want a tool? Start with silence. Just five minutes. Sit. Breathe. Ask yourself what you need to know. Then shut up and listen. Don't scroll. Don't reach for the answer outside of you. Let it rise. Your intuition is a skill. The more you use it, the stronger it gets. And once you trust it, you stop outsourcing your power.

Integration here means you stop brushing off the whisper and start following it. Even when it's scary. Even when nobody else gets it, the big decisions—the ones that change everything—usually come from that quiet place. From your soul, not your strategy. Build this wealth first. Let everything else take its place after. When you lead from your soul, money follows. Confidence follows. People follow energy. But you've got to lead from the inside out. Not because someone told you to. Not because a trend says it's time to "tap in." But because you trust yourself that deeply.

That's spiritual wealth. And nothing beats it.

This is the map. These five types of wealth work together. You don't need to master all of them overnight, and you're not meant to. But you do need to understand that they're connected. Real wealth isn't built in silos. You can't ignore your body, your peace, your relationships, your time—and expect your bank account to save you. It won't. If you're rich in one area but bankrupt in the others, it shows. It leaks through your mood, your mindset, your energy, your decisions. And over time, it costs you. More than money ever could.

That's why this matters. That's why this chapter comes early in the book. I need you to see the full picture before we get into the tactics, the rewiring, the deep mindset work. Because if you walk into those later chapters thinking it's just about earning more, working more, or manifesting a better paycheck, you'll miss the point entirely. That's not what this book is about. This is about aligned wealth. The kind that lasts. The kind that doesn't burn you out or box you in. And that starts with a new definition of what wealth really is.

Every chapter that follows will challenge a part of your identity, your story, your habits, and your beliefs. Some will push you financially, some emotionally, some spiritually. And as you go through it, I want you to keep coming back to these five types of wealth. Keep asking yourself: where am I in alignment? Where am I out of sync? Where am I trading my time, my energy, my peace—for crumbs? Where am I pretending I'm okay because the bills are paid, but I feel empty inside?

This isn't just a cute list. It's a framework to come back to. It's your compass. Because when things feel off—and they will—this is how you check back in. Maybe you've been focused on building financial wealth, and now your health is on the back burner. Maybe you've been pouring into everyone else, and your spiritual connection is dried up. Maybe your schedule is packed, but your soul is starved. This framework helps you see it, name it, and shift it. Wealth alignment means your life supports your energy, not just your bills. It means you're not hustling for your worth, burning out to prove a point, or chasing goals that don't even feel good once you get them. It means you're building something real. Something sustainable. Something that actually feels like yours.

So ask yourself—where am I wealthy right now? Where am I barely scraping by? What's costing me more than it's giving? That's the level of honesty that changes everything.

Because when all five align, wealth stops being something you chase. It becomes the way you live.

CHAPTER 4
Stop Cheating On Your Money

THAT MOMENT OF disbelief when our card is declined at the checkout is something we've all experienced. But if you're set on increasing your income, it's absolutely within your reach. Regardless of how many attempts you've made and fallen short, or if you're in a tough spot financially, there's a way forward.

Boosting your income and wealth might seem daunting now, but it's definitely achievable. We're talking serious wealth—like the kind that lets you spoil your loved ones with houses and perhaps some flashy gold teeth, if that's your thing. And hey, if you haven't mastered the money game yet, don't beat yourself up. Money is a complex beast, wrapped in layers of emotions: we covet it, loathe it, obsess over it, neglect it, resent it, stash it, yearn for it, and criticize it. It's so emotionally charged that discussing it openly, much less chasing it with enthusiasm, feels taboo, similar to how society treats discussions about sex.

Now, if you're reading this book openly, kudos for your bravery! This means you are ready to make peace with your money relationship and work on it. The good news is that you can repair this relationship if you struggle with financial woes. Imagine one day living the life you've always dreamed of, all because you faced your financial fears head-on. Boo-ya!

The first step in this change is to recognize and overcome your barriers, choose to focus on new, empowering beliefs about money, and pursue it with an unwavering enthusiasm. This book is your guide to doing just that. The real game-changer is taking bold, uncomfortable risks—doing things you've never done, stepping into the limelight, and embracing your worth. It's about craving wealth, committing to it, and, most crucially, allowing yourself to achieve it.

You're on a mission to transform your financial mindset and reality. Let's dive into why you think and feel about money the way you do, uncovering the origins and influencers of your financial beliefs. My goal is to craft a new narrative for your financial life, reshaping your perceptions of money beyond the labels of good, bad, or evil.

Be prepared to roll up your sleeves because actual change demands action. Without your active participation and effort, your financial situation will remain the same. It's time to make that shift happen. Talking about making money your bestie is a big part of my spiel. It's about seeing the connection–or lack thereof–between how badly we want money and how well we actually treat it. Think about it: if we treated our money like one of our closest friends, would we still be in the same financial spot?

It's like realizing there's a gap between our desire for more cash and the effort we put into maintaining a healthy relationship with it. It's kinda funny when you picture money as a buddy you've been neglecting, right? Time to step up and show our finances the same love and attention we give to our tight-knit circle.

When you see money as a vital relationship in your life, it transforms your interactions and connections. It's widely recognized that financial issues are at the heart of many couples' disputes and even lead to many divorces. The stress and arguments about money can overshadow the real essence of relationships.

However, imagine a scenario where money is no longer a source of tension. In such a world, your focus shifts to nurturing your relationships without the cloud of financial worries hanging over your head. Life becomes more enjoyable, and the space to cultivate deeper connections with others broadens.

You might wonder, "Alright, I get it. Improving my relationship with money sounds good, but how do I actually bring more of it into my life? We're definitely diving into that, as it's time to rewrite your money narrative. Everyone has their own money story, and mine was quite a shit show. Let me share a bit about the old money stories that used to define my financial life.

Having three amazing kids now, I often think back to that curveball life threw me at 18. Fresh out of high school, I packed up and moved to a new city with the out-of-town heartthrob. We'd been together since I was 16, so yeah, we've got history. Right after we settled in, bam—we found out I was pregnant. That's when things got really tough.

He had to trek across the country for work, leaving us in a long-distance setup. There we were, not even 20, and money issues were pulling us apart. He was in a different province, hustling for our growing family, while I was back with my folks in Ontario, rocking the pregnancy solo. It felt like a choice between love and money, which sucked because who wants to pick, right? We thought we were doing the best thing for our future, for our son.

After my son was born, I made the big move to be with my him, but life didn't get easier. Living costs were through the roof, and although we lived together, he had to spend long stretches working far from home.

Eventually, we were together with two little ones, but money still hung over us like a dark cloud. We moved back to Ontario, hoping it would help, but we were still scraping by, paycheck to paycheck. He had to leave again for work. We were stuck in a loop—fighting about money, missing each other, and struggling to give our kids everything.

It was an endless cycle of choosing between love and money, and honestly, it seemed like we couldn't have both at the same time. Money was always the root of our fights, a constant battle in our lives.

Arguments about finances became our routine. I was yearning for him to be home, and he felt the same. It wasn't about the amount in our bank account; it was about being together. Yet, in today's world, you can't ignore the fact that money is essential for survival. This created a never-ending cycle of stress and disagreement between us.

It felt like an impossible choice, a constant tug-of-war between love and financial stability. This struggle made it seem like having both a happy family life and a stable financial situation under the same roof were just out of reach.

It wasn't a great catch twenty-two. For Love or For Money story, right? We argued all the time about money because I wanted him home. He wanted to be home. I didn't care about how much money we had, but you need money to live. You need money to survive in this day and age. It was just this never-ending cycle.

I long held the belief that love and financial abundance couldn't coexist. Money seemed to always bring tension, turning every conversation about finances into a battleground within our relationship. This struggle made me believe that true harmony and financial success were incompatible. It always felt like love could only work when money wasn't in the picture, like the second bills showed up, and so did the arguments. It just seemed impossible to have both a healthy relationship and real financial success. From what I lived and saw, that combo was a damn unicorn.

However, having it all is indeed possible, though it took me a while to see that. For years, a cycle of scarcity trapped us, always feeling like we didn't have enough to support ourselves financially. I, much like my parents, worked tirelessly, embedding in me the belief that financial gain was only the result of hard work and sacrifices. It seemed like the only alternative to this relentless grind was a stroke of luck, similar to winning the lottery. But this mindset limited my view of the vast possibilities for acquiring wealth and living abundantly.

For a good chunk of my life, my financial mindset was pretty black and white. You could either have money or love, but never both. And making money?

Well, that was always a struggle. Whether we were arguing about how to spend it, stressing over not having enough, or bickering about the best ways to earn more, money was always at the center of conflict. This narrative dominated my thoughts and experiences for far too long.

Realizing this changed everything. I had to do the work—unlearn all the crap I believed about money and rewire how I saw it. I saw that love, money, and hard work didn't have to be tangled up in drama.

They could actually exist on their own, in harmony, without one dragging the others down. That shift? Game-changing. It marked the beginning of rewriting my entire money story and reevaluating my financial reality.

I've totally changed how I see money now. Wealth doesn't have limits, and it's not about luck—it's about owning who I am and letting the world see what's inside. We're not just bodies chasing paychecks. What's inside us? That's where the real value is.

I've realized that I can create endless wealth because of my inner value, which is limitless. Sure, my business is a way I show my worth and bring in cash, but it's just one path. Like me, you've got endless ways to welcome wealth into your life, and for me, running a business is just one option. Right now, we are as young as we will ever be, full of potential.

Being wealthy isn't just about having a fat bank account. There are countless ways to feel and live like a millionaire. You don't need stacks of cash to feel top-notch. You do not need a million bucks to feel like a million bucks. My life proves you can have both love and money.

The early days were rough—money worries sparked plenty of arguments between my husband and me. But for several years now, those money fights have stopped, and I can't recall the last time we truly argued about finances. This shift came when I rewrote my money story and embraced a mindset of abundance, impacting every area of my life. Now, I enjoy love, financial stability, a wonderful family, and genuine happiness. Changing my perspective on money has shown me that wealth isn't just about the cash—it's about creating a fulfilling life where love and financial well-being coexist beautifully.

I'm about to lay out everything I've learned and applied to boost my wealth. I was just like you, wrapped up in fear, guilt, and anxiety about money. I used to think there was never enough, and that talking about money was a no-go zone. Maybe you can relate to that. Did someone you respected growing up ever tell you not to talk about money, your earnings, or that wanting more was greedy or even evil? That was me, too.

I felt that way because I didn't truly get what money was all about. It's time to change that narrative and show you that talking about money, desiring more, and even asking for that raise isn't just okay—it's essential for creating the wealth you deserve.

Not knowing what something is can definitely set off the alarm bells in our heads. It's like when you hear a strange noise coming from your closet or a thump from the basement–your mind races with many scary possibilities.

The fear builds up because you're dealing with the unknown. But then, when you muster up the courage to check it out and realize it's just your cat goofing around, all that fear turns out to be for nothing. That's the power of the unknown–it can make things seem way scarier than they actually are, just like our misconceptions about money can.

Diving into the realm of money, I discovered a world of possibilities. Everywhere I turned, stories of financial success and online wealth creation filled the air. Despite the buzz, my self-belief was shaky—I couldn't quite grasp that such abundance could be within my reach. However, a shift in perspective changed everything. As I peeled back the layers of what money truly is, I realized it's more than just currency or numbers in a bank account; it's an idea, a concept that can shape and expand. This revelation altered my understanding of money, allowing me to see it as a limitless resource available to anyone, including me, including you.

Money, at its core, is just an idea. It's something we each make mean something in our own minds, and honestly, nobody taught us to believe that. When you see money differently, not how it's drilled into us, you stop feeling so desperate, weird, or stressed about it. Because money isn't this rigid thing, we've made it out to be.

I want to nudge you to set a goal during this book, maybe a financial one or anything you're aiming for, and start seeing it in a new light. Let's not view it as this massive, unattainable thing. Instead, think of it as just another figure, another milestone in your journey. To put things into perspective, consider celebrities like Oprah, Elon Musk, or Kim Kardashian. Imagine, for them, making $100k a month wouldn't even manage their business operations; their monthly expenses likely exceed that amount. This comparison isn't to overwhelm, but to normalize and scale your goals, showing that what might seem huge to us is just everyday business for others. It's all about context and perception.

Our past environments, upbringing, and exposure to financial perspectives shape our perception of what makes up a large sum of money. If we had grown up in the Kardashian family or a celebrity circle, our view of what makes up a large sum of money would drastically differ.

In such a world, we would likely deem an amount we currently consider substantial to be minor. This contrast shows how our upbringing and social circles penetrate our perspective on finances.

I recall hearing about someone whose husband had a friend receiving a $100,000 monthly allowance from his father. This substantial sum was merely his 'play money.'

Remarkably, the only time money even became a topic of conversation between him and his father was if he spent all $100,000 before the month ended. For him, such a financial lifestyle was just the norm.

Consider the idea that any view we hold, whether we see something as good or bad, large or small, is merely our perception, not the absolute truth. This notion of perception is projection, suggesting that we can only perceive things that are already within our consciousness. Carl Jung, a Swiss psychologist and founding figure of psychology, discussed this concept alongside Adler and Sigmund Freud. Jung proposed that our perceptions reflect our inner selves, meaning we cannot perceive anything externally that isn't already a part of us.

You know how sometimes you feel like there's this invisible thread linking what's going on inside you to the bigger picture of your life? Well, Carl Jung, this Swiss psychology genius, totally got into that. He talked about how our inner world—like our dreams, gut feelings, and even those "why did I do that?" moments—are more than just random thoughts. They're like clues to who we are deep down and how we see the world. It's like we're walking, talking collections of these stories and vibes we've picked up throughout our lives, shaping how we experience everything. So when we talk about identity shaping our reality, it's not just some fancy idea; it's about how the unique cocktail of our personal experiences and inner thoughts craft the life we live. It's fascinating, right? Just think, the way you see a sunset or react to a song, that's all you, painting your world with your own colors.

Money stories? Yeah, most of them are just recycled lessons from people who didn't really know how to handle money. They might have appreciated what they had, sure, but deep down, they didn't see more wealth in their cards, because of this or that reason—you know how it goes. We've all got those tales in our heads, reasons we believe we can't hit the next level of financial freedom or wealth. It's like a hand-me-down sweater of beliefs; it might not fit well, but we wear it because it's familiar.

Let's think about where this idea of hard work equals money really came from. If you ask your folks, they'll likely say they got it from their parents, who got it from theirs, and so on.

Makes you wonder, doesn't it? Who was the original author of this tired old script? Sure, there were times, like the industrial era, when folks pounded factory floors, believing that sweat and grind were the only paths to financial gain. That belief got baked into our collective mindset: more physical labor, more money.

But hey, we're not in the same boat today. We've got tech and automation easing our load, yet some of us are still running on this ancient hamster wheel, thinking hard work is the only way to fill our wallets. It's like trying to use a rotary phone to send a text message—exhausting and, frankly, silly in today's world. We need to update our mental software to match our current reality, or we're just spinning our wheels with a mindset from a century ago.

I want you to think about who taught you Your Money Story?
1. Where did it come from?
2. How were you raised?
3. Who taught you those beliefs?

Your money mindset often stems from lessons learned from

trusted figures or past experiences that slipped out of your control. These beliefs, however well-intentioned, might be holding you back. It's time to align energetically with the wealth you seek, embodying the confidence of someone who knows they can have it all.

Consider this: the financial beliefs you carry, are they lifting you up or weighing you down? We're diving deep into what money signifies for you and how it might block your path to success. We'll peel back the layers of your subconscious financial blueprint, pinpointing the automatic scripts shaping your reality. By tracing these patterns to their origins, we aim to break free from any inherited or past-life constraints.

The goal? To redefine your money narrative, craft a story that not only empowers you but also paves the way to the life you yearn for.

Now, let's explore the underlying beliefs that subtly dictate your financial journey.

Here's a powerful exercise to uncover and shift your deep-seated beliefs, not just about money, but all areas of your life. Get ready to expose the hidden thoughts that might hold you back from experiencing abundance, love, and fulfillment.

1. Grab a journal or open a voice memo app.
2. I'll prompt you with a statement and you'll immediately jot down or verbalize your gut reaction. Write or speak your thoughts as they come — unfiltered, raw, and without judgment. This isn't about crafting the "right" answer. It's about capturing your authentic reaction in the moment.
3. Once you've recorded your response, take a moment to reflect. Seeing or hearing your unfiltered thoughts can be eye-opening, revealing the subconscious narratives influencing your life.
4. Don't rush to fix everything at once. Aim to address one belief or thought pattern at a time, allowing space for genuine transformation.
5. While we're talking about money here, this method works across the board—your relationships, self-image, finances,

all of it. It's a go-to tool for growth, no matter where you use it.

By confronting these internal dialogues, you start the journey of reshaping them into empowering beliefs that support your goals and desires. This process is about gradual, sustainable change, creating a foundation for lasting abundance and happiness in your life.

I want you to think of what your first memories of money were? (Is it asking your parents for pizza money for school, getting a birthday card in the mail from a relative, asking for change for the candy store, bus fare, raising money for school fundraisers, parents figuring out bills at the table, friends asking to borrow money for cafeteria food).

Don't edit or judge your response; just let it flow naturally, capturing it precisely as it emerges, free from any notions of right or wrong. Got it? Great. Proceed:

Money is _____.
Money really is _____.
People who have a lot of money are _____.
People who don't have a lot of money are _____.
Money creates _____.
I would make more money if _____.
Rich people are rich because _____.
Poor people are poor because _____.
My mom thought money was _____.
My dad thought money was _____.
My high school friends viewed people with money as _____.
My college friends viewed people with money as _____.
My current friends view people with money as _____.
Money makes people _____.
I think money can _____.
I'm afraid money will make me _____.
If I had more money, I would _____.
If I did better than my partner financially then _____.
If I did better than my colleagues financially then _____.
If I did better than my father financially then _____.
If I did better than my mother financially then _____.

The best way you can spend money is _____.
The worst way you can spend money is _____.
I would never spend money on _____.
I could never afford to _____.
I would judge people if they used their money for _____.
I should spend my money on _____.
When people who are wealthier than me talk about money, I feel _____.
When people who are less wealthy than me talk about money, I feel _____.
If I could teach people one thing about money, it would be that _____.
I would feel comfortable with $_____ in my bank account.
I would feel uncomfortable with $_____ in my bank account.
I currently have $_____ in my bank account.

Reflect on your responses; they mirror the financial narratives looping in your mind, shaping your money dynamics and reality. As you revisit your answers, consider: What insights emerge that surprise you? What feelings or thoughts surface? What revelations did you discover that were perhaps previously hidden?

To change these money scripts, start by recognizing and acknowledging them. Here's a step-by-step guide:

1. Awareness: The first step is recognizing the existing money scripts. You've already begun this by identifying what thoughts and beliefs you have around money.
2. Reflection: Reflect on where these beliefs come from. Consider your upbringing, influential people in your life, experiences, and societal messages about money.
3. Challenge and Question: For each belief, ask yourself, "Is this really true? Does this belief serve my current goals and lifestyle? Where did it come from, and is it based on my reality or someone else's fears or experiences?"
4. Rewrite Your Narrative: Create new, empowering beliefs. For example, if your old script is, "Money is the root of all evil," you might reframe it as, "Money is a tool for doing great things in the world."

5. Action: Align your actions with your new beliefs. This could mean making financial decisions that reflect your new mindset, like spending in a way that brings you joy and aligns with your values.
6. Consistency and Patience: Changing deeply ingrained beliefs takes time and consistent effort. Regularly remind yourself of your new beliefs and why they are important to you.
7. Celebrate Progress: Recognize and celebrate changes in your financial behavior and mindset, no matter how small. This reinforces positive change and motivates you to continue.

By following these steps, you can transform your money scripts into empowering beliefs that support your financial well-being and goals.

Over the next few days, take a minute to think about how the stuff you saw growing up—or the money habits you picked up—have shaped where you're at now. Shifting those old beliefs into an abundance mindset can seriously change your relationship with money, and yeah, that shows up in your bank account, too. You have buried these beliefs deep. So, when you go back through your answers or listen again, pay attention—what jumps out? What emotions come up? What did you not even realize was sitting there before?

Perception Is Projection
—Carl Jung ♥

CHAPTER 5
Money, Often Seen As A Mirage, A Mere Reflection Of Something Deeper

UNDERSTANDING WEALTH IS a bit like Shrek's take on onions—it's all about layers. You know, like how Shrek famously says, "Ogres are like onions, they have layers." And guess what? So do we! Most people haven't quite figured out what wealth truly means, just like Donkey didn't quite get Shrek's onion analogy at first. So, let's cut through the confusion: what exactly is wealth? What sets the wheels in motion? And what lies beneath the surface? We started by examining the big player: money. It's the universal symbol of wealth, but trust me, there's more to it than meets the eye.

Let's get something straight—most of the money out there? It's not even real. It's numbers. Codes. Blips on a screen. Only about 8% of the world's money exists as actual cash. The other 92%? It's chillin' in banks, apps, and systems we'll never see.

I don't know about you, but I'm not walking around with stacks of cash. I've probably got enough on me for a coffee, maybe. The rest? It's floating in cyberspace, moving through apps, taps, and transfers like some invisible current. And it works because we all agreed it does. That's the game. Electronics are energy. It's all just energy shifting from one place to another.

Money's one tiny piece of your value—not the whole damn pie. Wealth consciousness helps you attract more of it, sure. But your self-worth? Untouchable. You were valuable long before your bank account caught up.

Riches in the mind are available to everyone, with no exceptions. Anyone willing to do the work can grow it. It's like air. It's all around you, but it's up to you to breathe it in. You've got the power to shift your mindset whenever you choose, and nothing can hold you back from that.

Myth Busting the Money Mirage

Money has many ironies, and here's a crucial one: wealth is what you don't see. Imagine someone driving a Dodge Challenger, a $100,000 car. You might think, "Wow, they must be rich!" But in reality, all we know is that they have $100,000 less than before, or they're deeper in debt by $100,000. Our society often equates wealth with visible consumption–the cars, homes, and Instagram-worthy moments.

Yet, true wealth is the spending you haven't done. It's the luxury cars left in the showroom, the diamonds left in the store; the designer watches never worn, and the expensive clothes never bought. Wealth is about financial assets that you haven't converted into visible, tangible things.

It's an untapped possibility. It gives you options, opens doors, and lets you create more than what you've got right now. That's the difference between being rich and being wealthy. Rich could mean you're making good money now. Wealth means you've built something that lasts and can grow.

Being rich can feel flashy. It's easy to fake. Wealth? That's the stuff you don't see—savings, investments, the quiet moves no one's posting about. It's the discipline, the "not right now" choices, that actually build it. Most people want the freedom that comes with wealth—the ability to live life on their terms without stressing about money. But society keeps mixing up having money with blowing it, and that noise drowns out the actual work it takes to build the wealth that lasts.

So, what's the real value of wealth? It's having options, feeling secure, and knowing you've built something that lasts. And I'm not just talking about money. Wealth is the energy, mindset, and freedom behind it all.

Real wealth isn't loud; it's not always something you can see. That's what makes it harder to learn from. But once you get that, once you respect the stuff that doesn't show up on a price tag, that's when you build true wealth on your terms.

Most money isn't even real; it's just numbers on a screen. If we tried to print it all? We'd probably run out of paper.

So, it's kind of like we're all playing this massive game of make-believe with money. It works because we all play along, believing in the same rules. It's not about the physical money we see, but about this entire system we've built around the idea of money.

Money isn't the same as wealth. It's just one part of the picture. Real wealth is bigger than dollars. It's how you think, how you live, and the freedom you create.

The numbers in your bank account are just a mirror of that. If you get too caught up in the money, you miss what actually builds a wealthy life.

Money is just one slice of the pie when it comes to your worth. It doesn't define who you are. It only connects to one part of you, your wealth, not your entire personal value. Just because someone has money doesn't mean they are worth more. It just means they have activated the part of themselves that understands wealth.

You need nothing fancy or anything outside of you to activate wealth consciousness. Everything you need is already inside. Maybe it's been buried or ignored, but it's still there. You just need to stop tuning it out.

It's time to stop dreaming about wealth and start living it. You have more wealth capability in your pinky finger than you can experience in a lifetime. Don't sweat it thinking you've maxed out your wealth potential or that some obstacle is blocking your cash flow. And don't fuss over how to morph your wealth consciousness into cold, hard cash. It's like magic. It'll just start happening. Think about the people who've built real wealth, the kind that goes beyond just money. Back when they were starting out, they didn't have some perfect, detailed plan.

Sure, they had goals and maybe a vision, but if you ask them now, most will tell you it was the unexpected twists, the timing, and those "how did that even happen" moments that pulled it all together. Their ambition lit the fire, but the path to wealth was messy, unpredictable, and full of timing they couldn't plan for.

Now it's your turn. You might not see every step ahead, but you can create the energy and mindset that brings those unexpected wins your way. Set yourself up so the good stuff has a reason to show up.

You're right on the edge of stepping into wealth consciousness. That means shifting how you think and feel about money and value. It's about seeing wealth as something you create from the inside out, not something you chase. And once you're in that mindset, avoiding success gets pretty hard. Opportunities, money, and freedom flow your way without the constant grind. You unlock parts of yourself and your life you didn't even know were there. And the happiness that follows? It's real. It's grounded. And it's yours.

Most of us want to make it big. We're chasing that dream of hitting it rich, becoming wealthy, and living a good life. But what exactly is wealth?

Is wealth just about stacking cash and buying things, or is it something deeper? True wealth is about having real freedom, the freedom to live how you want, build meaningful relationships, grow as a person, and enjoy life on your terms. It's not just the flashy stuff everyone shows off. It's the foundation that makes everything else possible. It's like that feeling you get when you're doing what truly lights you up inside, following your passions and living life on your own terms, rather than just chasing after things.

The way you live, the people you love, the peace you feel, and the drive that keeps you going. It's the moments that matter, the growth you go through, and the impact you make. As we move forward, stop looking at wealth like it's just cash or things. Start seeing it in every part of your life and decide to live from that place.

Money messes with many people. We're handed beliefs about it from the time we're kids. Some help us. Most hold us back.

Those beliefs shape how we think, act, and deal with money every day. And whether we know it, they're steering the direction our financial life is going.

You know, they say our minds are like sponges when we're kids, especially before we hit seven. It's during those early years that our subconscious gets its first big makeover. Everything we see, hear, and feel gets absorbed and shapes how we perceive things later on. So, by the time we're adults, a lot of those past experiences still hang around in the background, steering us in ways we might not even realize.

Here is the truth. Money is not good or bad. It is just a tool. It shows you what you value, what you want, and even what you fear. If you really want to understand your relationship with money, you need to look at what is going on underneath. The beliefs you have picked up over time are running the show, whether or not you realize it.

This is about figuring out how you really think and feel about money. You see where your beliefs come from and what needs to change so you can feel in control. When you strip away the conditioning and the noise, you get clear. You stop seeing money as something stressful and start using it as a tool to build the life you want. You make money your BFF. That is where freedom starts.

Why do some people seem to attract wealth effortlessly while others struggle to make ends meet? This age-old question has puzzled philosophers, economists, and psychologists for centuries, and probably you too. The answer to this head-scratcher varies just like the individuals who ponder it. We must acknowledge this undeniable truth: internal beliefs and choices, as much as external circumstances, profoundly shape financial struggles. Mic Drop! Money struggles usually come from a mix of what's going on outside and what's going on inside.

Things like lack of education, a rough economy, or your inner circle can slow you down. But most of the time, it's your own mindset and habits that hold you back the most.

Self-sabotage shows up when fear, insecurity, or a scarcity mindset takes over. It can wreck even the best financial plans.

Most of it comes from limiting beliefs about money, usually passed down from childhood, society, or experiences. Basically, everything you believe about money is just a mess, like that disaster of a Tupperware drawer we all avoid. But even in the chaos, there is hope. When you understand what is really behind your money struggles, you can start breaking them down, piece by piece. When you get honest about your beliefs and habits around money, you can start calling out the patterns that keep you stuck. And then you can change them.

You rewrite your money story by trading fear for courage, scarcity for abundance, and limits for possibility. Every old belief you break down clears space for more. And that shift? It doesn't just change your bank account. It changes everything.

Myths and misconceptions about money

These old-money beliefs hang around like a heavy fog, making it hard to see anything clearly.

They get passed down through generations, backed by society, and they mess with how we think and act around wealth. I'm here to clear that up and call out the lies that keep us stuck.

One of the biggest myths is that wealth is only for the lucky ones—the ones born into money or handed some magical opportunity. That kind of thinking feeds the scarcity mindset and makes people feel like if they didn't start with a silver spoon, they're screwed. You've heard it before, right? "If I didn't have bad luck, I'd have no luck at all." But the truth? Wealth has no limits. It is out there, growing, and available to anyone who's willing to go after it.

We all carry beliefs about money that shape how we think and act, like "there isn't enough to go around," "I don't deserve a lot of money," or "You need money to make money." Then there are the classics like "Money can't buy happiness" or "You can't change your financial future." These beliefs make people feel stuck, like they have no power. They feed into the whole "money doesn't grow on trees" mindset or the idea that "the rich get richer and the poor get poorer." And let's not forget "you have to work hard for money"—like money only shows up if you're grinding yourself into the ground. It is all just noise that keeps you from realizing you can actually take control. When you call out these money myths for what they are, you stop living in scarcity and start thinking in abundance.

Wealth isn't a game where someone else has to lose so you can win. There's more than enough for everyone. You don't have to scramble for leftovers. You get to create your own success and share it without taking from anyone else. Stop playing small.

Own the fact that abundance is already here for you. Forget the stories that hold you back. Wealth is real, it's yours, and it's waiting. With courage, determination, and a willingness to challenge the status quo, we can rewrite our financial destinies and create a future of abundance and prosperity for ourselves and generations to come.

You know, those sneaky little stories they fed us when we were knee-high to a grasshopper, telling us what we should believe about money and all things green. Let's dive into them more.

Myth 1: Money is the Root of All Evil

Let's kick things off with a classic: 'Money is the root of all evil.' Now, I'm not sure who came up with this gem, but let's set the record straight. Money itself isn't evil. Nope, not one bit. It's just a tool, like a hammer or a knife. It's all about how you use it that counts. And if you've ever thought that line came straight from the Bible, it didn't. The actual verse says the love of money is the root of all evil. Vast difference — and one worth remembering, because money will only ever magnify who you already are.

Myth 2: You Need Money to Make Money

Ah, the age-old saying, "You need money to make money." Sure, having some cash to invest can give you a leg up, but let me tell you a little secret: it's not the only way to get ahead. In fact, some of the most successful people out there started with nothing but a dream and some hustle. So, don't let a lack of funds hold you back. Get creative, put in the work, and watch those dollars roll in.

Myth 3: The Rich Get Richer, and the Poor Get Poorer

Now, this one's a real doozy. "The rich get richer, and the poor get poorer." Sounds pretty bleak, right? Well, I'm here to tell you it's not set in stone.

Certainly, there are challenges that can make it more difficult for some individuals to succeed, but that doesn't mean it's game over. With a little perseverance and some grit, anyone can climb the ladder of success. Don't let this myth get you down. You've got what it takes to break the cycle and make your own luck.

Myth 4: Money Can't Buy Happiness

Last but not least, we've got the age-old saying, "Money can't buy happiness." Now, I'll admit, there's some truth to this one. Money alone won't magically make all your problems disappear. It sure can make life a lot easier, though. From taking that dream vacation to finally being able to afford your favorite guilty pleasure, having a little extra cash in your pocket can definitely put a smile on your face. So, don't be afraid to chase those dollar signs. Remember to keep your priorities in check along the way. The truth is that money can't buy the emotion of happiness itself, but it can buy the things, experiences, comfort, and security that contribute to happiness.

Just because everyone's saying it doesn't make it true. So, keep an open mind, do your own research, and never be afraid to question the status quo.

What money myths have you heard? And now that you know the truth, how will you shut them down for good?

CHAPTER 6
Swipe Right For Wealth

Now that we've laid the groundwork, it's time to build on that foundation. We're going to explore your relationships and money mindset even further to unlock the wealth you deserve. We'll dive into how your personal relationships mirror your financial ones, shining a light on the link between wealth and well-being. Why does this matter? Because understanding this connection can revolutionize how you think about and handle money.

Let's break down what makes your money relationship either powerful or exhausting. I'll throw some real questions your way to shake up how you see your finances and help you start a no-BS conversation with your cash. Think of it as a straight-up heart-to-heart with your bank account — where truth leads to real change.

How will we do this? By reflecting on your past and present money stories, pinpointing the beliefs that serve you, and rewriting those that don't. This isn't just about getting to know your money better; it's about reshaping your financial future, one empowering thought at a time. So, let's get started and see how adjusting your money mindset can lead to a richer life, in every sense of the word.

- Think about all the different relationships in your life, like with your friends, family, co-workers, or partner. What's your idea of a fantastic, empowering relationship? What are the must-haves for you to feel supported and positive in these relationships? Now, think about what definitely

shouldn't be there. What are the big no-nos or things that just ruin a relationship for you, whether it's with a buddy or your significant other?
- When you think about the relationships in your life that just suck the energy out of you, what comes to mind? Describe what a negative or disempowering relationship looks like for you. What elements make it feel toxic or just plain bad? And on the flip side, what's usually missing in these relationships that leaves you feeling down?
- Our relationship with money often mirrors our interactions with people in our lives. It's like holding up a mirror to how we connect with others and how we handle our finances. Do you notice a connection between how you treat your relationships and how you manage money? For example, if you neglect spending quality time with your personal connections, could you also be neglecting your financial planning? Or if you shy away from difficult discussions with friends or family, do you also avoid facing financial issues head-on? What patterns do you see between your social and financial behaviors?
- When conversations around money come up, do you shrink or expand? Is it constant with anyone you're talking to, or does it change based on the other person's financial "status"?
- How much time do you spend thinking about money? What are your thoughts about it? Are they loving and grateful? Or stressed and frantic?
- Does money keep you up at night? Does it make you unable to sleep or eat?
- If I were to ask you to go into your bank account and look at your money, what comes up? How do you feel?
- Beyond your survival and basic needs, what do you desire money for? What will you do with it? In the present moment? In the future? (family stuff, home, luxury, experiences, travel, hobbies, self-care, health, charity, etc.)

- As you write those desires out, what thoughts, beliefs, reactions, judgments, or feelings are coming up for you?
- How can having more money allow you to contribute even more to the world and be more generous? What will you do as you make more and more money? Where do you want to give back?
- Imagine if you could dive into the most captivating relationship with money ever. I'm not just talking about some fleeting infatuation; I'm talking about a soul-deep connection that's rich, expansive, and fulfilling AF. How would that look and feel like for you? Picture the long-lasting and nourishing bond you crave with money. When you're dealing with it day in and day out, how do you want to feel? What expectations do you hold for this money romance, and how do you plan to have each other's backs? Let's dish—what's your dream money relationship all about?
- What's missing in your current relationship with money that shows up in your ideal money relationship?
- What's present in your current money relationship that you don't want in your ideal one?
- What needs to change to bring you closer to your ideal money relationship? What's your first move?
- What are your tendencies and habits with money? Do you spend it all—on yourself, on others, both? Do you "hoard" it?

If you save money for a "rainy day..."

- What does that mean to you? Describe what you envision a "rainy day" to be in terms of your finances.
- Think about the reasons someone might save money for a "rainy day." What do you believe are the benefits of having a financial safety net?
- Reflect on your own habits and attitudes toward saving money for unexpected expenses. Do you currently set aside funds for emergencies or unforeseen circumstances? Why or why not?

- Consider the emotions associated with saving money for a "rainy day." How does the idea of having a financial cushion make you feel? Are there any anxieties or uncertainties that come up?
- Imagine a scenario where you need to dip into your savings for a "rainy day." How would you feel about using that money? What criteria would you use to determine when it's appropriate to access those funds?
- Explore the concept of preparedness versus over-caution for saving for a "rainy day." How do you balance being smart with your money and still living your life right now?
- Think about the impact of saving for a "rainy day" on your overall financial well-being. How does having a financial safety net affect your sense of security and peace of mind?
- Consider how your upbringing or experiences may have influenced your approach to saving money for unexpected expenses. Are there any beliefs or attitudes inherited from family or learned through personal experience?

Saving for a rainy day is a common piece of advice, but it can hold you back if it turns into fear-driven hoarding or keeps you from investing and growing your wealth. Finding your own balance between safety and growth is where the real power lies. These prompts should help stimulate deeper reflection on the concept of saving for a "rainy day" and its significance in your financial mindset.

But, if you spend your money right away...

- Reflect on your spending habits. Do you spend money as soon as you receive it? What motivates this behaviour?
- Consider the immediate gratification of spending money versus the long-term benefits of saving or investing it. How do you weigh these two options when making financial decisions?
- Explore any emotions or impulses that arise when you have money available to spend. Do you feel a sense of urgency or excitement about making purchases? How do these feelings impact your spending patterns?

- Think about the consequences of spending money impulsively. Have you ever regretted a purchase made on a whim? What lessons have you learned from these experiences?
- Consider the role of budgeting and financial planning in managing your spending habits. Do you have a budget in place to help prioritize your expenses and allocate funds wisely?

These are the money scripts running on repeat, shaping your relationship with money and your financial reality. As you review your answers, some surprising insights might emerge. What's coming up as you dive deeper into your thoughts and feelings about money? Maybe you're uncovering hidden beliefs or patterns you didn't notice before. Jot down any revelations or shifts in perspective; this is all part of your journey to a stronger, more empowered money relationship.

The truth about money is as simple as a cat video on the internet. Just like how some people see cats and go 'OMG! So CUTE!!', while others run for the hills because of a terrible encounter, money is just a thing in this world. It's neither a saint nor a sinner, unless you decide it is. So, what's your verdict on the green stuff?

Now, let's get into how money shows up in your relationships. When it comes up, do you puff up like a peacock or shrink like a raisin in the sun? And be real, does the way you talk about money shift depending on who's flashing the cash?

How much headspace does money rent in your brain? Are your thoughts about it all lovey-dovey or more like a stressed-out parent at a kid's birthday party? Does money keep you up at night, tossing and turning, or worse, snacking? When you jump on Google looking for quick fixes or how-tos about money, what are you googling?

If I dared you to peek into your bank account right now, what would you see? Go on, feel those heart palpitations.

Beyond the essentials, what's your money mojo for? Dreaming of luxury yachts or just paying off student loans?

As you pen down those desires, what's popping up in your head? Guilt? Excitement? A sudden craving for chocolate?

How can stacking more dough make you the superhero of philanthropy? Where do you want to make it rain when the cash flow increases?

Remember, investing in a better relationship with money isn't just smart, it's a downright necessity for kicking your Wealthy Life into high gear!

HAVE A HEART-TO-HEART WITH MONEY

Imagine money is sitting right across from you, like a trusted friend, ready for a heart-to-heart chat. I want you to write a letter *to* money, pouring out your thoughts, feelings, and intentions about your relationship with it. Be honest, be vulnerable, and let it all out.

Once you've written your letter to money, I want you to flip the script. Now, imagine money is responding to you. What would it say? Write a letter *from* your perspective, addressing your concerns, acknowledging your efforts, and offering your perspective on your relationship.

Write a letter to money, then write a letter from money.

Here's an example to get you started:

Dear Money,

Okay, real talk. We've had a complicated relationship. I've blamed you, chased you, ignored you, obsessed over you, and honestly, treated you like crap. One minute I'm desperate for you, the next I'm pushing you away like you're the villain in some twisted drama I wrote in my head.

My stress, shame, guilt, and worth, I've made you responsible. I expected you to fix everything, then got mad when you didn't show up. I've judged people who had a lot of you, and I've judged myself for not having enough. That ends now. I am so sorry.

I'm not here to beg or play victim. I'm owning my part. I've made you the enemy when really, you've just been waiting for me to get my shit together and treat you right.

So here it is, I'm sorry.

I'm sorry for talking shit about you.

I'm sorry for acting like you're never enough.
I'm sorry for not trusting you to stick around.
I'm sorry for using you as a measuring stick for my value.
I'm sorry for thinking you only show up when I hustle myself into the ground.
I'm sorry for not seeing you as the generous, powerful, neutral force you are.

From now on, I'm choosing something different. I'm choosing respect. Partnership. Appreciation. I'll pay attention. I'll make room for you. I'll let you flow without gripping so tight. No more toxic patterns. No more hot-and-cold energy. Just truth, clarity, and trust.

You're not the problem. You never were. I was just scared to receive you without conditions. But I'm done playing small.

Let's rewrite this story together.

Love,

Me

Express yourself however feels right, whether it's a formal letter or just a casual talk. The point is to lean into this exercise fully and see what truths come up about your money relationship. Happy writing!

Here are some revised prompts for you to consider:

- Reflect on times when you may not have been fully truthful or honest with money. Is there something weighing on your conscience that you've been holding back? Now's the time to address it and clear the air.
- Consider what shifts and healing you're ready to embrace in your relationship with money. What limiting beliefs or negative patterns are you prepared to let go of in order to move forward with greater strength and clarity?
- Explore how you can foster a better partnership with money. How can money support you more effectively, and vice versa? What communication strategies and relationship dynamics do you envision for your future interactions with money?
- Recall instances when money has come through for you in

the past. Whether it was during a time of need or to facilitate an exciting opportunity, reflect on how money has been a reliable ally in your life.
- Celebrate the incredible adventures and experiences you've shared with money. From memorable trips to meaningful purchases, reminisce about the moments when money has enriched your life and opened up new possibilities.
- Acknowledge how money has made a positive impact on your life, as well as the lives of your loved ones. Consider the opportunities, comforts, and blessings that money has provided for you and your family.
- Envision the future adventures and experiences you look forward to sharing with money. From travel dreams to personal goals, dare to imagine the exciting possibilities that lie ahead in your continued partnership with money.
- Reflect on how you want to feel when interacting with money. Do you seek a sense of abundance, security, or freedom? Define the emotions and energies you wish to cultivate in your ongoing relationship with money.

Explore these prompts and any others that resonate with you as you compose your letters.

CHAPTER 7
Wealth From Within

A SIMPLE 5 letter word like Dodge shares more in common with money than you think. Take "money," another 5 letter word, straightforward. Both can hit hard—in the gym or in your finances. If you can dodge a wrench, you can dodge a ball. Similarly, if you can dodge limiting beliefs about money, you can dodge a scarcity mindset. If you can dodge those "I'm broke" thoughts, you can dodge the broke life altogether. Dodgeball and money can both sting. Dodgeball is physical in the gym class frenzy, and money metaphorically when it slips through our fingers.

Just like the red rubber ball that left a mark on my ribs, and probably yours too, back in the day, money can leave a lasting impact, be it positive or negative.

I remember those gym class days, the air thick with anticipation and fear. Everyone wanted to be on my brother's team in dodgeball, the game where being hit meant you were out, but also their strategy and skill could make you a winner. I dreaded being on his team, not for lack of love, but because I knew his competitive streak all too well. In a way, money is like that too. Money works the same way. If you don't know the rules, the moves, or the mindset to win, you're out before you even start.

Navigating finances without understanding money is like being the target of that red rubber ball in dodgeball—unexpected, often painful, and sometimes a wake-up call. If you can dodge money problems, money can dodge you, but when it hits, it burns like salt in a paper cut — you'll feel it; it leaves a mark. It's not just about dodging or avoiding, but learning to engage with it effectively, to understand its nature, and to make it work for you.

In this journey of discovering your wealth from within, let's explore how we can shift our perspective on money, learn its rules, and engage with it not as a feared opponent but as a potential ally in the game of life, like mastering dodgeball in gym class.

That sting of the dodgeball, I can remember it like it was yesterday, reminiscent of my brother's fierce throws in gym class, right in the gonads, mirrors the sharp encounters we often face with money. It's a game of strategy, awareness, and, most importantly, understanding the rules to succeed. Similarly, uncovering your wealth from within starts by seeing that the actual game of wealth is played inside you first.

Wanting to be someone else is a waste of the person you are. - Kurt Cobain

This journey is about more than financial gain. I want you to keep that in mind as you read through this chapter. It's about tapping into the vast reservoir of potential inside you, ready to transform every part of your life. Wealth from within means real abundance starts with you.

It's about dropping the pressure to prove or perform and tuning into what's already there: your strengths, your desires, your truth. In this chapter, we dig into what makes you truly wealthy, beyond just your bank account. Wealth From Within isn't about chasing the success the world told you to want. It's about getting clear on what lights you up and building a life that feels rich because it's real.

Connecting With Your Wealth Within

What are your unique strengths?

If I asked you this question, could you come up with lists of your unique strengths, or would your mind go blank?

We spend our whole lives trying to fit in, so to truly be yourself, whether that is in your life, relationships, or work, it can get hard to find your unique strengths that only you can bring to your life.

By beginning to connect with your wealthy self and the energy within you, you will be able to answer that question with crystal clarity sooner than later.

To embody your wealthy self—the version of you right now—and ignite your will to show up as that person, you have to get crystal clear on what you really want. Not what you should want or what you're "supposed" to want, but what you truly want at this moment.

What do you really want, the vision that lights you up and gives you purpose?

Step into your wealthy self right now. Own it with clarity, confidence, and no apologies. Be the version of you who already has what you want. Show up, make moves, and make an impact.

Channeling the Wealth in You

When you get unapologetically clear about your Divine Desires, what you really want, the universe shows up. Things align in ways you didn't expect.

The hard part? Most people feel guilty asking for more. Like wanting what you desire somehow makes you selfish. That's just conditioning. You're not robbing anyone by going after what's meant for you.

In this exercise, don't hold back. Say what you actually want. Don't let your inner critic chime in with crap like, "that'll never happen" or "be realistic." Shut that voice down.

Don't overthink it. The longer you sit with it, the more your self-sabotage kicks in. The fast answers, the ones that come without a filter, those are your genuine desires. That's your wealthy self talking. That's the divine part of you showing up.

The first thought that pops up in your head. Hold nothing back.

This exercise works best if you really pour your heart and soul out on these pages.

WEALTH FROM WITHIN: CHANNEL YOUR WEALTHY SELF

Who are you when you're fully tapped into your wealth? Not just money, but the version of you who knows they're rich in every part of life. The one who owns their power, trusts their magic, and creates what they want without second-guessing. That's your Wealth Self. Time to let them lead.

This work really begins with who you are BE-ING and how you affect who you are being. It all stems from your thoughts and beliefs and how you live those out daily.

Ask yourself, "Who is the person who gets the result?" What do they think? What are their beliefs? Their most common feelings are what? Who do they BE? If you already had $10K sitting in your account, what would you be doing right now? Would you move differently? Make bolder choices? Stop stressing over little things?

Who are you as the version of you who knows you're infinitely rich in every area of life and has the power to create what you truly want?

Before moving forward, tap into your wealthy self. This is the version of you who knows they're rich in every part of life. The big-picture, whole-person you who fully owns wealth from within.

Ask yourself:
- *What does your wealthy life look like?*
- *What is the energy of your wealthy self?*
- *What are your wealthy traits and qualities?*
- *What are you available for and ready to open yourself up to?*
- *What are you no longer available for and releasing?*
- *What are your values?*
- *How do you dress?*

- *What is your day like?*
- *How do you interact with people?*
- *What do you invest your time, money, and energy in?*

BE and then DO while embodying that being, you end up HAVING what it is you desire.

Now let's go deeper with embodiment.

This is about stepping into the version of you who already has what you want. It's reverse-engineering from that outcome. This part is more targeted and practical.

Ask yourself this:
- *What is the thing you desire to have?*
- *Who is the person who already has what it is you desire?*
- *What are their thoughts and beliefs?*
- *What are their predominant feelings?*
- *What are the actions they take?*
- *What do they do regularly?*

Do you see how this differs from how you are currently being and doing? What is the biggest thing that needs to shift?

Take a minute to journal on who your wealthy self is and how you can tap into that power starting now.

Now, let's go a little deeper into meeting the wealth from within.

Describe your wealthy self from when they wake up to when they go to bed, answering the following questions on a subcon-scious level - the first thing that comes to mind. Do NOT hold back. Include as much detail as possible.

(Think about all five senses: sight, scent, touch, taste, and sound.). The more time you devote to your answers, the easier the visualization becomes.

Who is your wealthy self?

The version of you who knows they're infinite and can create whatever they desire.

What is the energy of your wealthy self?

What vibe do they carry? Calm? Powerful? Magnetic?

What time do you wake up?

Is it early and intentional or slow and luxurious?

Describe your bed.

Is it big, soft, and full of pillows? Does it face a window? What color is the bedding? What do you see, hear, and feel when you wake up?

Where are you?
Are you in a city condo, a beach house, on a lake, an island, in the mountains, on a yacht, or in your dream home?

Who's with you?
Are you alone, with a partner, family, friends, or pets?

How do you feel when you wake up?
Energized? Grateful? Excited? At peace?

How do you dress?
What's your style? What fabrics, colors, or pieces make you feel wealthy?

What are you having for breakfast?
Where and what are you eating? What does the setting feel like?

What does your morning look like?
Are you doing yoga, meditating, journaling, walking, or reading?

What do your meals look, taste, and feel like?
Are they fresh, fancy, slow, indulgent? Where are you eating—out, home, patio?

What does your afternoon look like?
Are you meeting friends for coffee, going to the spa, shopping, reading, or relaxing?

Who do you surround yourself with?
What people are in your circle? Uplifting? Ambitious? Fun?

What is your day like?
What's your flow from start to finish? Are you working, creating, playing, or leading?

How do you interact with people?
Are you confident, kind, magnetic, calm, or direct?

How do you move through the day?
Do you walk with purpose, ease, or energy?

How do you celebrate?
Small wins? Big ones? Do you treat yourself? Share joy with others?

What does your evening look like?
Is it movie night, making a beautiful dinner, stargazing, time with loved ones?
What are you doing right before bed?
Are you meditating, journaling, stretching, winding down with tea? What time is it?
What were you grateful for when you went to bed the night before?
What moments stood out?
Can you visualize and feel yourself living this?
Is it vivid and clear? (if not, tweak the image in your mind until it actually hits.)
See what you would see, hear what you would hear, and feel all the feelings!
Take some time to journal about who your wealthy self really is—and how you can tap into that power and start showing up like them now.

Life threw me some serious curveballs that changed everything. From figuring out family, money, and identity at a young age to a sudden, life-shaking event that cracked me open. It taught me that no matter what hits you, true wealth and resilience come from within—anchoring and guiding you through the storm.

We've already dug deep into self-discovery and empowerment. My journey through big dreams, tough challenges like moving across the country and becoming a young mom, laid the foundation for what real inner wealth is all about.

When money got tight and an identity crisis hit before my 30s, plus facing a major life-changing loss, I had to rethink what wealth really meant. That struggle was tough, but it revealed the strength and abundance inside me that was waiting to be unlocked.

I encourage you to not just reflect on these words but to live them. Keep exploring and becoming your own version of wealth. My journey from deep lows to personal growth and success shows how powerful it is to align with your wealthy self. It's not just about money; it's about realizing the richness of who you are.

Embrace "Wealth From Within" and step into the abundance waiting for you. Let your experience guide you to a future where abundance isn't just a goal, but your everyday reality.

Wealth can hit hard, just like that dodgeball from gym class. But now you know the game better, the rules, the moves, and how to protect yourself. It's not about dodging wealth forever, but learning to face it with confidence. Keep practicing your strategy, challenge those limiting beliefs, and turn every hit into a chance to grow stronger.

In a way, money is like that too. It's a game where under-standing the rules, the strategy, and how to play can make all the difference between success and struggle. Just like the movie *Dodgeball*, if you can dodge a wrench, you can dodge a ball. If you can dodge limiting beliefs about money, you can dodge a scarcity mindset.

So, let's master the game of wealth, dodgeball style, and learn to navigate financial challenges with skill, strategy, and confidence. Grab your journal and write one thing your wealthy self would do today. Start small, but start. Show up for yourself and own your wealth from within.

CHAPTER 8
The #1 Cause For Success Or Failure In Your Life, Drum Roll Please

HAVE YOU EVER found yourself, after a little too much indulgence in adult beverages, in the most unexpected of places? Picture a warm summer night, the kind where the air is thick and carries the scent of blooming flowers mixed with the earthy aroma of freshly cut grass. In my life, there was a time when I pushed the boundaries of fun a little too far. I ended up passed out in the backyard, face down, with the cool, damp grass imprinting its texture on my cheek. The sky was just beginning to lighten to a soft blue, hinting at the dawn of a new day. Honestly, I think even the lawn was judging me. At 6 a.m., while the world was waking up, I was busy perfecting my 'human lawn ornament' look.

Success or failure comes down to how you see yourself—your self-concept. It's more than just belief; it drives every action and shapes what you get in life.

So, ask yourself: if your reflection doesn't make you happy, isn't it time to change the story you tell about yourself? Your power is inside you, waiting for you to use it. Loving yourself isn't fluff—it's the key to unlocking possibilities you can't even imagine yet. Change how you see yourself, and you change everything around you. The choice is yours. Own it.

Let's back this up with something real. Dr. Carol Dweck, a psychologist from Stanford, spent years studying what actually makes someone successful. And guess what? It wasn't talent. It wasn't intelligence. Mindset was the key. Dr. Dweck coined the term "growth mindset," defining it as the belief that one's abilities and potential are not fixed, but instead flexible and expandable.

People with a growth mindset see failure as feedback. They don't stop when it gets hard—they lean in. Her research shows that what we believe about our capacity directly shapes our outcomes. You think you can grow? You will. You believe you're stuck? You are. Boom—self-fulfilling prophecy.

So, if you're out here wondering why things aren't moving, check your mindset thermostat. Are you locked in a story that says, "I'll never figure this out"? Or are you the person who's like, "Let's learn, let's pivot, let's go again"? One creates resistance. The other creates results.

As I slowly came to, my senses hit me all at once, with the mix of the soft, dew-like damp grass against my skin, a pounding headache, and the stark realization of my vulnerable state.

The once comforting smell of the grass now seemed to mock my poor choices from the night before. Then, from above, a voice broke through my groggy awareness. My neighbor, peeking over the fence with a smirk dancing on her lips, couldn't help but chuckle and say, "Was it worth it last night?"

Her tone was light, tinged with humor. Rather than judgment, recognizing the oh so fresh feeling of youth and excess, rather than condemning it.

This moment, as embarrassing as it was, serves as a stark metaphor for the concept of self that we carry. How often do we overindulge, push past our limits, or find ourselves face down, not in grass perhaps, but in situations that force us to confront our choices and their impact on our self-image? It's in these moments, lying in the backyard of our decisions, that we're compelled to look at our lives from a different perspective, literally from ground level, the ground up.

Reflecting on this, I had to ask myself—was my self-concept so thirsty for escape, validation, or oblivion that it led me here? Isn't this the essence of our journey? Whether nursing a hangover or the fallout of bad choices, it's a chance to face our core beliefs. Do we drink to celebrate or to hide pain?

Have you ever found yourself metaphorically or literally face down in the grass, wondering how your night, your choices, reflect your self-concept? Have you ever clung to the porcelain god, not just from too much booze but from too much escaping reality, only to realize that reality is where your power to change truly lies?

The #1 cause of success or failure in your life is your self-concept.

This chapter's about owning your power, not just when you're killing it, but also when you're screwing up. It's in those messy, actual moments that your true self shows up, ready to drop the truth about how to grow and actually love yourself. It's not just about sobering up from life's chaos, but waking the hell up to the crazy potential and wealth you've already got inside.

Getting aligned with real wealth starts with owning your wealthy self—the version of you that knows abundance isn't just about money. It's about dropping the doubts, fears, and all that crap society feeds you, and tapping into the powerful, unlimited person you really are. When you connect with that, you unlock the ability to create not just financial success but a life that actually feels good—full of purpose, joy, and real meaning.

This is about leveling up to your highest self, breaking free from the usual, and living a life without limits.

Stop lying to yourself

Let's get real for a moment. How many times have you told yourself you'd do something, only to let it slip through the cracks? You know the drill: promising to tackle the laundry pile, scheduling a coffee date for 2 PM, but never showing up. It's a slippery slope we've all slid down at some point. Every time we bail on ourselves, we're sending a message to the universe. We're saying, "Hey, I can't even keep my word to myself, so why bother sending any abundance my way?" If you're wondering why the universe seems to hold out on you, maybe it's time to take a hard look in the mirror. Until we show up for ourselves, we shouldn't expect wealth or anything else to come knocking on our door.

When I first started writing this book, doubt and fear clouded my mind. We've all been there, haven't we? That place where every step feels uncertain, and it scares the hell out of you. But even in those dark moments, there's one thing I cling to with everything I've got—I am 100% committed and always true to myself.

But you know what the hardest part is? It's just showing up. Yup, you heard me right. Just showing up. Because the moment you do, you're not just making a statement to the world; you're sending a crystal-clear message to the universe. You are saying, "Hey, I'm here. I'm serious about this. What are you waiting for?" And when you're serious, when you're committed, the universe has a funny way of rallying behind you, providing the support and help you need to manifest your dreams.

But let's flip the script for a second. What happens when you decide not to show up? Maybe you bail on that 2 PM coffee date, blaming a lack of mood or motivation. Sure, you might think it's no big deal, but let me tell you—it's a trust breaker. Not just between you and the other person, but between you and yourself, and yes, even between you and the universe. And when trust goes out the window, confidence follows suit. Suddenly, you're stuck in a cycle of doubt and hesitation.

The realization that our words don't describe the world, but determine it. This means we can look at people who have done something incredible and not say, "Oh, they can do it, but I can't..."

Understand that anyone who has ever created success has left behind a trail of techniques. If you want to create the same results or even better ones, you can model their success. One of the first steps is to stop lying to yourself.

This ties into our beliefs about what's possible. Take Roger Bannister. He was a relay runner when nobody had broken the four-minute mile. During a race, the person passing him the baton said something he completely misunderstood.

He thought they said they were behind, but that was not what was actually said. So Roger Bannister started running as fast as he could and without even intending to...

He became the first person to run the four-minute mile, which is incredible. Before that, people thought humans could not run that fast.

They believed our bodies were not aerodynamic enough, or our hearts might explode. They just thought it was impossible. But after he ran a four-minute mile, there were a bunch of other runners who reported that they did the same. And now people who are in high school and college and all that stuff are running four-minute miles. We were told, back in the day, that it was impossible.

So often, just seeing someone else doing something and noting how they did it, and observing the techniques can help us go from saying, "oh, this is impossible", to believing and saying, "this is actually possible." All we need is to understand and learn the techniques to do it.

By pushing past what seems impossible, we create breakthroughs and prove that limits don't stand a chance. Think about the Wright brothers, who turned the dream of flying into reality, or Thomas Edison with the light bulb, or Alexander Graham Bell with the first working telephone. Today, we carry cell phones in our pockets that let us video call, record memories, and do things people once thought were impossible. None of it would exist if someone hadn't believed it could be done. Just because you haven't seen something done before, or you don't see anyone in your circle doing it, doesn't mean it's not available to you.

You can follow a model for success, or you can be the first to create one. Sure, you can follow the techniques someone else left behind, but you can also go first, push the boundaries, and lead the way. Here's where we shift gears, raise that financial identity, and step into a version of yourself that's not just surviving but thriving.

How do we do that? Through identity and collapsing timelines. Right now, you're living on a specific timeline. Imagine you are just going about your day, right?

There are different versions of you out there, living different financial realities. You've got your 80K-a-year self, your millionaire self, and maybe even your 30K-a-year self kicking it in the mix.

It changes everything when you realize this. All these versions of you are just floating around. You're only really experiencing one of them right now, consciously at least. It's like you're on this timeline, and each version of you is on a different track. Now, to shift consciously into a different timeline, you must slightly alter your identity. It's like bringing the timeline you're living right now and the one you want to be in together, collapsing them into one. And how do you do that? By changing up your identity.

Right now, you might be trying to manifest from the identity of an 80K-a-year earner, but you need to manifest from the identity of a six-figure or seven-figure earner — if that's what you want. How you do this is so, so simple.

I want you to answer this aloud right now: If you were already a six-figure or seven-figure earner—or whatever amount you want to call in—how would you think, feel, act, and speak to yourself and others? What would you declare? What would you ask for? And how would you BE? This BE-ing is the key. Your identity is BE-ing. You must BE this version of you NOW to create that reality and collapse the timeline.

Become that version of yourself who already has what you want. Act like you already are that person. Identity is the easiest way to lock in habits.

Let's get real for a sec. We've all had those days when hitting the gym feels like a chore. Who hasn't struggled to lace up those sneakers and just get moving? I knew deep down I needed to move, not for some big fitness goal, just to feel good.

See, I was a yoga instructor, but I wasn't practicing as much as I should've been. So, I wanted to dial up my game, clear my head, and tap into that post-workout high.

It wasn't just about burning calories; it was about finding clarity, processing emotions, and shedding what no longer served me. So, I started affirming to myself, "I AM a fit person. I AM an exerciser. I work out all the time." It wasn't about faking it 'til you make it; it was about stepping into that version of myself and owning it.

Your identity sets the tone for everything. If you want that six-figure lifestyle, set your thermostat there. BE that person. Ask, "If I already had that wealth, how would, I think, feel, act? What choices would I make today?"

Imagine a world where everyone loves themselves so much they don't care what others think—about opinions, skin color, sexuality, talents, education, possessions, religion, or just being real. What if every day started with self-love and knowing your value?

If we shook off shame, guilt, doubt, and embraced what we want without hesitation—that's the world I'd sign up for. It's about living that vision and making it real, step by step.

BE DO HAVE MODEL

Many people have this backwards, so they believe that when they **HAVE** the wealth, then they will **DO** the things, then they will act like they have the wealth they want, then they will **BE** wealthy.

People are out there chasing ways of being. They want to be wealthy, but what they don't get is that when you embody that wealth now, everything around you starts reflecting it. It's about being that version of yourself first, then making moves that prove it.

How often have you caught yourself saying things like, "Once I **have** $5k in my bank account, **then** I'll finally go on my honeymoon or **once** my kids move out, **then** I'll **be** successful," or "Once I **have** the beach-ready bod, **then** I'll go out on dates and then I'll **be** happy and in love!"

GREAT SCOTT!

You're essentially saying, if the money doesn't come in, then you won't pursue your dreams and be successful. Or if you don't have a smokin' hot body, then you won't allow yourself love and happiness.

This is a broken model.
This is living in effect and being a victim of your external reality.
This takes all your power away and is very limiting.

The Be, Do, Have Model

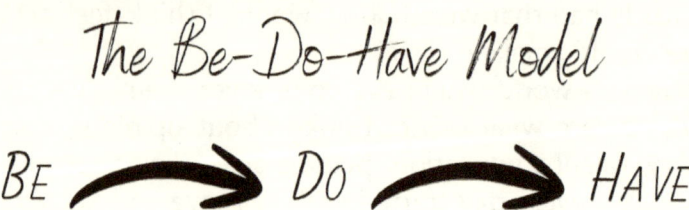

Create a way of BEing in alignment with your goal → Your way of BEing will propel you into action → The results of your actions will bring YOU to your goal

Many people have it backwards. They think external stuff creates the feeling inside, like, "When I have the money, I'll feel like a millionaire" or "I'll be happy once I have X." That mindset doesn't work.

Real success and happiness start from within. It's BE-ing first, then DO-ing, then HAVE-ing. When you own that version of yourself now, your actions align, results follow, and your reality shifts.

Most people try to fix the outside first, but real change comes from within. When you fully embrace who you are right now, everything else starts falling into place. You do things that vibe with that version of you and before you know it, you're living a reality that matches your vibe. Dig deep into who you are and watch your life ripple outward. Trying to change the outside first won't shift what's inside. That is not how it works. It's all about identity. That's where the magic happens. Dive deep into who you truly are and watch your reality shift right before your eyes.

I invite you to approach your goals using the BE, DO, HAVE model. It's way more powerful and guaranteed to create results.

The Be-Do-Have model is a simple yet powerful framework for achieving your goals and manifesting your desires. It basically breaks down like this:

1. **Be:** This is where you start. You embody the qualities and characteristics of the person who already has what you want.

It's like stepping into the shoes of your future self. Want to be wealthy? Start thinking, acting, and feeling like a wealthy person. It's all about mindset.

2. **Do:** Next up, you take action! You can't just sit back and wait for the universe to hand you everything on a silver platter. You roll up your sleeves and get to work. Take consistent, focused action toward your goals, and let nothing hold you back.

3. **Have:** Ah, the sweet, sweet payoff. Once you've done the work and embodied the right mindset, the universe lines up to give you what you desire. Whether it's wealth, success, love, or happiness, you'll see your dreams becoming reality.

Ask yourself, "Who's the person who gets the result?" What do they think? What do they believe? What are their strongest feelings? Who are they BE-ing? As the person who already has $20k in their bank account, what would they be doing? When you BE and then DO while fully embodying that BE-ing, you end up HAVING what YOU desire.

Give this a try:
- What is the thing you desire to have ?
- Who is the person who already has what you desire?
- What are their thoughts and beliefs?
- What are their strongest or most important feelings?
- What actions do they take? What do they do regularly?

Do you see how this differs from the way you are currently being and doing?

What is the biggest thing that needs to shift for you to uplevel —your mindset, your beliefs, your story, or how you relate to money and your relationship with it? Your results start with who you decide to be. When your actions match that identity, wealth becomes inevitable.

You control what happens next. So, stop waiting, stop questioning, and start deciding. This is your moment to rise, to claim it, to become it. No more playing small. Own your power and make it undeniable.

You've just taken your first step into the Sequence to Aligned Wealth by diving deep *within* — into the most powerful place you'll ever explore.

Everything starts here. Before the money, before the clients, before the business, before the dream car or house, *before anything external*, you must know and own the version of you who already has it all. That version lives inside you right now.

You are not separate from them. They're not a future goal. They're already here, buried under layers of old programming, limiting beliefs, and outdated paradigms. The wealthy version of you doesn't hustle for worthiness. They don't question if they're enough. They don't shrink to make others comfortable. They walk into a room like they own the energy because they are the energy.

Wealth isn't something you chase—it's something you *embody*.

This "W" section reminds you that your external results are a direct mirror of your internal reality. If you aren't seeing money or opportunities flow in yet, it's not because you're broken—it's because your identity hasn't fully aligned with the version of yourself that receives easily.

So, who is that version of you?

They're bold.

They're unapologetic.

They walk with certainty.

They don't wait for validation because they know they're already powerful.

They don't hope wealth will show up; they expect it. You've always been the source of wealth; it's just waiting for you to claim it. You are the energetic match to everything you desire. But it won't activate until you stop seeking wealth outside of yourself and start reclaiming it from within.

It's time to *decide* that you're that person now.

Not next year.

Not after summer.

Not after the next job or the next promotion.

Not when you've lost 10 pounds or gained 10 followers.

Now. Right now.

That decision? That's what flips the switch. That's what opens the floodgates.

Wealth has never been about what you do. It has always been about who you are. Identity is the engine behind every result you see in your life. When you see yourself as broke, stuck, or unworthy, life mirrors that vision back to you. When you see yourself as powerful, capable, and worthy, life responds with opportunity.

The truth is that you have never been broken, and you have never been behind. You have only been living in a version of yourself that felt smaller than the truth of who you are. That version served its purpose and taught you lessons, but it no longer defines you.

You do not need to search for wealth, and you do not need to wait for it. You are the source. Wealth already lives within you, flowing through your choices, your energy, and the way you decide to show up each day.

You are not walking a path of becoming someone new. You are remembering the truth of who you have always been. Each time you choose to live from that truth, you expand the level of wealth and possibility available to you.

And when you live fully from that truth, wealth will rise to meet you without hesitation.

E
ELICIT

THIS IS WHERE THE REAL SHIFT STARTS

Always, always believe in yourself, because if you don't, then who will, sweetie?
— Marilyn Monroe

THIS IS THE part where we stop lying to ourselves, because real wealth demands honesty — and that honesty starts now.

This isn't about manifesting with moon water or journaling your feelings into oblivion. This is about pulling the curtain back and finally getting honest with yourself about what's actually going on under the surface.

I'm talking about the habits that blow your bank account up before payday. The way you fantasize about your "someday" life while ignoring what's in front of you right now.

This section is your permission slip to stop pretending and start paying attention. To finally break the cycle and see what's really going on behind the scenes. No blame, no guilt. Just straight-up owning your part.

We are not here to sugarcoat your habits. We are here to call them out, because once you see the truth, you can change it. And when you change it, your whole life shifts. Grab a pen and get honest with yourself. You cannot fix what you refuse to face, and you will never level up while carrying baggage you will not name.

Ready? Let's ELICIT.

CHAPTER 9
Calibrate Your Compass: True North Or Bust

My due date was supposed to be a day brimming with anticipation and joy, but instead of a serene birthing experience, chaos unfurled on the day I was due to give birth to my second son. Life, with its twisted sense of humor, had other plans.

Of all days, my brother and Daryll hit up the bar. This wasn't just any bar visit—this one turned into a scene straight out of a wild west movie. A brawl broke out, and amidst the chaos, Daryll got tasered. Talk about bad timing and worse luck. There I was, on my due date, pissed off, home alone, and expecting to cradle a newborn. Instead, I got a late-night call from the police station. "Is this the sister of Travis and the girlfriend of Daryll?" the officer asked. My heart plummeted. I thought, "This can't be happening!" After the officer told me they had been arrested and I could come bail them out, I lost it. I was fuming mad they had gone out at all, and the thought of bailing them out made me even angrier. I didn't want to go.

Furious and ready to unleash nine months of pent-up hormonal rage, I found out they were arrested for their part in the bar fight. I was there not to bail them out, but to give them a piece of my mind.

However, the sight of me, heavily pregnant and fuming, must have struck a chord with the officer. He let them off the hook. No bail required—just a $200 donation to Santa's Anonymous. Irony at its finest.

Daryll actually missed my second son Tatum's birth because of this chaos. And it wasn't the only time he wasn't there for a major moment. When my first son, Phoenix, was born, Daryll was miles away, racing back on a bus from a job out of town. He was working hard, always on the move to provide for us, but it meant he missed the most critical family moments of all.

Now, Daryll's track record with timing wasn't exactly stellar, and not just because he liked to live on the edge, but because sometimes life just gets in the way.

There I was, ready to welcome our second child, while Daryll sat in jail on my due date. Thankfully, I didn't deliver that night while my brother and Daryll were busy getting cozy in shackles. Guess the baby was waiting for a less eventful welcome party. Two weeks later, we had to drive two hours to the nearest city because I was scheduled to be induced. But that same afternoon, Daryll had to drive back to our town to get his fingerprints taken because of the bar fight. All alone... I didn't have to get induced after all. I guess Tatum couldn't wait for his dad or a doctor, because an intern delivered him less than an hour after Daryll left.

Looking back, all that chaos and missed timing wasn't random — it was a wake-up call. These weren't just stories. They were reminders of how quickly life can knock you off balance if you let it. Chaos, bad timing, and unexpected curveballs will always show up, even when you're supposed to feel the most grounded. This is your reminder to find your center when life throws chaos your way. It's time to go Back to the Future, not the one built from other people's timelines, but the one that's actually yours to live.

Then there was my daughter, Raya, where history painfully repeated itself. Daryll was out of town for work again, same script, different day. Just hours after he flew back to work, my water broke, and once more, he missed another birth by mere timing. Life felt like a cruel joke, testing our resilience at every turn. But despite these absences, it was clear Daryll was grinding hard for us, chasing a better financial future —even if it meant missing moments he didn't even know he was sacrificing.

It's impossible not to feel a mix of frustration, laughter, and acceptance over what we gave up for stability. Daryll's constant absence wasn't planned or taken lightly. It was the heavy price we paid trying to balance life's demands with our financial goals.

Through the lens of humor, we can see the absurdity of the situations we find ourselves in. Yet, beneath the laughter lies the raw, unvarnished truth of our journey, marked by missed moments and the relentless pursuit of financial security. These stories aren't just anecdotes; they are the vivid, emotional chapters of our lives, illustrating the profound sacrifices made in the quest for stability and success.

Just like you, just like me, every one of us has lived through chaos and moments that tested us. Like any journey, you need to know where you're starting, where you're headed, and have a compass to keep you on track.

This book cuts through the noise and focuses on what actually moves the needle. This chapter is about your "Divine Desire", your life's cheat code. Spend 20% of your time here, and you'll get 80% of the wins everywhere else.

Divine Desire vs. Outcome Goal vs. Process Goals — What's the Difference?

Your **Divine Desire** is your big, soul-level vision, the life you're truly meant to live. It's your why, your purpose, the ultimate thing that lights you up and drives you forward. Think of it as your personal North Star guiding everything you do.

Your **Outcome Goal** is one specific, concrete result you want to hit that supports your Divine Desire. It's measurable and focused, like a milestone on your journey. For example, if your Divine Desire is *vibrant health*, a Top Outcome Goal might be *losing 10 pounds in 3 months* or *running a 5K*.

Your **Process Goals** are the regular actions or habits you commit to that keep you on track toward your Top Outcome Goals. They're the daily or weekly steps that build momentum and make your milestones achievable. For example, if your Top Outcome Goal is losing 10 pounds, your Process Goals might include exercising 3 times a week, tracking your meals, and getting 8 hours of sleep nightly.

In short: Divine Desire sets the vision, Outcome Goals mark the milestones, and Process Goals are the consistent actions that get you there.

Start by locking in your Divine Desire, then break it into clear outcome goals that move you forward step by step. Once the vision is set, momentum builds naturally, and success begins to stack in your favor.

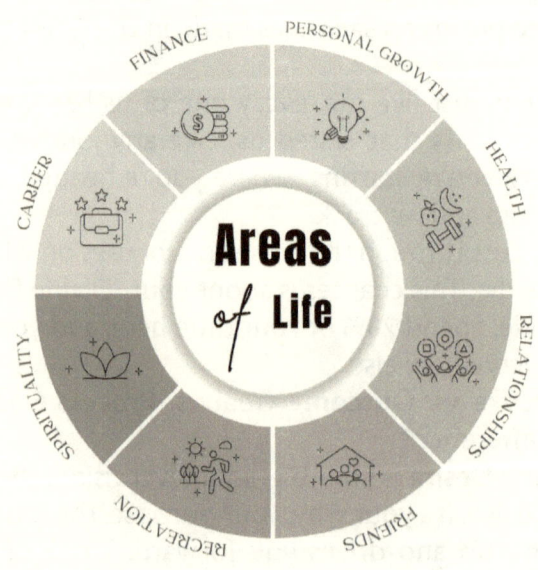

What Each Area really Means

HEALTH
Fitness
Sleep
Nutrition
Self-Care
Wellness

RELATIONSHIPS
Connection
Love
Support
Communication
Intimacy

FRIENDS
Quality Time
Bonding
Laughter
Support
Community

PERSONAL GROWTH
Mindset Work
Education
Learning
Reading
Reflection

CAREER
Purpose
Clients
Workload
Fulliment
Leadership

RECREATION
Play
Hobbies
Adventures
Leisure
Joy

FINANCE
Income
Budgeting
Spending
Savings
Investments

SPIRITUALITY
Nature
Source
Faith
Giving Back
Gratitude

THE GOAL LADDER

- Divine Desire → The North Star. Your big, soul-level vision.
- Outcome Goal → The milestone. A measurable result you can track and celebrate.
- Process Goals → The steps. The daily or weekly actions that keep you moving.

Health Example
- Divine Desire: Vibrant health and energy
- Outcome Goal: Lose 10 pounds in 3 months
- Process Goals: Exercise 3x weekly, track meals, sleep 8 hours

Business Example
- Divine Desire: A thriving business that creates freedom
- Outcome Goal: $20k in monthly revenue
- Process Goals: Launch one new offer, grow email list weekly, post consistent content

Relationships Example
- Divine Desire: Deep connection and love
- Outcome Goal: Weekly quality time with partner
- Process Goals: Schedule date nights, communicate openly, practice gratitude daily

IDENTIFY THE BIG VISION FOR YOUR LIFE

THINK BIG AND limitless as you consider these questions. Imagine all the endless possibilities waiting for you.

- If no one's judgment or side-eyes could touch you, what bold thing would you bring into the world that's guaranteed to rock?
- What wild dreams are you hiding deep inside — the ones you haven't even dared to whisper to yourself?
- If you could guarantee your own success and build your

perfect world, what would it look like? What would make you feel truly amazing?

Now, ground those big visions into specifics. Ask yourself:

- When you think about the bigger vision for your life, what is it you desire?
- What's the legacy you want to leave?
- What's your 5-year goal?
- Your 1-year goal?
- What are your 3–6 month goals?
- What are your top goals and desires for this book's experience?

UNCOVER YOUR DIVINE DESIRE

Step 1: Lock In Your Outcome Goals

For each area of life, write 1–3 outcome goals—the big results you want to create in the next 3–6 months. Think of outcome goals as the end game or what success looks like. If anything was possible (spoiler: it is), what would you make happen?

Heads up: I'll explain the "Rate Yourself" column in Step 2. Leave it blank for now!

Example Goals

Health + Wellness:

- Weigh 145 lbs
- Eliminate all gluten and dairy
- Feel sexy in a bathing suit
- Sleep 8–9 hours a night
- Exercise 5x a week

Business + Career:

- Launch my first product into the world with 5 paying customers

- Create consistent $20k months
- Be a guest on 5 podcasts
- Grow my email list to 5k customers

YOUR TURN

You don't need to fill in every category right away. Start with the areas that feel most important to you now, then expand over time.

Finances

Rate Yourself	Outcome Goals
	1. 2. 3.

Health + Wellness

Rate Yourself	Outcome Goals
	1. 2. 3.

Personal Growth & Spirituality

Rate Yourself	Outcome Goals
	1. 2. 3.

Relationships (Partnership, Family, Friends)

Rate Yourself	Outcome Goals
	1. 2. 3.

Career / Business

Rate Yourself	Outcome Goals
	1. 2. 3.

Lifestyle (Fun, Enjoyment, Home Environment)

Rate Yourself	Outcome Goals
	1.
	2.
	3.

Step 2: Rate Yourself

On a scale of 0 to 10, rate how far (0) or close (10) you are to achieving your outcome goals in each area of life. Just flip back and drop your rating in the "Rate Yourself" column.

Step 3: Get Clear On Your Priorities

Look at where you're at in each area and reflect on what you want to prioritize in the next 30 days. Rank each one in order of priority — 1 being most important, 10 being least important.

Step 4: Determine Your Divine Desire

These big goals across your life are powerful and will make an impact. While you could scatter your energy, focus on the one area that, if you really locked in on it now, would make everything else easier or fall into place.

Don't worry about right or wrong here. Trust what feels true. Just because your big vision might be to create $20k or even $50k months, it doesn't mean your Divine Desire has to be business. If focusing on health or wellness first helps you hit those numbers later, perfect. You can set outcome goals in every area of life, but ask yourself: If you made one area your #1 focus, which one would naturally lift the rest?

Once you've chosen it, the way you phrase your goals matters. Always state your outcomes positively. Most people can list what they don't want, but few can say clearly what they do want. That's why they stay stuck on the problem instead of the solution. When you focus on what you don't want, you stay stuck in the problem. But when your attention is on what you desire, energy flows there — and your mind starts spotting solutions.

For example:
- Instead of saying, *"I don't want to fight with my partner,"* say, *"I desire open, loving communication with my partner."*
- Instead of saying, *"I don't want to live paycheck to paycheck,"* say, *"I desire consistent overflow and financial security."*
- Instead of saying, *"I don't want to feel tired all the time,"* say, *"I desire vibrant energy and a strong, healthy body."*

Once you know your Divine Desire, ask yourself: *Which area of your life does it touch the most?*

Outcome Goal Clarity

- **Define it clearly.** Looking at the area of life that is your Divine Desire, what is the top outcome goabut of the three you want to focus on? Be as specific as possible.
- **Describe success.** How will you know you have it? Is it money in the bank, a number on the scale, or the way you feel?
- **Imagine it fully.** What will you see, hear, feel, and experience once you've reached it?
- **Take stock.** Where are you right now in relation to your desired outcome?
- **List your resources.** What personal strengths, tools, or support do you already have to help you reach your goal?
- **Find expanders.** Do you know someone who has achieved what you want? What resources did they have to get there — and how might you apply those to your own journey?
- **Apply what you see.** How can you use these resources or strategies yourself?
- **Know your why.** Why is this goal so important to you? What will it make possible in your life?

- **Notice the ripple.** Who else will be affected by this change, and how will their lives improve?

Process Goal Clarity

Process goals are the regular actions or habits you commit to that will help you hit your outcome goals. They're the daily steps that turn your big vision into reality. Write down a few process goals that will keep you on track toward your top outcome goal.

Example (Wealth):

- Divine Desire: Financial freedom and overflow
- Outcome Goal: Consistent $20k months
- Process Goals:

Track income and expenses weekly (numbers as feedback, not judgment).

Create one piece of value-driven content daily that connects with potential clients.

Schedule 3 sales conversations or follow-ups each week.

Review money mindset affirmations or visualizations every morning.

Set aside 10% of all income into savings or investments.

Celebrate every win — no matter how small — to reinforce momentum.

Example (Health):

- Divine Desire: Vibrant health and energy
- Top Outcome Goal: Lose 5 lbs
- Process Goals

> Do a quick daily mental scan, notice where your thoughts are wandering, and redirect them to match the version of you who's already 5 lbs lighter.
>
> Track your weight (use the number as feedback, not failure).
>
> Try on your bathing suit daily and anchor a state of confidence.

Exercise 3x per week.

Walk 10,000 steps daily.

Grocery shop and prepare healthy food every Sunday.

Keep a food journal or use a food tracker app to notice what you ate and how it made you feel.

Align With Your Bigger Vision

Do your Divine Desire, outcome goals, and process goals line up with the bigger vision you just clarified at the begining of the chapter?

If they do, keep moving forward. If not, pause and adjust — choose the desire and goals that truly match the vision you want to live.

Overcome Whatever's Held You Back

I'm willing to bet this isn't the first time you've set goals like these. There's a reason (or three) you haven't created the results you wanted up to now — so it's time to dig deep.

Why haven't you achieved what you desire (yet)?

- Reflecting on your outcome goals for your divine desire, why do you think you haven't achieved your goals up to this point?
- What current thoughts, beliefs, feelings, habits, patterns, actions, or behaviors are getting in the way?
- Be honest: what fears come up? What are you afraid of if you were to hit these goals?
- What are you afraid of losing if you reach these goals?
- Which parts of the process or journey intimidate you the most?
- What are you afraid will happen if you DON'T hit your goals?
- What are you afraid will happen if you DO hit your goals?
- What has not having or creating these goals cost you so far?

Turn It Around

Imagine all the *good stuff* that could happen when you follow through on your process goals and hit your outcome goals.

- List the positive things the process goals will create.
- List every amazing thing that becomes possible when you hit those outcome goals.
- How does your life change? How does it ripple out to others?

Dive Deeper: Create New Non-Negotiables

What are your non-negotiables for hitting your top outcome goal? What are you committed to experiencing along the way — and how do you want to feel, not just when you arrive, but every step of the journey?

For example:

I want to feel energized, so I'll get 8 hours of sleep and eat nourishing foods.

I want to feel connected with family and friends, so I'm only available to work 6 hours a day.

Use this moment to call out the old "rules" you've been living by and choose what's true for you *now*. *I used to live by the rule that the harder I worked, the more money I made.*

Now, I live by the rule that the more fun I have and the more I trust, the more wealth and impact flow in.

Who Do You Want to Be?

Before you chase any outcome, ask yourself this: **Who do you want to be while creating it?** How do you want to show up? Get crystal clear on the version of you who owns their thoughts, feelings, actions, and energy, and knows limitless possibilities are always on the table.

Reminder: It's who you become in the process that makes your goals inevitable. When people stay scared and never try, they stay stuck. But in the doing — in the messy, brave action — you change, you shift, and you level up.

Why is now the time to change?

If you've been second-guessing the Divine Desires you already defined or struggling to focus on one area, remember this: a Divine Desire doesn't mean you're only focusing on that one thing. For example, when my Divine Desire was Health + Wellness, I wasn't just eating healthy, working out, and staying calm. I was also working on my business and making time for my husband and kids. HOWEVER, my Divine Desire came FIRST. No matter what.

My process goals were non-negotiable — like walking 10k steps, eating veggies, and working out a set number of times a week. And if I was ever torn between getting something done or going for my walk? It was the walk EVERY SINGLE TIME. The truth? After that walk, I felt more inspired and ready to handle whatever needed doing.

Another way to think of this is to ask: what's the one thing that will have a domino effect on the other areas of life? It's not about choosing one over the other, but about deciding which one will best support everything else.

Clarity means nothing without commitment.
Are you ready to commit to all of this now?
Check one:
☐ Yes
☐ Hell Yes

CHAPTER 10
The Gamble: More Than Just Loose Change

As a teenager, every Friday night felt like stepping into a casino. It was a gamble of choice and chance that went beyond pocket change with my dad. The ritual was simple, yet full of life lessons about money's elusive nature. I would ask for money for the weekend, and he would give me a choice: the change in his pocket or the money in his wallet. It was fun and thrilling, and I waited all week for the weekend to hit so I could ask my dad for a couple of bucks to go out on the town on a Friday night. This weekly gamble was more than a game; it was a lesson in choices, risk, value perception, and financial decision-making.

By having to pick between the change in his pocket or the bill in his wallet, I was:

- **Learning to weigh risk and reward.** One option might have been safer (I could hear the jingle of coins, so I knew something was there) while the other felt riskier but had the potential for a bigger payoff.
- **Learning about value perception.** What looked like the better choice might not always be the better choice. Sometimes the pocket change could've been more than the single bill.
- **Learning decision-making under pressure.** I had to choose without knowing for sure, which mirrors the kinds

of decisions I face with money later in life — investing, spending, saving.

So the real lesson? Money isn't just about what's in front of you, it's about how you see it, weigh it, and decide.

Some weeks, his pockets were stuffed with coins, like a mini treasure chest, sometimes even worth more than the crumpled bill in his wallet. But other times, it was the opposite. That small pile of change didn't come close to the surprise bill hidden in there. This back-and-forth of luck and choice was always a bit of a rollercoaster.

This childhood experience with my dad was more than a playful exchange; it shaped how I saw money and the importance of making smart choices. It taught me that monetary worth isn't always visible at first glance and that the allure of apparent abundance can sometimes lead to overlooked opportunities. These early lessons in financial decision-making laid the groundwork for understanding the dynamic and often unpredictable nature of money.

Transitioning into the story of growing up and dealing with money, the fun and clever lessons with my dad really stood out against the serious, life-changing experience with Daryll.

The Crash That Changed Everything

The day I received the call about my husband's accident was a day that forever altered the trajectory of our financial life.

I was sitting at the dentist's office, waiting to get my wisdom tooth pulled...and my cell phone rang...

The person on the other end of the line informed me of his accident. The stark reality of a 4,000-pound machine crushing him underground was a nightmare turned into reality, a moment where time stood still, and the situation painfully highlighted the fragility of life and financial stability.

I couldn't comprehend what was being voiced to me on the other end of the phone call, people staring at me in the sitting room of the dentist's office, not knowing why I turned white as a ghost.

My husband, the primary breadwinner, is now bedridden and wheelchair-bound, bringing our income to a grinding halt. Extra costs piled up fast, equipment, supplies, and everything insurance didn't cover, on top of our regular expenses, stretching our financial reserves thinner by the day. Our living room became a makeshift hospital room, a constant reminder of the accident's toll on our lives and finances.

Money was tight, and the pressure was real. We faced the dual challenge of managing a health crisis and a financial downturn. Not knowing if Daryll would recover and the bills piling up every day had stress hanging over us like a damn storm cloud. This all happened just a week after we drove across the country to our best man's wedding. Flights were too expensive, so we made it a road trip and brought my mom along since she had never been to beautiful British Columbia. We danced, laughed, and soaked in every moment.

Money wasn't even a thought until Daryll's pelvis shattered thousands of feet underground, and everything changed. It was a time filled with tough decisions, constant sacrifices, and the harsh reality of how vulnerable we really were. We had a six-month-old, a six-year-old, and a nine-year-old, and suddenly, no income coming in. This chapter of our life was not just about the physical healing from Daryll's injuries, but also about facing the curveballs life throws at you when you least expect it. It showed us how strong we really are, taught us the real value of health, how unpredictable life can be, and why having a solid financial plan is non-negotiable.

These experiences, both the playful yet insightful lessons with my dad and the profound life-changing event with Daryll, have helped to shape my understanding of money. One was fun and the other scary. They have taught me about the inherent risks, the importance of preparedness, and the profound impact financial decisions can have on our lives.

Understanding Your Money Story

A belief is just a thought you keep repeating until it feels like the absolute truth. Those thoughts shape your beliefs, and those beliefs create the stories and habits you carry around money. Can you recall a time when money's absence hit hard, like when that accident left Daryll bedridden and our finances in chaos. Being a caregiver, mother, and anchor during that period was a heavy chapter in my money story, showing just how fragile financial security is and how much strength it takes to get through it.

What Does It Mean to Elicit Your Money Story?

Elicit means to bring something hidden to the surface—like a feeling, memory, or truth. So, when we say "Elicit Your Money Story," we're talking about uncovering all those beliefs, emotions, habits, and experiences about money that you picked up growing up, whether from your family, culture, or past moments.

What matters is shining a light on what's driving how you think, feel, and act around money. Because until you know what's really going on beneath the surface, you can't change it or take control of your financial story. This process helps you get real, so you can rewrite your money mindset and start making choices that actually serve you.

The First Step: Eliciting Your Money Story

Eliciting your money story involves exploring the emotions and beliefs about money formed in childhood and carried into adulthood.

Questions to Think About:

- What are your current beliefs about money, and how do they trace back to your childhood experiences?
- When you think about money, what emotions come up? Where do you feel them in your body—stomach, throat, head, or heart?
- What do you believe about money right now? Where did those beliefs come from?
- How did your family talk about money when you were growing up?
- What money habits did you pick up from your parents or caregivers?

- What's a money memory that still sticks with you—good or bad?
- How do you really feel about spending money compared to saving it?
- What fears or worries pop up when you think about your finances?
- How has your money story shaped the choices you make and the opportunities you've had?

Digging into these questions will get you closer to the truth behind your money mindset.

Adding to Your Story

My money story was shaped by playful lessons, painful crises, and unexpected events that happen in our lives, all of which build the beliefs we carry about money. Missing births and accidents happened because of tough financial choices made out of necessity, not want. These moments remind us how much power money can have over our lives. Money doesn't run the show. You do.

One way to reclaim that power is by paying close attention to your money story. These experiences, both the playful lessons with my dad and the life-changing event with my husband, have helped shape my understanding of money. They taught me about risks, the importance of being prepared, and the serious impact financial decisions have on our lives. It's not just about journaling or positive thinking; it's about who you become through the process.

Positive thinking is everywhere, but negative subconscious beliefs hit just as hard. Our thoughts shape our reality; what you believe, you create. Settling for less than you want is selling yourself short. You made your current money story with your thoughts, so you can rewrite it the same way. Believing in what you can't yet see is where the real shift happens. Change your mindset first, and the proof will follow.

Money is energy, plain and simple. It responds to the way you think, feel, and act. We've been conditioned to grind for it, but the truth is money flows when your energy matches abundance. How you show up on the inside shows up in your outside world. Your thoughts shape your beliefs, and your beliefs shape what you experience. If a bad minute can wreck a good day, then why can't a good minute fix a bad day? Shift the focus. Put your attention on what's working, on what you want, and on what you already have. That's when your frequency rises, doors open, and opportunities show up.

Two Tips to Change Your State

Did you know you can flip your emotions in seconds? Shifting your state doesn't just change your mood, it changes how you show up for wealth. The Wonder Woman pose, standing tall with hands on hips for 16 seconds, fires up confidence and authority — the same energy you need to make bold money moves. Another way is recalling a time you felt unstoppable excitement and stepping back into that feeling. That surge of energy can instantly remind you that one bad moment doesn't get to hijack your whole day. When you shift your state, you shift your decisions — and your financial reality follows. (I'll share a powerful NLP mindset-shifting technique designed to elicit a vivid state in Chapter 22: The Frequency of Money)

My dad's fun gambling lessons mixed with the hard hit of my husband's accident show how money stories get made. It's all about experiences, mindset, and energy, the real drivers of our financial path. After those big shifts, I saw just how much my beliefs, especially the negative ones, had quietly shaped my money reality and steered my life without me even noticing. Think about that nagging thought in your head, saying success is out of reach or financial stability is just a pipe dream. That belief, probably born from scarcity or tough times you've seen, might not hold up when you step back and look at the whole picture. It's like climbing a mountain and realizing what felt huge before is just a small part of a much bigger view.

Sometimes when you're stuck in your money struggles, it's hard to see the bigger picture. What you believe feels like fact, but most of the time it's just stories you keep telling yourself. Getting a fresh take, whether from a friend, a mentor, or just stepping back and being real with yourself, can show you where those stories fall apart. That's where the real shift happens. Start questioning those beliefs. Ask yourself, "What if I just haven't figured it out yet?" That one word "yet" turns a dead end into a new possibility. It flips stuck thoughts into a fresh chance to move forward.

This isn't about crunching numbers or hunting for some magic formula. It's about shifting how you see money and success. Breaking down the old beliefs that boxed you in and building new ones rooted in truth. That shift is what sets the stage for a future that feels richer, freer, and fully yours.

CHANGING YOUR BELIEFS

What's one negative belief you have about wealth?

- What changes when you zoom out and see the bigger picture?
- If a fly on the wall watched how you think about that belief, what might it notice?
- How silly or surprising would your money belief look from its perspective?
- What if you challenge that belief?

Example of a challenged belief:
Belief: *I'll never be financially secure.*
Question: *How do you know you'll never be financially secure?*
Belief: *Because I've always struggled with money.*
Question: *You've always struggled?*
Belief: *Yeah.*
Question: *Not even when you had a good month or got a raise?*
Belief: *Well, I guess there were a few times.*

What if you change the wording of your belief and pay attention to your way of communicating? Avoid words like, can't, or never.

What happens if you add the word "yet"?

Reflecting on those Friday nights with my dad and the tough times with my husband, it's like life's been teaching me the value of money in its own unique way for a while now. From the simple coin tosses with my dad to the complex challenges we faced during my husband's recovery, it's all been part of a bigger lesson. These stories aren't just about money; they're about the choices we make and how we deal with the cards we're dealt. They taught me that even when things seem out of control, we can still move forward, make smart choices, and keep our eyes on what we want our financial future to look like. It's about taking those lessons, whether they come from a game of chance with change in our pockets or navigating life's bigger storms, and using them to build a better, more secure future.

As you think about your own money stories, remember that it's in your power to change the narrative, to shift from simply getting by to truly thriving.

CHAPTER 11
The Great Goal Heist - Busting Goals Like You Own The Joint

I STARED DOWN at yet another list of goals. Ambitious, sparkly, and just as unattainable as spelling supercalifragilisticexpialidocious.

But staring at goals and knowing how to actually hit them are two very different things. What's the first step to be hitting those six- or seven-figure months? You might be thinking, "If I knew, I'd already be there, Christina."

We all want more money, freedom, and to hit our goals But most of us are stuck at square one, unsure of where to begin. Goal-setting isn't about dreaming big and hoping. It's about breaking that dream down into clear, actionable steps, and I'm here to take you from "What the hell do I do?" to "Hell yeah, I'm on it!"

I wasn't born with an entrepreneur badge. I hit my Big 3-0 and had a full-on identity crisis. I thought, "Now what?" Fast forward, and here I am, a proud NLP trainer, helping people turn their financial dreams into reality. I grew up in chilly Northern Ontario, where seniors outnumber the young and the cold bites deep. Along the way, I cracked the code on how to embed goals deep into your subconscious so they actually stick and grow—no fairy dust needed.

Ever met people so vague about their goals? It's almost comical. "I want, um, happiness?"

"I don't know what I want."

"I know what I don't want—I don't want debt, I don't want anxiety, I don't want this, I don't want that."

But that's not what I'm asking you. I'm not asking what you don't want. I'm asking what you do want.

If you don't know your destination, you'll end up going in circles. I'm here to cut through the bullshit and help you find your financial North Star.

Most people set boring goals like "Make more money." Yawn. Get specific. Name the exact amount, down to the last cent. And don't make it just about cash. Pick goals that light a fire in your belly and make you jump out of bed, ready to conquer the world.

During my NLP training, I discovered techniques that help you embed goals like a pro. That's one of the reasons why I became a trainer. Suddenly, my goals weren't just wishful thinking—they became clear, doable, and damn satisfying.

I wasn't born with a silver spoon, but I figured out how to turn vague dreams into real results. That invisible income ceiling holding you back? It's about to get smashed. You're not alone if you think everyone else has the cheat code. The real power lies in changing what's inside you.

Ever set a goal, then forget it two weeks later? That's what we're fixing. It's not about trying harder. It's about changing how you go after them. We're going to find your number one goal for the year, embed it deep in your subconscious, and lock it in so tight it has no choice but to happen. This method is powerful. Your future self will want to thank you. Now ditch the distractions and let's get real about why your goals haven't stuck. Most people set goals as vague as a horoscope. Full of wishes, zero clarity. "I want more money" doesn't cut it. How much? Be specific. That fuzzy dream that keeps slipping away? That's because your goals aren't clear.

Your goals need to become part of who you are. This is brain science mixed with real-life action. Are you ready to turn your dreams into cash? Let's map it, lock it in, and make it real. No more drifting.

That stops today.

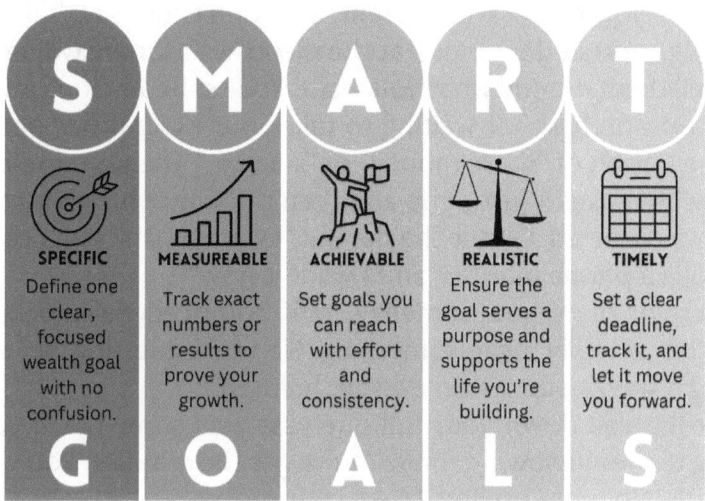

- **Specific, Simple, Sensory:** Don't just mumble, "I want more money." Say, "I want $111,300" with the confidence of a toddler demanding candy. Keep it clear. Make it vivid. Feel it.
- **Measurable, Meaningful and Magical:** If you can't track it, it didn't happen. No guesswork. Know your numbers.
- **Achievable, Actionable, and Attractive:** Your goals should pull you out of bed, not make you want to hide under the covers.
- **Realistic, Relevant, and Responsible:** It has to matter to you, but not wreck your sanity or blow up your life.
- **Timed and Transformative:** Deadlines create momentum. Make it more than a checkbox— make it transform you.

Imagine your life as the goal-smashing badass you were born to be. Visualize not just the end game but each step, each triumph, feeling so real you could almost taste it.

So, you're sitting there, contemplating the first step to wealth or becoming a six-figure superstar, right? If only it were as simple as finding a penny on the sidewalk. "Yay, more money," says the universe, patting herself on the back. But let's get real, you're not here to collect loose change.

When you go to a restaurant, you don't just say, "Give me anything." You sit down, look at the menu, wait for the waiter, and then tell them exactly what you want. Your subconscious mind is like a top-notch waiter waiting to take your exact order, not just a vague notion of "more money" or "success." The waiter tells the cook, who makes it just right, and then the waiter brings it to you exactly as ordered. Give it the details: "I want a bank balance that looks like a phone number, and I want it now!"

Let's cut the vague "someday" talk. You need clear, locked-in goals that actually mean something. No more guessing. No more hoping it works out. It's time to get focused.

We'll break down your full one-year goal soon, but if you're itching to dive in now, go for it. You've got the mindset. You've got the tools. No more stalling. Make your move.

1. **Define Your Dream:** Get crystal clear on what you want. Write it like it's already happening.
2. **Break It Down:** Use the SMART method. Make every step count.
3. **Set the Date:** Deadlines, not suggestions. Put them on your calendar and commit.
4. **Take Action:** Move daily. Small wins stack fast.
5. **Reflect and Adjust:** Check in, pivot if needed, and keep going.

You're not waiting for success. You're building it. Let's get to work.

It's time to get serious about the future you're creating. Pick a bold goal you want to bring to life this year. This isn't about busywork or another checklist—it's about growth, identity, and stepping into your wealthiest self.

The next chapter walks you through setting a one-year goal that actually aligns with your vision. The win isn't just hitting the number. It's who you become in the process.

So here's the choice: play small, or prove to yourself just how capable you really are.

CHAPTER 12
Conjuring Cash With The Seven-Step Sorcery System

CRUSHING GOALS ISN'T about chasing big dreams and hoping they land. It's about getting clear, focused, and actually doing something about it. In this chapter, I'm giving you my 7 Step Sorcery System. It's simple, it works, and it'll help you break those big goals into steps you can actually stick to. We're going to figure out what you really want and why it matters. Then you'll train your subconscious to back you up, not hold you back. No nonsense. No waiting. You've let goals slide before. That stops now.

If you feel stuck or like you're not living up to your potential, consider this your wake-up call. I'm here to help you lock in on your goals and break them down into manageable steps. My goal is to guide you toward your dreams and make the process effective and actually doable. Today, we'll break down goal-setting in a way that increases your chances of hitting what you're aiming for.

When goals work, they drive you straight to success. When they don't, it's usually because:

- You're crafting vague goals that lack a clear outcome. Like saying you want to travel "somewhere nice"–how do you pack for that?
- You're unsure about what you really want. It's like walking into a restaurant starving and telling the waiter, "Surprise me."

- You're stuck in the goal-setting stage and never actually start. It's like revving your car's engine but never putting it in drive.
- You're waiting for the 'right time' (like when the kids are older). Spoiler: Perfect timing is a myth, like unicorns.
- You're not engaging your subconscious mind, the powerhouse behind your actions. Ignoring it is like trying to drive with the parking brake on.
- You have no clue if you're getting closer to or further from your goal. It's like going on a treasure hunt without a map. Good luck finding that chest of gold!
- You're setting goals to please others (like friends or family), which is like wearing someone else's too-tight shoes. Ouch!
- You're clueless about the next steps. It's like assembling furniture without instructions.
- You're aiming too low. Shoot for the moon. Even if you miss, you'll land among the stars.

By spotting these common traps, you can reset your approach. So, what's the fix?

The solution is simple. I'll break it down so you can:

- Specify your outcome and identify the crucial last step before hitting your goal, giving you clear direction.
- Write it down to make your goals real and visible.
- Program your subconscious to keep working on your goals, even when you're not focused on them.
- Track your progress closely.
- Pinpoint immediate actions for next month, next week, tomorrow, and today.
- Commit to massive action NOW, pushing forward with unstoppable momentum.

Put it all together, and you're not just setting goals, you're shaping the life you actually want.

CLARITY IS KEY

Getting clear on your desires is like setting the GPS for your life's journey. Imagine you got dropped off in the middle of a forest with no map in hand and were told to find your way to New York. You wouldn't get too far, now would you? That's why specificity is your roadmap. When I was searching for our family's perfect home, I just didn't want any house. I pictured a fenced backyard where the kids and dogs could run, a cozy fireplace for cold Canadian nights, and a spare room for my office—or for when my husband ends up in the doghouse. The clearer your vision, the easier the path.

Consider the time I wanted to increase my income. Saying "I want more money" and then finding a penny might give the universe a laugh, but it's hardly the payday I had in mind. When you ask for more money and find a penny on the ground, the universe thinks, "Job done" and moves on. You asked for more money, and that's exactly what you got. Lack of specificity makes your subconscious lazy. Our subconscious, that tireless worker behind the scenes, needs precise instructions. Without clarity, you're sending a muddled message and wondering why nothing's landing.

When you picture your goal as if it's already real, your brain can't tell the difference between imagination and real life. This can trick your mind into thinking the goal is already done, so it stops pushing you to go after it. That's called "early closure."

I teach a simple way to fix this. You do want to imagine your dream, but there's a trick to how you do it. First, picture it like it's already real, so you can feel if it actually hits and make sure it's what you really want. Then, take a step back and watch yourself doing it—like you're sitting in a theater watching a movie, and you're the star. This helps your brain see it as something you're still working toward, not something already done. It's not that you don't imagine it—it's about how you imagine it. That little shift tells your brain, "This is where we're going," not "We've already arrived." That simple switch keeps your goal active in your mind and keeps you taking action.

We're getting clear and focused on what you really want, and this tool helps lock it in. Your dream isn't some feel-good fantasy. It's the path you're walking. Watching yourself win like you're watching it play out keeps you focused, hungry, and actually taking action.

It sounds weird, but it makes a difference.

GOAL SETTING + GOAL GETTING

We're stating our goals as if they are already achieved: "I have a million dollars in the bank," "I'm soaking up the sun at my beachfront property," "I'm making a massive impact on my business."

For years, I was my own biggest obstacle. I used to second-guess myself and shrink my own power. I believed success was reserved for others, not for me. It was a cycle of self-doubt that kept me stuck until I realized the only one holding me back was me.

Everything changed when I started believing in myself the way I believed in everyone else. I became unstoppable. You will, too, the second you decide you're built for this. If you can picture it, you can create it. Most people stare at the big dream like it's a poster on the wall, forgetting it's made up of small daily moves. That was me in the beginning, focused on the huge financial goals and missing the steps it actually takes to get there.

To hit your goals and hold them, you've to dig up the subconscious programming, calling the shots. The mindset blocks, the sabotage, the stuff that keeps you spinning your wheels It clicked when I realized my money choices had to match my values. And every major goal I've hit in the last decade came from this exact method. Your conscious mind sets the goal, but your subconscious is what goes after it. You've got to train both to work together. When they're aligned, your brain starts filtering everything through the lens of your goal. That's w hen m omentum takes off.

Ever wanted a certain car, dog, or purse, and suddenly you see it everywhere? That's your subconscious tuning in. The same thing happened when I got clear on my financial goals; opportunities I'd never noticed started showing up.

So how does this relate to hitting your goals?

Many of us default to thinking about what we DON'T want. We look in our bank account and think, Ugh, I don't have enough money. I can't afford x, y, or z. Or maybe there's something about our partner that we don't like and focus on...and then we feel like they do the thing more and more. We're essentially training our subconscious to look for the things that we don't want, and it's, therefore, creating a reality that we're not vibing with. So instead, I suggest using your subconscious to work for you!

It's easy to focus on what's missing—the empty bank account, the annoying fights, the crap that keeps piling up. You've got to shift your focus toward what you actually want, not what you're trying to escape. That's how you start changing the story your subconscious is running.

So why not train your subconscious to start working for you instead of against you?

Tell your brain what you want

For example, many people set goals and forget them. They don't come back to review them regularly. So the brain forgets the destination and just wanders. But when you're super clear on what you want and you keep checking in with it, you're way more likely to hit it. That's why it's important to feel into your goals daily.

Every day, think about the resources, people, experiences, ideas, feelings, and actions that will help you get there. Expect them. This is Law of Attraction 101. What you focus on, you pull in. I go deeper into that in Chapter 31: *Life Is a Game — And There Are Rules...or Should I Say 12 Laws to Be Exact*. What you think about, you magnetize. And since timing matters, the most powerful moments to review your goals are first thing in the morning and right before bed.

So let's start strong. What's the money goal you want to manifest by the end of this book? Write it down now. Not totally clear yet? No worries. We'll dial it in together. The exercises ahead will help you sharpen that goal and get your subconscious locked in to make it happen.

SEVEN STEP SORCERY SYSTEM

Let's lock in the one money goal you're ready to call in.

The Process

1. **What money goal would you like to achieve?** Yep, the one you just thought of a second ago. Write it down.
   What will you see, hear, and feel when you have it?
   - Make it compelling to you and write your outcome with positive language (Not what you <u>don't</u> want)
     - If it's a boring goal (like doing taxes), link it to something compelling. "Once I finish filing my taxes, I will book my vacation to Hawaii!"
   - State your outcome with positive language.
     - "What specifically do you want?" (Not what you don't want)
     - Example: Not "get out of debt," but "have a positive balance of $10k in my bank account. "

2. **Where are you now in relation to your desired outcome? Draw out all the details.**
   - You can't get to an end location without knowing where you're starting from. If someone were to blindfold you and fly you out to an unknown location and then hand you a map and say, "Get to New York," A map will do you zero good unless you know where you're starting from.

3. **How will you know you have your goal/desire?**

- -What will need to happen to make you feel certain it is a done deal?
    - Ex: If you're booking a vacation to Disney Land, how do you know it's a done deal and happening? Is it when you purchase your flight? Book your hotel? Get on the plane? Arrive at the hotel? Get on a ride at Disney Land? Etc.

4. **What will this outcome give you?**

   What will this goal make possible for you? For what purpose do you want it?
   - What will this goal let you do or experience?
   - Why do you want it?
   - What will change in your life if you get it?
   - What might you lose or have to let go of to reach it?
   - Does this goal feel aligned with who you are and what matters to you?

   A couple of things to check in on:
   Sometimes people chase a goal because everyone else is doing it, or because their parents, friends, or society expect them to. Make sure you're doing it for yourself.
   - If you say it's for you and your partner, ask yourself, *"Which part of the goal am I personally responsible for?"* You could always create a joint goal later, but this one is for YOU. It's important to own the part that's truly in your control.
   - **Are there drawbacks?**
     - If so, look at how you can adjust the goal so it feels right in every part of your life.
     - For example, if you feel like making a million dollars might mess up your relationship with your best friend from high school, it's worth examining that. Get to a place where you feel good about your goal. Maybe it's seeing how the extra money could actually support and strengthen your relationships. Maybe it's realizing

you have to do what's best for you and your family. Or maybe it's creating a new version of the goal that feels right all around.

5. **Establish resources**

   What personal resources do you have that will allow you to achieve this?
   (look at this from the present moment forward)
   - Internal resources are the most powerful because they're always with you and available to tap into.
     - Examples: motivated, smart, driven, creative, committed.
   - If you list external resources like money or personal connections, that's fine—but the focus should primarily be on your internal strengths.
   - When you run out of ideas, ask yourself:

   Do you know anyone else who has achieved it? What resources did they have?
   (this perspective is from an outside, 3rd-person view)
   - Doesn't have to be someone you know personally—it could be someone you've seen on TV, read about, or heard of.

   Close your eyes and imagine you already have it. Other than those mentioned, what resources did you use to get it?
   (this perspective is from the goal backward)
   - Future pace yourself: see the moment when the goal is already achieved, then look back and ask, *what got me here?*
   - Write down: *"I achieved this because I am..."* and fill in the qualities and resources that made it possible.

   All of this helps your subconscious mind lock in the resources it needs to support you in achieving your outcome. Make sure to write everything down.

6. **Why now? Why did you choose that amount of money?**

7. **Put yourself in the future and write it in the present tense**

    - *Pick a specific future date and put it down on paper.* "Next month" is too vague.

        - Write it like this: "It is now August 12th, 2026, and …"
    - **Always write in the present tense: "I have…" "I am…" or "I do…"** (not "I will have" or "I will do").

State your outcome with positive language

This is where you put in writing the exact goal you're going after, based on what you just learned. Fix in your mind the exact amount of money/goal you desire. Be Specific.

Re-Write your money goal here: _____

Remember…put a specific future date down here for your goal. "Next month" is a sliding target and vague. Be exact.

- "It is now _____ (date, month/day/year)"

Write it in the present tense

- "I have…" "I am…" or "I do…" (not I will have or I will do)
- I have _____

Put it all together in a sentence: Example: *It is now August 12th, 2026 and I have $* _____…"

YAY! You've just gone through the 7-Step Sorcery System and applied it to a money goal. That is so amazing.

Additional Questions to Test Your Goal

"As you think about the goal you came up with…"

1. **What will happen if you get it?**
    - How will your life look or feel different?
    - What new opportunities will open up?
    - What thoughts or feelings come up when you imagine it happening?
2. **What will happen if you don't get it?**
    - What will stay the same if nothing changes?
    - What challenges or frustrations will keep showing up?

- How will that impact you long-term?
3. **What won't happen if you get it?**
    - What struggles or problems will disappear?
    - What patterns will no longer control you
4. **What won't happen if you don't get it?**
    - What possibilities will you miss out on?
    - What experiences will you never have if you stay where you are?

Wrap-up instruction:

If these questions make your goal feel stronger and more aligned, keep going. If they weaken it or raise doubts, that's a sign to adjust your goal so it fully supports you. Go back to Step 1 and refine it until it feels right.

Wealthy Magic Script

Channel your wealthy self who already is the person who has the thing you most desire.

Create a gratitude/goal statement—what I call a Magic Script—that connects to the Seven Step Sorcery System you just applied. Write it in the **present tense** and in **positive language,** affirming your goal as if it's already true.

- Start with a longer version that lays out the foundation of everything you're calling in. Write it three times so you really feel it sink in.
- Then create a shorter version you can say or write often, so you stay connected to it daily.

Example:

It is now August 12th, and I am so grateful to have [insert your goal statement here]. I am grateful that this extra income flows to me with ease. I welcome it with vibrant health, confidence, and joy, and I know it will keep showing up in my life because I am abundant. Money flows to me easily, and I receive it with fun and freedom.

Write your gratitude statement and say it out loud, DAILY.

- Set alarms on your phone throughout the day, and when

they go off, check in with yourself in that moment to see how close you are to embodying your wealthy self. And then, take a minute to channel your wealthy self and carry out your current activity in that energy.
- Call your goal statement a "Magical Script". Play motivational music while you are writing it, and make sure it is filled with emotion! Write it, giving thanks as if your goal has been achieved. What language would you use if all your dreams suddenly came true? It wouldn't be formal, would it? Use swear words if you normally swear! Be yourself!

Embody It Fully

Create an internal representation of your goal:
- *See what you'll see*
- *Hear what you'll hear*
- *Feel what you'll feel*
- *Taste what you'll taste*
- *Smell what you'll smell*

Step into that version of you. Notice your posture, your energy, your movement as you live it. Embody the mood and feeling of achieving the goal (e.g., confident, happy, excited).

Putting it all together: Write your full version with all the details, then anchor it in a shorter daily version:

Long version example: *It is now August 12th, 2026, and I have $50,000 in my savings account. I feel powerful, confident, and calm, knowing I'm financially secure. I see myself booking my dream vacation, hearing the confirmation email hit my inbox, and feeling the freedom in my chest. I taste the champagne I'm celebrating with, and I smell the ocean air from the trip I'm now taking with ease. I'm so fucking grateful that this money flowed to me easily, joyfully, and in total alignment with my purpose. I feel free, empowered, and abundant as hell.*

Short version example: *I'm so grateful I have $50K saved. I feel free, powerful, and totally aligned. Money flows to me easily, and I'm living it up in full abundance.*

Write both out, keep them where you can see them, and speak them daily.

Have your script typed out on your phone for easy access, and read it out loud every day. Yes, putting pen to paper has a certain magic, but so does your voice. Your subconscious mind will hear you and will take it all in. SPEAK your dreams into reality! Words have so much power.

Most people go about setting long-term goals the wrong way. They set their big goal and then think about what their next step is to get there.

Question: What's the first step to achieving six or seven-figure success?

If everyone knew, they'd be doing it!

Most people want this for themselves, but they simply don't know what to do first. So they do nothing.

When setting goals, the most important thing you can do is work backwards from the big vision.

You already set your money goal using the **Seven Step Sorcery System**. That's the one we're sticking with.

Now let's **reverse-engineer** it.

This next part will break it down into clear milestones over the next year, so you're not just dreaming it, you're building it.

You've got your number in mind?

Now, double it.

Yeah, seriously.

Here's why. Most people either hit their goals or fall short. That's why I tell my clients to aim way higher than they think they can. If you shoot for the moon and miss, you're still way ahead. And listen, this isn't just about hitting that exact number. It's about who you become while chasing it and what you unlock by actually doing the work.

As long as you're taking the steps towards your big dream, results will follow. And hey, if you only get 70% of the way to your $100k goal, that's still $70k, right? Compared to 100%, $50,000 is still $50,000.

Write down that bold new number. Let's see it. What's your bigger goal now?

1 YEAR GOAL

Let's say you create a one-year goal of earning $100,000 as a highly sought-after entrepreneur. It's challenging to figure out the first step, and if you already knew, you'd have achieved it by now. But if you work backwards, you have a much better chance of devising a plan that helps you get to your outcome.

Let's start with the 1-year goal as a highly sought-after and successful 6-figure entrepreneur who has exceeded $100,000, for example. Let's say today is August 12th, 2025, and your goal is for August 12th, 2026.

9 MONTH GOAL

At nine months in, you'd be just three months away from hitting your goal and already closing in on $100k a year. By then, your income would be stacking up toward that milestone, and you'd be confident in what you're doing, with people actively seeking your services or products.

Your nine-month goal could be: "It's May 12, 2026. My business services are fully booked with a growing waitlist. I've secured four major contracts, each bringing in $1k/month for the next six months. I've successfully launched a high-demand product or service, selling out its first release to 8 clients at $500/month for three months. This success has me nearing $8k/month, putting me on track to surpass my $100,000 annual target."

Write your 9-month goal.
Now think back—how did you get there? What choices, actions, and support made it possible?

I've built real marketing skills by showing up online, creating content, and building a loyal crew of clients. Every day, I sharpen what works and ditch what doesn't so I can grow my visibility and impact. Mornings are for focused action. I use that time to move the needle, connect with my audience, and grow my business in ways that actually matter. And having the right people in my corner? Game-changer. That support shifted everything and took this to a whole new level.

Write how you got to your 9-month goal.

6 MONTH GOAL

Where would you have to be in 6 months to set up your 9-month milestone?

For example: "It's February 12th, 2026. My business is consistently generating $4.5k/month. I've attracted 6 clients at $750/month each for a 4-month package. This momentum is building the foundation for my $100k year."

Write your 6-month goal.

What helped you reach your 6-month goal? What actions, learning, or support made it possible?

"I've immersed myself in digital marketing webinars and e-commerce strategy workshops, crafting a product line that resonates deeply with my target audience. My social media presence has become a magnet for my ideal customers. I've honed my skills in online marketing and sales, and after implementing what I've learned, I'm seeing a real uptick in traffic and conversions."

Write how you got to your 6-month goal.

3 Month Goal

What needs to be true in 3 months to set up that 6-month goal?

"It's November 12th, 2025. My e-commerce store is thriving. I've landed 3 contracts at $500/month each and raised my product prices from $111 to $222, leading to 10 sales. This growth is boosting my confidence and proving the potential of my online store."

Write your 3-month goal.

Now reflect: What actions, choices, or support helped you get here?

"I dove headfirst into the digital world, reaching out and networking nonstop, which led me to secure 3 contracts at $500/month each. I also took a bold step by doubling the price of my products. This wasn't just a guess; I knew my value and stood behind it. That move paid off, bringing in 10 strong sales.

Seeing these results has boosted my confidence and confirmed the potential of my e-commerce strategy."

Write how you got to your 3-month goal.

1 MONTH GOAL

Where do you need to be in 1 month to move toward that 3-month milestone?

For example: "It's September 12th, 2025, and I've just completed my first 90-minute client session for $111. It went so well, and now I have 5 more people interested in working with me."

Write your 1-month goal.

Now think: what helped you get here?

"Last month, I enrolled in a social media marketing course. It felt like a big step, but I knew it was what I needed to level up online. That course sparked new ideas, fresh offers, and gave me the clarity to map out everything—who it's for, why it matters, what to charge, and how to sell it."

Write how you got to your 1-month goal.

1 WEEK GOAL

Once you have the one-month goal written, then ask, Where do you need to be a week from now in order to hit that 1 month goal?

"It's Monday, August 19th, and I'm fully immersed in the Social Media Marketing Course. I've mapped out my target audience, refined what I want to sell, established some pricing structures, and devised effective marketing strategies."

Write your 1-week goal.

How did you achieve your 1-week goal?

"I prioritized and blocked off some of my time by scheduling dedicated slots in my calendar for attending the Social Media Marketing Course sessions and completing the assigned tasks."

Write how you achieved your 1-week goal.

DAILY GOALS

Then you can break it down DAILY. What are you committed to doing today (and every day for the rest of the week) to make sure this one-week goal becomes your reality?

"It is Monday August 18th, and I am committed to dedicating specific time slots each day to attend the course sessions and complete the assigned tasks. I prioritize these activities by sched-uling them into my calendar, ensuring I stay on track and make steady progress towards achieving my goal. It's already a done deal."

Write today's goal and how you plan on making it a done deal!

Finish strong and commit fully today, and watch how those small daily wins stack up into unstoppable momentum toward your big goal.

> *Wealth is not his that has it, but his that enjoys it*
> — Benjamin Franklin

CHAPTER 13
Blurring The Lines Between Spending Reality Vs Spending Fantasy

IN THE NOT-SO-QUIET corners of my life, I had to get real about my spending, and you should too. Getting real about your spending habits might not sound sexy, but let me tell you, it's one of the most powerful moves you can make.

If you want that dream life you've been picturing to actually become the one you're living, then this part is non-negotiable. Trust me, I've been there. Sitting down, cracking open the bank statements, looking at what's going in, what's flying out, and wondering how the hell I was paying for five different streaming services I barely used. It wasn't fun, but it was the wake-up call I needed. Once I got real with my money, I finally had the clarity to change it.

This next exercise is going to help you figure out what you're actually spending (hello, reality check) and what you *want* to be spending in your dream life. You'll get a clear look at your personal expenses and map out what needs to shift to bridge the gap between the two.

Make it your own, add things, delete what doesn't apply, and customize it to your world. This is about getting crystal clear so you can make empowered choices and start *living* that fantasy life you've been dreaming about. Because clarity = power, and this is where your next-level money story begins.

Getting into the nitty-gritty of your spending habits might not be your idea of a wild Friday night. But getting honest about your cash flow is non-negotiable. Dreaming big is great, but if you actually want that life, this part can't be skipped.

I started reviewing my finances to see what was coming in and out of my account, including all my subscriptions: Netflix, Spotify, Amazon Prime, and Disney. I'd rather clean my baseboards, but it was something I finally did for me.

I've been there, feeling the fear of facing my financial truth. But once I did, I finally had the power to change it. Let's get into it and take control.

HOME

Investment	Current Amount	Desired Amount
Mortgage/rent payment		
Utilities		
Homeowner's insurance		
Repairs/Maintenance		
Decor		
Cleaning service		
Other:		
TOTAL:		

TRANSPORTATION (CAR, BUS, TAXI, SNOW MACHINE, BOAT)

Investment	Current Amount	Desired Amount
Payment(s)		
Vehicle Insurance		
Fuel		
Repairs/ Maintenance		
Other:		
TOTAL:		

HEALTH + WELLNESS

Investment	Current Amount	Desired Amount
Groceries		
Eating out		
Ordering in		
Coffee		
Gym membership		
Private chef		
Other:		
TOTAL:		

FUN + SELF-CARE

Investment	Current Amount	Desired Amount
Travel		
Gifts		
Clothes		
Mani/Pedi/Facial		
Massages/Spas		
Yoga		
Other:		
TOTAL:		

CHILDREN (AND/OR PETS)

Investment	Current Amount	Desired Amount
Daycare		
Clothes		
Healthcare		
Food/Supplements		
Toys		
Schools/Activities		
Other:		
TOTAL:		

PAYMENTS

Investment	Current Amount	Desired Amount
Credit card payments		
Student loans		
Personal loans		
Other:		
TOTAL:		

BUSINESS INVESTMENTS

Investment	Current Amount	Desired Amount
Coaches/Teachers/Trainer		
Courses/Memberships		
Travel		
Team/Employees		
Client gifts		
Marketing/Advertisement		
Software		
Other:		
TOTAL:		

MISCELLANEOUS

Investment	Current Amount	Desired Amount
Charities/Donations		
Savings account		
Taxes		
Retirement		
Life insurance		
Bank fees		
Other:		
TOTAL:		

How was that?

Take a second to check in. What came up for you during that exercise? Any realizations or holy sh*t moments? This is about getting honest with yourself. No judgment. Just clarity. Now let's get real. Can you actually handle your current money game? What feels off? What's screaming for a change? What's essential right now, like food, housing, and bills? And what's more of a want than a need while you're getting things sorted?

Even if you're nailing your financial scene right now, why not play detective with your spending? Scope out your expenses. Is there anything you could ditch? Spot anything that's not really sparking joy but still munching away at your wallet? Stumbled upon a cost you forgot existed and can axe pronto? (Netflix, Spotify, gym memberships, skip the dishes, Uber Eats, subscriptions, bank fees...etc.) Could there be a better place to channel that saved-up dough?

What's the gap between your current spending reality and your dream spending spree? Is it a tiny hop or a giant leap? Calculate the extra cash you need each month to turn your spending fantasy into your daily lifestyle. How big is that number?

What's the top priority that you believe needs your immediate attention to catapult you into your dream lifestyle? *(The #1 thing you feel you need to focus on)*

After getting real about your spending and mapping out what you want, it's time to check in. I remember the days I tracked every single dollar, deciding between what we needed and little extras like streaming services I thought I couldn't live without.

We've peeled back the layers of your financial reality and uncovered the gap between where you are and where you want to be. It's not just about cutting back on coffee or Netflix. It's about aligning your spending with what actually matters to you and building a future where every dollar fuels your goals. So, let's wrap this up by committing to more than just dreaming about wealth. Let's start building it. Now that you've looked at where your money's going and what you really want, you can make bold, intentional moves that close the gap between your current reality and your dream life.

CHAPTER 14
Habits - The Automatic Actions For The Financially Fierce

LET'S REWIND TO the very start of money, way before it became the complex thing it is today, a time when there was no cash or coins, and people had to trade items to get what they needed. Think about trading a chicken for a sack of potatoes. Sounds straightforward, right? But it was anything but easy. Agreeing on what's fair value was a headache, and you couldn't exactly slice a cow in half for a loaf of bread!

So, who had the brilliant idea of inventing money? It's tough to say who exactly, as money kind of evolved in different spots around the globe. The Lydians, way back in 600 BC in what's now Turkey, were some of the first people to get the ball rolling with coins. This was a total game-changer, making it a lot simpler for people to trade and set a standard for what things were worth.

Now, fast forward to our time, and money has taken on a whole new face. We've moved from actual coins and notes to digital numbers, think credit cards, online transfers, and even cryptocurrencies like Bitcoin. The way we see and use money has transformed, doing a whole one-eighty. It started as a simple way to trade things, but now, it's this massive network of value, trust, and transactions that keeps the world's economy spinning.

The way we view wealth has changed big time as well. Back in the day, being rich meant having tangible things like land, livestock, or gold. It was all about what you physically owned and could pass down through generations. But now, it's also about the intangibles, like owning shares in a company, investing in bonds, or even having digital currency.

Wealth today goes beyond money in the bank or physical assets. It also includes intellectual property—anything you create with your mind that holds value, like books, courses, logos, inventions, software, or even music and videos. We've shifted from an economy of tangible goods to one that's digital and complex, where the value of money isn't in what you can hold but in the trust and systems that back it. Wealth isn't just money.

Wealth, in its simplest form, is the abundance of valuable resources or possessions — including money, assets, health, relationships, knowledge, and emotional well-being. True wealth means richness in all parts of life, not just your bank account.

But not all wealth is created equal. That's where aligned wealth comes in.

Aligned wealth means your money, time, and energy are all working together in a way that feels right for you. It's not just about having more; it's about living better. When you redefine wealth to include time, freedom, health, peace, and connection, it changes how you make decisions. You stop chasing just income and start building a life that actually feels good. Aligned wealth isn't just about stacking cash. It's about creating a lifestyle that matches who you are and what matters to you.

Most people are still chasing the old version of wealth. They think more money, more stuff, and a bigger status symbol equals success. That's what we were taught. Old wealth looked like material possessions, corporate ladders, and retirement plans. Aligned wealth looks like spaciousness, doing meaningful work, having time for your family, and being mentally and physically well.

People chase money because it's what they've been taught to chase: status, a bigger house, a nicer car, the next promotion. But real wealth isn't about any of that. It's in the choices you get to make every day. The ability to live life on your terms. The freedom to say no. The power to work less and live more. Most people are grinding for numbers without realizing they're already rich in the ways that matter. Wealth isn't just earned, it's built with intention. And you're the one building it.

Digging into the history of money gives you a real look at why dealing with finances today feels so damn complicated. It's not just about what you spend or save; it's tied to a long history and centuries of evolution that have shaped how we think, feel, and act about money. Centuries of change and personal experience have wired the way we handle it now.

Allowing the money in is one thing; being comfortable with the money sticking around is another. In my early adulthood, I found myself in debt. As most people would, I stuck my head in the sand when it came to my finances. I did not want to know what was in my bank account, how much I owed on my credit cards, or how much the bill was that I just got in the mail. That scared the crap out of me, but so did actual money.

For months, I ignored looking at the exact number in my bank account or on my credit card statements. I just knew the approximate number, squinting my eyes when opening up statements, and making sure to look at the minimum payment due so I would not miss it. I never knew what automatic withdrawals would come out of my bank account. Any automatic withdrawals like memberships, apps, gym fees, or music subscriptions would come out of my account, and I'd just hope the money was there to cover it.

Budgeting weekly expenses can feel scary, annoying, and frustrating. If that wasn't enough, many of us overdraw our bank accounts at least once a week, sometimes twice. Those letters from banks about every overdraft and the NSF fees probably make up most of your mail, aside from grocery flyers.

Sound familiar? Maybe you're going through this right now, burying your head in the same sand I did. Finally owning up to my money was a major shift. After years of struggle, it was time to face it. My gut told me I had to deal with it to change it. I did not realize how much straight-up neglecting my finances was affecting my money game. I did not like to spend time with my money, and so it was no wonder money did not like to spend time with me. That was a powerful realization for me. I was irresponsible. I showed my money no love. No respect. I did not even acknowledge it when it did come around.

This is something I need you to realize: you and your money are in a relationship. In many ways, it's one of the most important relationships you'll ever have. Money is often the reason for divorce and the reason for misery among families. When money is hard to come by, there is nothing else to do but stress and worry about money from morning to night. Where is the fun in that? I want you to see your money as an extremely important relationship, a relationship between you and your finances. If you neglect your spouse, partner, or any of your close friends, do you think the relationship would succeed? I bet you are shaking your head right now because it's a big fat no. Like, the hardest no possible.

I don't have to be a psychic to predict that whatever your relationship is with your finances right now, it is exactly what's reflected in your bank account. Your relationship with money also determines how easily it can manifest in your life.

Manifesting money can be easy, but most people block it without even realizing it. We overthink it, stress about it, and make it harder than it needs to be. However, I have really great news for you. We can make a choice right now to own up to our neglect and rebuild our relationship with the dollar bill. It's time to open every single credit card statement, bank account, and wallet you have cash in, and assess how much money you have and where it is going. This may sting a bit, but start tracking when you receive income or get paid.

Figure out when your expenses come out of your account, like when you pay your mortgage, rent, child care, groceries, insurance, etc. Track down as much as you can. You want to know the dates, the amount, and all the details in between. This also includes looking at your debt if you are in debt. Yes, I know, this is some scary shit. But so worth it. This is not a bad thing. Debt does not defy you. You are not a bad person for having debt or not having a clear idea of where your money is going. I want to make that super clear.

People get into the vibration of guilt and shame when it comes to money, and my goal is not to shame you here or make you feel guilty of your past spending history. It's quite the opposite, actually. There is no guilt or shame involved here. The choices you have made are now in your past. We are letting it go and creating a compelling, exciting, financially free future. Just like anything else in this universe, what you focus on expands. What you track increases. What you are grateful for, flourishes and multiplies. The same goes for money. Repeat that to yourself as you own up to your own money relationship.

Say it with me, what I focus on expands. What I track increases. What I'm grateful for, flourishes. Focus on your money, track your money, be grateful for every penny, and watch it grow.

TRACK IT LIKE YOU MEAN IT

This is where the magic gets real. Tracking your money doesn't have to be boring, stressful, or feel like punishment. It's not about obsessing over numbers. It's about building a relationship with them. And like any good relationship that matters, it needs attention, respect, and a little quality time.

Track what's coming in. Track what's going out. Know your dates. Know your numbers. Know your worth. Because when you treat your money like a priority, it starts treating you like one too.

Light a candle. Blast your "I'm a rich bitch" playlist. Open that spreadsheet or bank app. Let's go. Stop checking your bank account hoping something suddenly changed. That's not a strategy. It's avoidance. We're talking intentional, badass money tracking like your wealthy self already does.

And while we're here, let's shine a spotlight on those sneaky habits that quietly suck up your time and energy like a financial vampire. Tracking is a habit. It's not just a task, it's a ritual. One that builds your financial power every single day. You can't build fierce habits without cutting the lazy ones that drain your time and energy.

James Clear in *Atomic Habits* says lasting change isn't about giant leaps. It's the tiny, steady improvements, like one percent better every day, that add up big time.

Success isn't about goals. It's about building systems that actually work. If your system is broken, motivation won't save you.

Flip the focus from what you want to do to who you want to be. Every habit you build is a vote for that identity. Be the person who *automatically* hits those goals. Want to run a marathon? Become the runner who never skips a run. That's the real system.

Forget willpower and motivation. They're unreliable because they fade fast and fluctuate.

They're unreliable because they fluctuate. What actually keeps you on track is structure, your environment, your triggers, and your routines.

Make good habits easy and bad habits hard. It's a strategy, not fluff. You don't need to be perfect. Just show up and choose who you want to be every day. The results? Guaranteed. That's the math of tiny gains.

Habits aren't luck. They're the muscle behind every win. Get your habits right, and everything else follows.

Lazy habits sneak in, looking harmless, but rob you blind. They kill your focus, drain your energy, and stall your momentum.

Lazy Habit List:

- Scrolling your ex's cousin's dog's Instagram (why tho?)
- Checking your phone notifications 97 times a day like it's a lifeline
- Watching one video, then realizing it's dark outside
- Rewriting your to-do list instead of doing the damn thing
- Cleaning the fridge when you said you'd go over your budget
- Saying "I'll start tomorrow" every single day

These sneaky habits add up. Replace them with intentional habits that move your money forward. Start tracking like the financially fierce person you are. Pick one. Call it out. Shift it. Every hour you take back is a chance to lock in a habit that actually moves you forward.

One thing you can start doing today is checking your bank account daily. Yes, every single day. Something that really helped me turn this into an exciting, uplifting, positive experience was to put on a high-vibrational upbeat song, make a fancy drink, and light a candle when checking my accounts. The point is to make the process enjoyable so that you can associate money with having fun. You want your nervous system to link money with ease, not stress. And no matter what the number says, be grateful for it.

Once I started watching, tracking, and appreciating my money consistently, it started growing. Even before I raised my income, unexpected money would show up. Month after month, my balance kept rising. The principles I share really work. They are laws of the universe, after all. Take ownership of your money. Take care of it. Show it love and respect, and money will take care of you in return.

We are what we repeatedly do. Excellence, then, is not an act, but a habit." - Aristotle

Over 90% of the actions we take each day are not conscious decisions, but unconscious habits running on autopilot. And guess what? Every time you repeat a habit, you strengthen it and make it even more automatic. This is great news if your habits support your goals and the version of you you're becoming. But if they're working against you, it's time to shift them. You're here to build strong, aligned habits and rituals that support the life you actually want. You're about to start one powerful journey, and like any journey, it's important to know where you're starting, where you're headed, and how to stay on course.

If you're spending just 1 hour a day on bad habits, whether that's scrolling on social media for a half an hour, opening and closing the fridge and cupboards figuring out what you want to eat for 20 minutes, or feeling groggy because you didn't get a good night's sleep so you're unfocused for 10 minutes, then that quickly adds up. That's an hour right there.

Freaky fact—Losing one hour a day to bad habits adds up to one month per year.

Imagine what you could do with one month of your time each year?

If you don't like the reality you're creating, change it. And maybe that freaky fact alone will be enough to shock you out of those old habits. Every decision, even the small ones, shifts the direction of your life. Every choice stacks. The Fusion Reaction is about paying attention and making moves that expand your life, not shrink it.

You already know your mind absorbs whatever you feed it. Ask yourself if you're pouring in power or pouring in poison. The inputs matter.

That podcast you play, the post you linger on, the conversation you replay in your head—they're all shaping how you think, feel, and act. Feed your mind the good stuff, the bold stuff, the aligned stuff. Because what you take in becomes how you show up. Every. Single. Time.

Swap the mindless scroll for voices that light a fire in you. On your drive out and about, skip the drama and queue up something that fuels you. What you consume is shaping what you create. Choose wisely.

And if you lose hours of focus every day from the flood of notifications on your phone, set boundaries. Check them only in the morning and evening. Turn off the alarms, shut down the auto-receive functions, and take control. Your attention is currency—protect it.

When your phone keeps dinging and you instantly check it, you're conditioning yourself to believe that everyone and everything on the other side of that notification is more important than what you're doing at the moment, who you're with, where you are, or even more important than you.

Check your phone and notifications when you choose to, not when your cell phone tells you to.

Even one hour a day lost to bad habits like scrolling social media, standing at the fridge trying to decide what to eat, or dragging through the morning because of poor sleep adds up fast.

If your reality isn't cutting it, you can change it. Realizing how much time these habits steal can be the wake-up call you need to drop them. As you cut the noise and bring in better inputs, your energy rises. The less negativity you feed your mind, the more space you create for positivity to grow.

Remember this freaky fact: losing just one hour a day to bad habits adds up to one full month each year. How many times a day do you check your notifications?!? I bet you don't want to do the math on that and add it up.

You might be wondering where the heck that time's even going. Like... What are these habits, really?

Let's call them out, shall we?

Lazy (a.k.a. sneaky) habits that steal your time + energy:

- Mindlessly scrolling social media (you said 5 mins... it's been 47)
- Reopening the fridge like it's going to magically restock itself
- Starting five tasks and finishing none (hello, tab chaos)
- Watching one YouTube video that becomes a Netflix episode binge
- Snoozing your alarm five times and then starting your day in panic mode
- Refreshing your email every 3 seconds
- Obsessively checking stats, views, likes, or followers
- Overthinking instead of doing (aka "researching" for the 100th time)
- Complaining but not changing anything
- Waiting for the "perfect" moment to start

If you're mentally checking these off like a scavenger hunt, good. Awareness is your golden ticket. Now flip them. Tiny shifts. One at a time. And yes, make it fun.

What's one habit you're ready to change today to take back your time and build real wealth?

Back in the day, wealth wasn't measured by the gadgets we owned or the apps we had on our phones. It was about the simple pleasures of life that kids today wouldn't understand. When the phone rang, we had to dash to the wall to pick it up, and there was an element of surprise in every conversation because we had no caller ID.

Friends didn't just send texts; they knocked on your door to see if you were home, and hanging out meant going outside to play hide and seek with neighbors until the street lights came on. Drinking water from the hose outside was a refreshing treat, and getting up to change the channel on the TV guide was just a part of daily life.

Wealth was in the genuine connections we made, the laughter we shared, and the adventures we embarked on without the need for screens or devices.

I remember when I would just go to a friend's house for coffee. No text, no call, just knock on the door, and someone would answer, and we'd spend an hour or two just talking, sipping coffee, and enjoying the moment. That was normal. Now? When the door rings or someone knocks, what do we do? We duck, barrel roll, and hide behind the couch like we're in a spy movie, praying they don't see us. We whisper, hoping they don't realize we're actually home. Even delivery drivers don't knock anymore. They drop the package and peel out of the driveway so fast you barely have time to unlock the door. The world's changed, hasn't it? We've become so disconnected, and yet we crave that connection more than ever.

Before nonstop notifications and distractions, our minds were clearer. Had real conversations over coffee, and focused on the moment. And we didn't pencil it into a day planner or squeeze it between meetings. It just happened, naturally. Today, with tech overload and endless noise, we have to protect our mental space. That means flushing out negativity and choosing what we let in. Less scrolling, more real life. Less noise, more joy. Simpler times had it right—and it's on us to bring that back.

Every day, we get to choose, cling to old memories, emotions, and beliefs, or step into new ones that actually serve us. Most people try to change habits by tweaking their environment or behavior, but they often overlook the underlying root cause. Real change starts deeper. It begins with identity. That's the base of it all.

Everything you do is either moving you closer to aligned wealth or pulling you further from it. It's not about being perfect. It's about getting honest. Habits don't lie. They reveal who you've been showing up as. So, let's cut the noise, ditch the excuses, and start acting like someone who actually wants more.

What's one habit you can change today?

CHAPTER 15
Rituals - The Intentional Actions For The Financially Fierce

EVERY DAY, YOU'VE got a choice: keep clinging to old stories that hold you back, or start acting like the version of you who actually gets what they want. And here's the truth—tweaking routines won't cut it, because that's surface-level. Real change starts with who you decide to be. Your identity runs the show. If you want to live wealthily, your habits and rituals better match the version of you who already is.

Rituals aren't just routines. They're intentional and on purpose. You've got to bring awareness to everything you do. That's how you train your subconscious to work for you, not against you. Because if you're running on autopilot, you're letting old programming call the shots, and that won't get you what you want.

DAILY RITUALS: Setting the Tone for Success

AM Rituals are the daily morning money-making journal prompts. Try to say that three times fast!

Journaling when you wake up is one of the best things you can do to get a head start on your day. The morning is when your subconscious mind is most active, making it a great time to get your thoughts down on paper. By journaling in the morning, you make sure you start the day on a positive and grateful note. When you add in the incantation-3 practice (more on that in a sec), you'll notice your mornings start a lot happier.

Most people focus on changing their environment or behavior when trying to shift habits. But the real change? It starts at the identity level. Who you believe you are drives everything. If you want different results, you need habits and rituals that match the version of you who already has what you want.

Being aware and intentional with your daily habits helps you choose the thoughts, beliefs, feelings, and actions that actually support what you want. Do it enough, and it becomes automatic. If you're not paying attention, that old programming, the stuff that probably doesn't even serve you anymore, just takes over and runs the show.

Crafting a Day of Intention

My mornings are sacred, built around rituals that align with how I feel and what I need to start the day strong. These practices vary, sometimes focusing on just one or blending several to match my mood. Here's a glimpse of some AM rituals:

- Breathwork
- Reading
- Journaling
- Writing content
- Pulling tarot cards
- Meditation/Visualization
- Listening to podcasts
- Running
- Walking my dogs
- Being in nature
- Yoga/Stretching
- EFT (Tapping)
- Affirmations
- Daily Incantation: 3 powerful statements each morning to set your tone for the day.

(Sometimes I do just one of these things, a mix, or all, depending on how I'm feeling.)

What morning rituals do you want to add to your routine that could shape who you are and push you closer to success?

Ending the Day with Intention

Just like mornings kick off fresh starts, evenings are your time to slow down and reset. PM rituals help you separate the chaos of the day from the calm you need. These are some that supported me the most when life felt heavy:

- Log out of social media
- Play music and light a candle
- Go for a walk
- Yoga
- Make and enjoy a nourishing meal
- Connect with your partner
- Read
- Bath with essential oils
- Journaling/Affirmations
- Personal development reading
- Meditate

Wrap up by reflecting on your day, whether or not anything big happened. Processing and releasing the day is powerful—it clears space and resets you, just like we do with the wins and lessons in our money journey.

What evening rituals could you add to bring more calm and purpose to your nights?

The Real You Is Getting Loud

There's a version of you that's done waiting. You can feel it. That dream life isn't some Pinterest board fantasy. It's sitting inside you, tapping its foot, wondering when you're finally going to move. You've got the skills. You've got the fire. Some of it you already own. Some of it is untapped, but it's in there—and it's time.

Clear the noise and get real about what you want. Grab your

notepad, pick up your favorite pen, and get yourself into a distraction-free zone. You're about to get clear.

Craft Your Affirmations

Daily identity affirmations are positive statements you say to yourself that reinforce the person you want to become. They help reprogram your mindset and align your thoughts with your goals. Think about your ideal self before you sleep. Picture the person you want to be, living the life you want. This nightly habit trains your subconscious to bring those goals to life. The more you commit to this vision, the clearer your ideas, motivation, and path become, leading you closer to making it real.

Consider setting a reminder on your phone for morning and evening affirmations, or partner with a friend to exchange motivational voice notes, keeping each other's spirits elevated.

You're here because some part of you knows you're meant for more than the 9–5 grind, the same meals, the same days on repeat. You're craving freedom from the rinse-and-repeat routine. Honestly, who isn't?

WHEN IS THE LAST TIME YOU HEARD A 'YES'?

- YES to spending your day doing what you love.
- YES to turning your passion into a paycheck.
- YES to finally hitting that goal you can't stop thinking about.

Whether it's landing that raise you've earned, launching the business you've built, turning your passion into profit, or booking that dream trip, getting the yes starts with one thing. Asking for it.

Be Honest.

When's the last time you actually did that? Like, really, ask for what you want?

I can't watch one more person shrink to fit into a 9 to 5 life that drains them. Stuck in a loop, waiting for a sign to move forward. When you let others call the shots, they'll make choices that serve them, not you.

That's how you end up underpaid, overworked, building

someone else's dream and retirement, then waking up one day wondering what happened to your life.

The first key to getting a YES is...Drum roll, please... Asking for it.

This is about taking ownership. Stop handing your power away. Decide what you want, speak it out loud, and go after it.

What Makes Your Heart Tingle

We're going after EXACTLY what you would do in a perfect world. Grab a pen and a piece of paper...

- Write ALL the things you love to do, BIG or SMALL.
- Write ALL the things you do not enjoy doing, BIG or SMALL.

Take a minute and picture yourself waking up in *that* life, your ideal one. Coffee in hand, maybe you're meditating, doing yoga, or just sitting in peace. Walk yourself through your day. What's your routine? How long are your workdays? Who are you spending time with? Make it vivid. Make it real.

See what you're going to see, hear what you're going to hear, and really feel all the feelings you will be feeling.

Shiny object syndrome is a trap. You're focused on your goals, then boom—someone else's success flashes in front of you, and suddenly you're questioning everything.

You think, "Maybe I should do that instead," and now you're down the scroll hole, Googling like crazy, polling your friends, and second-guessing your entire plan.

The ones winning aren't jumping from one thing to the next. They stay locked in on what they want and keep going. Every time you switch gears, you lose hours to research, second-guessing, and asking everyone else what they think. You end up starting over again when you could have been mastering the thing you said you wanted. Cut the noise, get clear on your goal, and commit to it. Back yourself like your future depends on it, because it does.

These rituals you just went through set the tone for a day that feels aligned with you. What's one small, powerful move you can use to anchor your day in the identity you want? In the morning, strike a power pose, Wonder Woman style, or fists up, stance strong. Just 16 seconds in front of the mirror to lock in that energy.

Before bed, release anything that isn't helping you. Let go of stress with EFT tapping, deep breaths, journaling, meditation, yoga, or whatever you'll actually stick to. Then drift off picturing your wealthy self living that life. Play the movie in your head. Feel the joy, breathe in the success, hear abundance all around you, and see the numbers you want in your bank account. Write it down to lock in the vision and let it run in your mind until you fall asleep.

WEEKLY RITUALS: LOCK IT IN

Pick one weekly ritual that keeps you locked into your vision. Start by letting go of doubts and limiting beliefs. No judgment, just release. As the week goes on, old patterns might try to sneak back in. Notice them, call them out for what they are, just old stories, and let them go. Stay present with your thoughts and shift what needs shifting. Your energy sets the tone for your wealth. Own your beliefs, feel them in your body, speak them out loud, and move like they're already true. When your inner script shifts, your outer results follow. This is the real work. The internal reset that makes success automatic.

Habits are automatic. They're the unconscious, repeated actions you do without thinking, like brushing your teeth, scrolling your phone first thing in the morning, or pouring coffee as soon as you wake up.

Rituals are intentional. They're habits with meaning attached. You do them on purpose, with awareness, to set energy, mindset, or identity. Journaling in the morning, lighting a candle before work, or repeating affirmations are rituals because they carry significance and intention.

Put simply: **A habit is what you do. A ritual is how and why you do it.**

Habits and rituals are your real power moves when it comes to building wealth. Habits are the daily deposits, like conscious spending, tracking your money, or planning ahead, that stack your financial foundation. Rituals are what keep your mindset on point, morning visualizations, and nighttime gratitude. That inner work that keeps your energy aligned with what you're actually working toward. Together, they connect how you think and act with where you want to go.

Wealth isn't going to explode just because you bought a cute planner or lit a candle. That stuff can set the vibe, sure, but what actually changes the game is deciding that your daily habits matter. When your rituals aren't just feel-good fluff but the actual structure that supports the wealthy version of you, that's when things shift. Every time you check your account with clarity, say no to chaos, or visualize that next-level life before bed, you're not just manifesting, you're building it from the inside out. Pick rituals that mean something. Stick to them like your future depends on it, because it does. This is where mindset meets movement. And when those two line up, you're unstoppable.

You've done a lot of heavy lifting in the Elicit section. Like a money detective, you pulled back the curtain on the sneaky beliefs running the show. In *Calibrate Your Compass*, you got clear on where you are and where you want to go. You unpacked your thoughts, feelings, and actions around money and finally saw what's been running in the background.

You looked at your habits and rituals to see whether they were setting you up for success or keeping you stuck at the same level.

In *Spending Reality vs. Spending Fantasy*, you stopped pretending and faced the truth. From there, *Smash Your Goals* broke those dreams down into steps you can actually follow. You rewrote the story you've been telling yourself about money. You've started to change the way you speak about your situation, and that shift alone has power.

The *Seven Step Sorcery System* gave you a rock-solid foundation to keep moving forward, even when things feel uncomfortable.

You've done the work. You've told your subconscious mind exactly where you're going. Now it's time to match your energy with action. The next section is all about Attract, and that's where things get fun. This is where you stop building the dream board and start living like the dream is already here.

This part of the journey is about becoming the person who

naturally calls in what they want. You've built the clarity. You've laid the foundation. Now it's time to fully step into it and move like the wealthy version of you is already running the show. Keep going. You're building momentum, and what's coming next will blow your mind.

A
ATTRACT

BECOME A MAGNET FOR WHAT YOU WANT

> *The future belongs to those who believe in the beauty of their dreams.*
>
> *- Eleanor Roosevelt*

Let's get one thing straight before we dive in. You *are the one who creates your reality*. Not your boss, not your past, not your bank account. You.

This section, *Attract*, isn't about learning how to wish for a better life. It's about owning the fact that you already have the power to create it. It starts with what's going on in your mind. Your imagination, your vision, and the version of you that's already living it.

This is where most people get stuck. They want more money, more time, more freedom, but they're still thinking like the version of themselves that doesn't have it. This section flips that script. We're diving into the real work that starts before the money shows up, before the business grows, and before the dream house is even pinned on a Pinterest board.

You're about to meet the part of you that dreams without limits, wants more without guilt, blocks out the noise, and turns every setback into a bigger vision.

This section is about waking up your ability to attract from within. It's about shifting your mindset, raising your standards, and calling in what was always meant for you. If you're ready to build a life that feels like it's actually yours, from your first thought to your last dollar, then let's begin.

CHAPTER 16
Imagination: Understand The Power

WHAT YOU PICTURE in your mind is what shows up in your life. Your imagination sets the tone. Let me show you how that played out for me.

The first half of that year felt incredible. We bought our first home, settled in, and even picked up a camper trailer to enjoy as a family. I was soaking it all in and finally starting to feel like things were coming together. We capped it off with my honeymoon in Mexico, eight years after getting married. No stress, just sun, ocean, and freedom. It was total paradise. I came back glowing, refreshed, and energized.

But by fall, life hit hard. Years earlier, my mom had already beaten the odds. Out of nowhere, her kidneys failed. One day she was fine, the next she was on dialysis. Then a miracle happened—not one kidney, but two. A double transplant. We were grateful, and for a while, life felt steady again. But in 2014, things shifted. My mom started getting sick, and this time it was different. No slow build-up, no warning signs we could prepare for. Just hospital after hospital with no answers and no direction. Then came the phone call, right after Labor Day weekend. A call that still echoes in my mind.

It was a Thursday, the kind of call that changes everything.

My parents were on the line, and I could hear it in their voices before they even said the words. The doctors had finally figured out what was wrong. It was a rare and aggressive blood cancer. They told her she had a year.

That call didn't just shake me. It cracked something open. I sat there holding the phone, trying to breathe, trying to make sense of what I was hearing. I was already questioning everything—who I was, what any of this even meant.

Four days later, she was gone. No warning. No time to process. No time to say everything I needed to say. The call shattered me. Her death rewired something in me I didn't ask for. Everything I thought I knew about life, time, and what really mattered started to unravel. That moment changed everything. Life, wealth, time, none of it made sense anymore.

So when I talk about imagining the life you want, I'm not just talking about the material things. It's not the "nice car" or the designer bag. It's the full picture. I want to be clear. I'm talking about intentional imagination for growth, not unhealthy disconnection from reality. This is practical imagination, not denial. You're building, not hiding. This isn't about escaping reality, it's about creating it on purpose. It's about training your mind to match what you want in life and using imagination to create results in the real world. The kind of wealth that includes time, health, and the people you love. Because your imagination doesn't just shape your reality, it reflects your soul. It's the compass you use to steer through chaos, loss, and change. It's how you remember what matters and how you create what's next.

Starting this chapter with my mom isn't random; it's the foundation. Losing her forced me to reimagine who I was, what mattered, what wealth really meant, and how I defined wealth. Not just in money, but in time, in presence, in memories. The wealth of a phone call, of a warm voice on the other end, Moments you can't get back.

What does wealth really mean? It's not just money, but time, presence, memories...

It's a voice you wish you could hear one more time.

It's the moments you didn't know were the last.

It's being there, fully there, while you still can.

It's having the space to grieve without worrying about bills.

It's being able to say yes to healing, to therapy, to time off.
It's not having to rush through your pain because life won't let you pause.
It's the moments you didn't know you needed until they were gone.
That's wealth. The kind you feel in your chest, not your wallet.

This chapter exists because, in the middle of my grief, imagination is what kept me going. I had to picture a version of me who could survive this, rise from it, and turn the pain into something that mattered. Imagination isn't about dream cars or big income goals. It's about finding meaning when everything falls apart. It's about visualizing who you want to become when everything familiar is stripped away. It's not just survival—it's rebuilding with purpose. That's the kind of wealth we're talking about here. The kind that starts in your mind and becomes the life you build on purpose.

This chapter, *Imagination*, isn't about fantasy. It's about facing the truth that life is short, and imagination is sometimes all you have when everything else falls apart. Losing my mom and finding myself in the wreckage showed me how powerful your mind really is. I didn't use imagination to escape. I used it to survive. To make sense of the pain. To rebuild from nothing. Because real wealth isn't just money in the bank. It's time. It's health. It's the people you love. It's having space to grieve without guilt. The freedom to heal without rushing.

It's not just about being present. It's about learning to breathe again when life won't slow down. That's the kind of wealth that keeps you grounded when everything else falls apart. That's wealth.

The kind you feel in your chest, not your wallet. This chapter is about using your imagination to face the hard stuff, to heal, to stay grounded, and to figure out who you are when life rips everything away.

The entire ride with my mom, from the shock of her kidneys failing to the miracle of her transplant to the gut punch of her cancer diagnosis, showed me how imagination becomes a lifeline. When nothing makes sense, your mind is where you start piecing it back together.

It's where you choose who you'll become and how you'll move forward, even when the ground under you feels shaky.

Imagination is where we go to make sense of chaos. It's not about escape. It's about learning how to hold both the good and the hard without losing ourselves. It's how we remember what mattered and still give ourselves permission to want more. Imagination reminds us that life isn't only measured in dollars or possessions, but in the moments that shape us and the visions that carry us forward. It's the bridge between pain and possibility, between what was lost and what can still be created.

Duality is about holding two truths at once — the joy and the grief, the abundance and the lack, the presence and the absence. When you think about wealth as both time and memories, both love and loss, you're already pointing to that dual nature of life. Duality means opposites exist together, and life is about balancing them.

Duality is key because life and wealth are never just one thing; they're always both, and learning to hold both sides is what gives you true power.

Life isn't just happening to you. It's being created by you, from the inside out. Every thought, every mental picture, is shaping what shows up in your world. Be intentional and make sure what you're picturing is actually worth building. Then show up for it. Every day.

People say things like:
"It's all in your head."
"You're overthinking."
"You're imagining things."
"You're making it worse by thinking about it too much."

Let me be clear, it's often used to dismiss what someone's feeling, as if what's happening in their mind isn't real or valid. What's "in your head" is powerful.

Your thoughts shape your emotions, your actions, and your reality. This isn't about living in your head or disconnecting from reality. You're not here to float off into fantasy land or pretend the hard stuff doesn't exist. This isn't about denial. It's about direction.

Imagination isn't where you hide; it's where you decide. You still live here, on this earth, paying bills and showing up.

When you use your mind with clear intention, you stop reacting to life and start creating it. This is grounded in reality and rooted in personal power. You are not running away from your life or pretending challenges don't exist. You are designing a future that actually feels like yours. Direct your own blockbuster vision and commit to showing up for it every day. Picture it in full high definition, with every detail dialed in. Spend intentional time in that mental cinema, watching the version of life you want to live. Your thoughts must match that movie with clarity and consistency. The universe does not cut scenes or revise your script. It delivers whatever plays on a loop in your mind.

Saying you want a "nice car" doesn't cut it. That's too vague and gives the universe nothing clear to work with. It's like placing an order and forgetting to say what you actually want. Stop treating your imagination like it's a joke or some throwaway concept. It's the most powerful tool you have for shaping what comes next. Your imagination doesn't just entertain thoughts; it builds the foundation for your reality. Every image you hold in your mind becomes a signal, and that signal starts shaping what shows up. So feed your subconscious something detailed and vivid. Picture yourself waking up in a home that matches your highest vision. Walk into your sleek kitchen and pour a hot espresso from that red machine that makes you feel like you've already arrived. Look out the window and decide what's there. Maybe it's a garden, or maybe it's the ocean, but either way, you're not just seeing it. You're building it. This is not just your morning routine. It's your future, already set in motion by your thoughts.

Everything begins in the mind. Every invention, every breakthrough, every success started as a single thought. Your imagination holds power, but like a muscle, it only grows when you use it consistently. No one else can do the mental work for you. You have to hold your vision and repeat it with intention. Keeping that mental picture alive throughout the day is where the real transformation begins. No one can take it from you unless you abandon it. Trying to change your external world without shifting your internal one is a losing game. Neville Goddard said it best: "An awakened imagination works with a purpose." This isn't about fantasy. It's about using your mind as a tool. Picture the moment you're after—the date, the stage, the promotion. Feel the nerves. Feel the pride. That emotion is what makes it real.

Now do a quick body check: heels, elbows, ears, nose, wrists. Feel them without moving. That's focus. That level of awareness? That's how you access imagination. When you think of your elbow, you don't need to touch it; you just know it's there. That's the level of presence you bring into your visualizations. It should feel just as real.

Drop into the vision like it's already happening. Let yourself play it out in your mind with emotion, clarity, and detail. What brings it to life isn't money, it's imagination. If you believe something is in your way, remember that belief came from your own mind. You imagined that obstacle. Change the picture, and you'll change the result.

Your imagination is where everything begins. It's where you create what's next. When you picture yourself thriving, successful, energized, fulfilled, you begin to make that version of yourself real. Not in some far-off future, but now. Your thoughts guide your actions, and your actions create your outcomes. Wealth is not just a number in your bank account. It's an energy you embody. If you want to feel rich, you have to live in the energy of abundance before the proof shows up. That's how you become a match for what you want. You don't wait to feel wealthy once it arrives. You choose to feel it now, so it has a place to land.

Being wealthy is an emotion you can tap into anytime. Be in the state of wealth if you want to be wealthy.

Can you remember a time when you felt totally wealthy?

Can you remember a specific time?

Go back to that moment in your mind.

Now imagine dropping fully into that memory, like you're there again.

See what you saw, hear what you heard, and really feel what it felt like to be completely wealthy in that moment.

Imagine being whoever you want to be just by using your

mind. Whatever you consistently picture, you can become. If you've ever caught yourself daydreaming about a different life or a new version of you, that vision isn't random—it's your future trying to get your attention. Everything around us started as someone's idea. Every invention and breakthrough began with someone imagining something more. The future belongs to those who are bold enough to see it before it shows up. Hold the vision in your mind and refuse to let it go. The only way to lose it is by deciding it's not possible.

Every dream you carry has the potential to become real, but you have to live it internally before it shows up externally. Imagination isn't about escaping life; it's about stepping into the reality you're meant to create. It's about feeling your desires like they're already happening. Think, "I've made it," not "I hope I do." Start thinking as the version of you who already has it, not someone hoping it might happen.

Think from the end, not of the end.

Imagination is more important than knowledge, Albert Einstein.

Your imagination shapes who you are. Say it out loud if you have to: *I am my imagination*. The more you believe that, the more everything shifts.

Picture a life where fear doesn't run the show and limits don't hold you back. That's the power of imagination. Every invention, every breakthrough, every bold move started as a thought. Don't just think about your dream life, step into it. When you're making your morning coffee, visualize yourself in your dream kitchen. Look out the window and actually see that perfect backyard in your mind. Let yourself feel it like it's already yours.

Knowing the work isn't enough. Change happens when you live what you've learned. That's when you see real results. Nothing will change if nothing changes. Embodying what you want isn't about being fake or dramatic. It's about stepping into the version of you who already has it.

That version thinks differently, feels differently, and makes bolder choices. Your self-image drives everything. No shift on the inside, no change on the outside. Start showing up like it's already yours. That's how things begin to move.

Crank up your imagination because that's where the power is. You want happiness, wealth, success? Then see it. Feel it. Picture it in detail. Smell the coffee in that dream house. Feel the cash in your hand. Step into the vibe like it's already here.

Neville Goddard taught that Imagination is a spiritual sensation. Step into the image of your wish fulfilled, add sensory detail, add texture, color, and sound. Let it be real in your mind, then live it because we become what we imagine.

Here's something people don't tell you: if the picture in your head is blurry or too far away, your body won't believe it. So, make it clearer. Make it brighter, bigger, and closer. Add movement. Turn up the color—if it's black and white, flip it to color, and if it's color, drain it to black and white. Layer in sound until it feels like it's happening right in front of you. Don't overthink it or force it. Keep adjusting the picture until it feels real, like it already happened. Once your brain locks in, your body and life follow.

This concept is based on neuroscience and psychology, especially how the brain processes mental imagery:

- **The brain responds to imagined experiences similarly to real ones.** Brain scans show that visualizing an action activates many of the same areas as doing the action. This is called functional equivalence.
- **Mental rehearsal improves performance.** Athletes, surgeons, and performers use visualization to improve skills. Research shows it strengthens neural pathways just like physical practice does.
- **The reticular activating system (RAS) filters information.** When you visualize something clearly and emotionally, your RAS tunes your awareness to spot opportunities that match that vision.
- **Embodiment and neuroplasticity.** When your mental image is vivid and repeated, it helps "rewire" how you think, feel, and act. That's neuroplasticity—your brain's ability to change based on input.

So yes, imagining in detail can influence your beliefs, emotions, and behaviors. It's not just "woo." Your brain takes it seriously.

Never lose the imagination within you.

How many times have you rolled your eyes at someone saying, "It's just their imagination"? That's where everything starts. Everything we use, wear, drive, or live in was first an idea in someone's mind.

Most people stop using their imagination. Don't let that happen to you. It's one of the most powerful tools you have. Now let's break down how imagination works and how it shapes your reality. It's not about daydreaming or wishful thinking. It's about using your mind on purpose—with clarity, emotion, and intention.

You're not just glancing at that vision, you're stepping into it. Feel the energy move through your body as you stand in your dream kitchen. Hear the hum of your coffee machine brewing that perfect cup. Smell the coffee, the clean air, maybe even the scent of your favorite candle burning nearby. See the space around you: big, bright, and vivid. If it feels dull or distant, adjust it. Pull the image closer. Make it louder, sharper, more detailed. Add texture. Let it feel so real that your brain doesn't question it. That's how you train your mind to believe it's already yours.

Want more money? Then see it. Picture your bank account with an extra zero. See the deposit notification pop up on your screen. Replay that image like it's already happened. That's how you flip your brain into receiving mode. Think it. Feel it. Walk like it's yours already. This isn't just theory. People like Oprah, Jim Carrey, Beyoncé, and Denzel didn't just daydream. They used their imagination on purpose. They created vivid pictures of their future and held onto them until the world caught up. That's the energy. That's how you build it before it exists.

They soaked in every detail, every sensation, every emotion. It wasn't just a quick thought—it was a full-time mind movie. They lived the success before it ever showed up. If you want the money, the fame, or that next-level life, get vivid. Feel it. See it. Breathe it. The more you practice, the stronger the connection between your mind and body becomes. That's what gets you ready for the real thing.

Visualization: The act of creating a mental image. You *see* the picture in your mind as if it's playing like a movie.

Imagination: Going beyond just seeing — you *live* it in your senses. You feel the emotions, hear the sounds, smell the scents, even taste the experience as if it's happening right now.

Don't mix up visualization with imagination. Visualization is seeing it. Imagination is living it, feeling it, hearing it, smelling it, tasting the win like it's happening now. Most people skim the surface, but when you pull in every sense, your brain locks in and starts shifting your reality to match. So stop treating goals like distant dreams. Step into them now. Live them in your mind as if they're yours already. That's how you build momentum, collapse time, and make success inevitable.

Think FROM the end, not OF the end. Sounds cryptic, right?

You're on the edge of something new, a fresh home, a sleek car, or finally getting those bills handled. Don't wait for the future to taste it. The moment you open your eyes, dive into your vision: stepping into your future kitchen. See yourself there, now, brewing your morning coffee on a glossy red machine that screams luxury. Hold that vivid image. Feel the space as you make your coffee. Feel the aroma wrap around you, hear the hum of the brew, and take in the view outside, whether a peaceful river, a buzzing oceanfront, or a quiet garden, each with its own rhythm. This isn't just seeing, it's living your future life, down to the gritty sand of your beach backyard or the rustling leaves of your forest retreat.

Your daily visualization doesn't just feed your subconscious, it strengthens it with vivid, powerful images.

Each morning, immerse yourself fully. Feel the cup's weight, hear the pour, smell the brew, watch the dawn light spill across your dream space, and taste your future in every sip. Use your imagination all day, every day. Live inside it. We don't imagine to escape. We imagine to create. Reality is imagination amplified. Everything you see once lived in someone's daydream. The entire universe is built from imagination.

Right now, I want you to do something for me. Be fully present for a second and just listen to my voice. Put your attention on your elbows. Not touching them—just bring your focus there. Are you feeling your elbows through your hands, or are you feeling them with your mind's energy? Now move that energy up to your shoulders. Feel where they are without physically doing anything. You're just tuning in. If I asked you to feel your knees, your focus would shift there. If I said feel your ears, your energy would go there too. That's how powerful your awareness is. It happens automatically without effort. It operates deep within your subconscious mind. And it's the same when you imagine. You fall into the image in your mind's eye. You don't just see it—you enter it. Fully.

That's your subconscious working. If I said knees or ears, your energy would go there. That's what imagining really is, feeling into the image in your mind's eye.

This isn't a game. It's training your mental muscles to flex on command. So when you visualize, don't just watch, dive all the way in. Feel every detail as if it were happening now. Tune in so completely that your mind can't tell the difference. That is the exact process of how imagination transforms into lived reality.

Here's what "feeling into your imagination" really means, because let's be honest, people throw that phrase around and never explain it.

Say you want to perform on stage. Maybe it's guitar, singing, a mic drop moment, whatever. You know fear's gonna kick in: goosebumps, belly flips, flushed cheeks. Now, when you're imagining it, actually feel that. Let your body react like it would in real life.

That's what "feel into it" means. If your face gets hot or your hands sweat on stage, feel that in your visualization. Don't just see the moment, experience it.

Same with calling in wealth. It is not just a number. It is a state of being, a way you choose to live. So step into that. What does the wealthy you, see, hear, touch, smell, and wear? Feel the calm, the freedom, the power in your body. Let your system believe it's already here. That's how you lock it in. Hold the image and hold the feeling with you all day, every single day.

No one can take your imagination. The only way to lose it is to stop using it. You have the power to embody anything: money, love, or success. But if you only think about it and never step into it, it stays out of reach. Think from the vision itself, not just about it. That simple shift changes everything. Unless you enter the image in your mind and think from it, not about it, it will not happen.

If you're imagining yourself on a first date or asking for a raise, and you know you'd feel nervous, then bring up those exact feelings while you visualize. Let the butterflies kick in. Feel the heat rise, the adrenaline move through you. That's how you connect to it. That's how you activate your energy. Over time, this gets easier. It becomes natural, like muscle memory. And once that level of intensity lives in your imagination, your external world starts to catch up—fast. I've seen it. I've watched clients shift their reality just by learning how to feel their vision fully. That's the real power of imagination.

I've trained in subconscious work, and let me tell you—imagination is the tool. Just like a trainer can't do your push-ups for you, I can't visualize your dream life for you. You've got to show up and do the reps. Your imagination, your effort, your results. It's all you. This isn't about escaping life. It's about designing it from the inside out. Let your imagination be the first thing you lean into when you wake up and the last thing you connect with before bed. It's not fluff. It's the foundation. What you create within becomes what you live out loud.

Stop obsessing over what's missing. Start visualizing wealth, joy, and freedom. That version of you that you keep thinking about already exists. Step into them now.

Use all your senses when you imagine. Don't just see the goal, feel it, taste it, move through it like it's real. If your imagination feels rusty, shake it off. It hasn't gone anywhere. Einstein said imagination is more important than knowledge, and he was right. Your imagination is your edge, and it becomes the advantage that separates you from everyone stuck in old patterns.

Holding your vision daily is not just a casual suggestion, it is a powerful practice. Your imagination is yours, and no one can take it from you unless you let it go. Neville Goddard said that when your imagination has intention behind it, it pulls in what you want and clears out what you don't. That's how you shift your life.

I want you to grab your journal or a piece of paper and write down what your dream life looks like in full color right now. Describe it with all your senses. Make it real on paper, so your mind can start making it real in life.

Imagination is everything. It is the preview of life's coming attractions.

— Albert Einstein

CHAPTER 17
Map It. See It. Practice It Daily

You've already seen how imagination changes the way you see life. Now I want to show you how to practice it daily, step by step, so it becomes second nature.

Imagination makes things possible. When you see yourself living with wealth, success, and freedom on your terms, you're not just daydreaming, you're leading. The more clearly you feel that vision, the faster your subconscious accepts it as truth. Walk yourself through that day like it's already here, grounded, calm, and aligned. Each time you return to it with focus, that version of you grows stronger and closer.

Neville Goddard once said, imagination is spiritual sensation. Enter the image of the wish fulfilled, then give it sensory vividness and tones of reality by mentally acting as if it were a physical fact. We become what we imagine. Visualization is when you form a mental image or concept using only your sense of sight. It's seeing a scene in your mind. But imagination is something else entirely. Imagination goes deeper. It activates all five senses and connects to your emotions. You can imagine something you've never seen before and still make it feel real. That's the power of it. Imagination allows you to step into an experience before it exists in the physical world. You don't just see the moment, you feel it, hear it, smell it, taste it, and react to it. Imagination is not about watching from a distance, it is about living the moment so completely that your mind believes it and your body follows. That belief is what begins to shift how you show up.

One of the most effective ways to practice imagination is to think from the end, not just think of it. This is where you stop hoping and start living in the result before it shows up. Most people wish, talk, or wait. You train yourself to step inside it. When you do, your mind and body catch the shift, and you begin showing up as if it is already here. That practice moves your focus from what is missing into what is already done.

When you picture something with clarity and intensity, your subconscious takes it as direction. The quality of those pictures shapes the quality of your results. What you hold in your imagi-nation shows up in your life. This is why I teach daily mental rehearsal. Wake up each morning and place a vivid image on the screen of your mind. Make it real. Make it specific. Anchor into the details. Train your mind to see it until it no longer feels like a fantasy; it feels like a memory from your future.

When you use your imagination, the clarity of the picture decides the clarity of the result. Hold a vague image and you get vague outcomes. Hold a strong image and your life starts to line up with it. That is why practice matters. Each morning give your mind one powerful picture to work with. See it, feel it, and keep repeating it until it no longer feels like fantasy, it feels like memory. Imagination becomes reality when you train it daily with precision.

Let me break this down even more. Maybe you want a new home, a new car, or paying off debt with ease. Don't think of it as some far-off goal. Imagine it now, like it's already yours. If it's the house, see yourself unlocking the door, stepping inside, running your hand along the countertop. If it's the car, feel the wheel in your hands, the seat beneath you, the sound when it starts. Make it real in your body and your mind. You're not waiting. You're living it mentally now, so your reality can catch up.

When you wake up in the morning, drop into the scene like it's already real. You walk out of your front door, keys in hand, and slide into your dream car. The leather is soft. The engine purrs the second you start it. You adjust the mirror, grip the wheel, and let yourself sit in that moment. You're not trying to feel successful. You are successful. The car smells like new leather and power. You pull out of your driveway without a second thought, because this isn't new to you. You've done it in your mind so many times, it feels like second nature.

Then your phone lights up. A notification hits. "Deposit Received: $50,000." You look at it, calm and grounded. You don't freak out, you don't second-guess it. You expected it. You open your business dashboard and watch the numbers climb with more sales, more growth, and more impact. You are not hustling from panic or scarcity anymore. You are moving from power. You already saw this before it happened because you trained your mind to expect it.

This is what it means to think from the end. You're not begging for results or wishing things would change. You're anchoring into the reality you've already chosen.

Every detail matters, from the sound of the engine to the touch of the steering wheel to the exact number in your bank account. The more specific you get, the more real it becomes. Your subconscious does not know the difference between what is real and what is imagined, it only responds to what you feed it consistently. So feed it power and feed it precision. Whether it is your dream car, your ideal income, or a business milestone you have been working toward, stop treating it like it is out of reach. Bring it closer and make it the default setting in your mind. Keep showing up to that same mental scene until it no longer feels like a dream, it feels like a memory from your future.

Imagining creates reality. Everything that exists today was once an idea in someone's mind. But imagination only turns into results when you use it every day. Most people stop too soon. They imagine once or twice and then quit when they don't see instant proof. The ones who keep showing up, holding the same picture until it feels real, are the ones who watch their lives shift. This isn't about hoping. It's about training your mind to live in the scene until it feels like your current reality.

No one can take your imagination from you. You're the only one who can shut it down by refusing to use it. Most people don't persist long enough to imagine their ideal life as already done. Every image you hold—money, wealth, success, love—can be imagined and embodied. But unless you step into that image and think from it, not about it, nothing happens. You have to feel into it. Live in it. Walk through the scene in your mind like it's your current reality, not some distant goal.

Let's say you're picturing a first date or asking for a raise. You already know you'd be nervous, right? So bring that same feeling into your imagination. Feel the butterflies. Feel the rush. Tap into the actual energy your body would respond with. That's how you pull your attention into the moment. That's how you activate it.

Over time, this starts happening on autopilot. You'll start slipping into your imagination with more emotion, more clarity, and way more power. And when you do that consistently, the physical world begins to shift fast. I've seen it happen. As an NLP trainer, I've helped people unlock massive changes just by tapping into this one tool.

I want to give you an example of what using your imagination feels like.

I would like you to close your eyes, (but of course you can't when you're reading this, but play along, read this part once and really feel into the words on this page, the black ink that created the words, the way the words roll of your tongue when reading the words, the way the words feel when you see them).

I would like you to "close your eyes"...

And I would like you to focus on my voice (the words on the page).

I want you to go ahead, and I want you to close your eyes. Imagine yourself sitting in your most favorite place at home. Feeling the familiar feelings of home. As you look around, you see all of the things that make your home yours. Feeling the familiar smells, feeling the familiar feelings of home. And allow yourself to get more and more comfortable where you're sitting, noticing how it feels to be there.

Then go ahead and stand up and, as you do, feel how your

clothes shift on your body when you stand up from where you were sitting. Now, using your imagination, picture yourself making your way into your kitchen and heading towards your fridge. Go ahead and reach your hand out and feel the handle of your fridge underneath your hand, noting its texture and the cold temperature of the handle...

Tugging on the handle, you hear that sound a fridge makes when it opens, and you can see the light turn on and feel the cold air flood out onto your skin from inside the fridge.

And as you observe all the items inside your fridge, you see something that maybe you hadn't noticed or known was there before.

Right in front of you, inside the refrigerator, is a bowl of perfectly ripe, yellow lemons. And as you reach into the fridge, you put your hand around one of the cold lemons, and you can feel the chill and texture of the rind on your skin as you pick it up.

Closing the fridge, you walk over to the counter where there is a cutting board and a knife. Pick up the knife and slice through the lemon, and listen as the knife tears through the rind and flesh of the lemon. *Ssschhhh*. Hear the lemon getting sliced in half.

Now take one of the halves and cut it again, and watch as the light glistens off the flesh of the lemon. You can already smell that lemony-citrus smell fill your nostrils.

And I want you to pick up one of the pieces of lemon...

And I want you to bring it up to your face...

And inhale...

The smell gets stronger and stronger.

And go ahead and take a nice juicy bite *sslpppppp* *mm mm mm.*

Good. Now go ahead and open your eyes. (or Yes, bring your focus back to reality).

Did you notice that there's more saliva in your mouth now than when we started?

Was there really a lemon? No, of course not, but your mind thought there was. The reason imagination works so well is that it creates thoughts so realistically that the body reacts biochemically.

The key to using your imagination is to turn it into a daily

Map It. See It. Practice It Daily

practice. Each time you create a mental scene, make it vivid and detailed enough to activate all your senses. It should feel real, not like a daydream. Use specific details so your mind can lock onto it. The more grounded the image, the easier it is to live from it instead of chasing it. Picture the money in your account, the freedom in your calendar, the peace in your mornings, and hold that vision no matter what is happening around you. This is how you train your subconscious to expect it.

Don't just hover over the image in your mind. Step into it every single day until it feels familiar. Walk through the scene and let it become second nature. Bring the same picture back again and again until it feels normal, not far off. That is how you close the gap between where you are and where you want to be.

Most people underestimate the power of imagination. But the truth is, we're creating all day long. We either do it on purpose or by default. If you're not paying attention, your imagination goes dormant, like a muscle you forgot to flex. But once you wake it up, everything changes. You become the one shaping your life, not just reacting to it.

I can't clock in at your job, answer your emails, or show up for your dreams, that's your responsibility. You've got to show up and do the work. I can't imagine your wealthy life for you. You've got to feed your mind the vision and feel it like it's already real. When your imagination has purpose behind it, that's when it moves mountains.

Every image can be embodied. You already know how to put your attention somewhere. When I ask you to feel your elbows or your ears, you don't have to touch them—you just know where they are. That's the same muscle you use when you feel into your imagination. At first, it takes focus. But keep doing it, and it becomes second nature. You'll start stepping into your mental images automatically because everything starts in the mind.

That dream you're chasing, that business you're building, that house you want, that moment where it all clicks, someone imagined it first, and now it's your turn.

Imagination lays the foundation before the world ever catches up. We waste too much time looking outside for answers, forgetting the power was always inside. So start using your imagination with intention. Wake up ready to step into it, carry it with you throughout the day, and let it guide your actions. At night, fall asleep inside the scene you've built. Let your mind replay it as if it already happened. Walk through the vision slowly, with feeling, like it's your truth. This isn't something you do once in a while. It's a daily practice, a rhythm. When you repeat it often enough, it becomes part of you. It stops feeling like a fantasy and starts feeling like a fact.

It's not your circumstances holding you back. It's the attention you keep giving them. The more you focus on what's wrong, what's missing, or what's not working, the more power you give it. Your imagination was never meant to fix your current reality. It was meant to build the next one. Maybe your imagination feels rusty because you haven't used it in a while. That doesn't mean it's broken, it just needs practice. You can reactivate it by seeing what you want, not how or when it will show up, but as if it is already here. Your imagination doesn't run on logic. It runs on belief, emotion, and repetition. Train it to work for you again. Start with one clear vision, not twenty. Just one.

CHAPTER 18
The Treasure Hunt Is Back On

THINK BACK TO those childhood days, where every corner of the world seemed sprinkled with a bit of magic. You know that smell right after a summer rain? Wet pavement, fresh air, like something new is about to start. That's when it would appear: a magnificent arc of colors stretched across the sky, a natural masterpiece painting the horizon. As a kid, spotting a rainbow wasn't just about seeing pretty colors in the sky; it was a signal that an adventure awaited, a hidden treasure just begging to be discovered. With eyes wide and a pounding heart, you'd set off, convinced that at the end of this luminous arc lay a pot of gold, a reward for the brave and the hopeful. That childhood belief in endless possibilities is what we're reigniting today as we move toward our own pots of gold in life.

The rainbow chases from childhood, those moments when every color in the sky was a promise of treasure, and all you needed was a rain shower and sunlight to kick-start the adventure. Remember that electric buzz, that thrill as you spotted a rainbow stretching across the sky, a kaleidoscope of red, yellow, pink, blue, purple, orange, and green?

Your heart just didn't beat when you saw those colours. It came alive. Back then, you didn't question it. You just knew that somewhere beyond that rainbow was something waiting for you. It wasn't some cute little game; it was a mission. Every step you took toward that glow in the sky felt like anything was possible. The world felt wide open, and you were all in.

Fast forward to now—when was the last time you felt that same electric pull to chase something big? To find that metaphorical pot of gold? This isn't about some childhood fantasy or fairytale daydream. It's about reigniting that fire, that drive to seek out treasures in your adult life. Today isn't about nostalgia—it's about activation. Spot wealth the way you used to spot rainbows, with eyes wide open and a heart full of anticipation. See opportunity everywhere, like it's waiting around every corner. Don't stop at dreaming about wealth. Go after it with the same bold energy you once had chasing that rainbow, because the end of the rainbow isn't the end at all—it's the beginning.

Wealth doesn't always show up as a giant check. Sometimes it starts small, in places you wouldn't think to look.

I want you to look everywhere. In your car, underneath the cushions, in the crevices of your couch, and in the pockets of your clothes. If you've put away winter clothes because it's summertime, you might find something in those boxes. Every day, I want you on the lookout, like an adult on a mission, eyes peeled for pennies, dimes, crumpled bills, or anything the universe tosses your way. This is your adult treasure hunt. Stay alert, look down, and expect the unexpected, because money shows up when you're open to seeing it.

Check your washer, your dryer, the bottom of your purse—anywhere. Today, I want you to find money because we love that thrill, that excitement of discovering something. We adore the chase, that treasure hunt, seeking the pot of gold at the end of the rainbow. And if you find money, holy shit, that's amazing!

Think about the money that's coming in. If you find a penny on the ground, don't just kick it aside. If you dismiss that penny, you're telling the universe that you're not ready to receive more. Our subconscious mind doesn't see the difference between a penny, a dollar, or a hundred-dollar bill. It just understands the concept of value. So, if you're disregarding a penny, your subconscious believes you're rejecting money in general. It doesn't care if it's a penny, a dime, a nickel, or a toonie if you're in Canada, a $5 bill, or a $10 bill.

Today is about finding money. If you spot a penny on the ground, thank that money and really feel into it. Pause for a moment and just visualize. Remind yourself of that feeling. When was the last time you felt that jolt of excitement from discovering something?

Was it when you were a child, chasing after that pot of gold at the end of the rainbow, or on a beach treasure hunt, convinced gold was buried beneath the sand?

Remember those days when we'd stash treasures behind bushes or bury secrets near picnic tables? That was our mission: to uncover hidden gems. That thrill didn't die. It just got buried under adulting. Today, we're bringing it back. We're reigniting that flame, tapping into the lost thrill of treasure hunting, even as adults navigating the chaos of everyday life, full-on adulting 101.

In the daily grind of nine-to-five routines, running errands, playing taxi for our kids, and managing the never-ending cycle of responsibilities, we sometimes lose sight of the joy in life's little surprises, like finding an unexpected dollar in the laundry. Let's set out on a quest today, with eyes wide open, because the universe has a quirky way of revealing treasures when we actively seek them. Your subconscious is always listening and responding, and when you find even a single penny and respond with gratitude, you're sending a clear signal that you're open to receiving more. That moment of appreciation triggers a ripple effect, attracting more wealth and abundance because your energy is aligned with it. It's not about the amount; it's about the message you send by how you react. Treat every find like it matters, because it does. That small spark of excitement fuels a bigger fire, and the universe will match it.

Each dime you spot is a stepping stone to more. Overlook a penny today, and you might miss out on the bounty waiting just around the corner. Money, in its essence, is energy, ever-flowing and omnipresent, waiting to be acknowledged and welcomed.

So, as you journey through today, let each coin you find be a reminder of the abundant universe we're part of. Feel the rush, the childhood excitement of discovering hidden treasures, whether it's a shiny quarter under the couch cushion or a forgotten bill in a winter coat pocket. Today is your treasure hunt, a grown-up search for the pot of gold at the end of the rainbow. Let the thrill of discovery be your guide and let your heart light up with the joy of each find, as if each penny, dime, or dollar is a secret nod from the universe, whispering, "There's more from where that came from."

It's not just a hunt for cash, it's a hunt for those little moments of real joy. Get out there, explore with the enthusiasm of your younger self, and let each find, no matter how small, fill you with that excitement. Go on, start your treasure hunt and rediscover the thrill of the find!

Carry that treasure hunt energy into real life. Treat every coin, crumpled bill, or surprise find like it matters. Finding money isn't random, it's proof that your energy is moving. You asked, and the universe answered.

Money shows up for those who notice it. And when you treat the small stuff like it matters, you're telling your subconscious you're ready for more. Every coin counts. Every find builds your belief. This isn't just about the cash—it's about the energy you hold when you spot it, the meaning you give it, the gratitude you feel in that moment.

From Seeing Coins to Seeing Possibility

Finding pennies is one way the universe plays with you. Now, let's take that same energy inward. Move through the world like wealth is waiting for you because it is. Imagination shapes your reality. So when you're thinking about how you want things to be, don't just think it—see it. Feel it. Build it in your mind first.

Your imagination holds the power to reshape your external world. Don't get stuck on what your senses are showing you right now. Use them inside your imagination instead. See it, feel it, hear it, smell it, taste it as if it's already here. Step into your imagination and write the story from desire, not from default. Stop thinking of the thing. Start thinking from it. That's how it works.

You can't stand in two realities at once. You're either inside the image of 10k a month or you've shifted into the image of a 20k a month earner. You can't hold both. So, if you want 20k, you have to live there now. Think from that space. Be in that image.

If you doubled your income right now, what would actually change? What would you do differently? What would your day feel like, look like, sound like? Would you finally hire that house cleaner? Would you pay bills without that tight chest feeling? With 20k, there's no "I can't afford this." It's just "Pay it."

Still clinging to that job you hate? In the 20k version of you, you wouldn't just quit it—you wouldn't even have it. That job wouldn't even exist in your world.

You wouldn't be thinking about what you're trying to escape. You'd be focused on what you're building. When you shift the image, everything shifts with it.

Don't lock your focus on just one thing, like the new car. Zoom out. Think about your full identity, your dream home, your steady income, and the way you walk through life. The money is just a measuring stick. It's never just about the money, it's about what that money makes possible.

What does that income actually give you? What does it bring into your world? What does it feel like? What kind of experiences does it allow? What does it upgrade? Luxury isn't just a thing, it's a feeling. Wealth isn't only money. It's the freedom, the choices, and the upgrades in how you live and feel every day.

Wealth is something you can step into at any time.

Here are a few daily practices you can use to bring imagi-nation into your body and your reality. This is about making it real. Making it physical. Giving your nervous system something to lock onto, not just something to think about. Do you want imagi-nation to show up in your life? Then show up in it first.

5-Minute Future Self Embodiment

This one's fast but potent. Choose a time of day when you can commit to five focused minutes. No distractions. Sit still, close your eyes, and see your future self living the life you're calling in. Imagine them walking through their day. How do they move? How do they talk? What do they wear? What do they say yes to? How do they respond to stress, to success, to everyday decisions?

Now here's where most people stop, but you're not most people. Don't just watch. Step into them. Be them. Embody their energy in your breath, your posture, your face, your voice. What does confidence feel like in your body? What does wealth feel like in your skin? Stay in that version of you for the full five minutes.

This daily five-minute practice begins to hardwire your nervous system for the version of you that already has it all. Repetition creates identity. Identity creates action. Action creates results. You're not trying to get there—you're already there. This isn't about fantasy, it's about frequency. This is about giving your body a new normal. Your brain learns through experience, not theory, and this is you teaching it who you really are.

If you skip a day, fine. Start again the next. But keep showing up. When you do, the world starts to shift around you.

Nightly Playback

Right before bed is when your subconscious is wide open. What you think about in that window stays with you longer and sinks deeper. You've spent all day in your current reality. But you don't have to go to sleep in it.

Replay the day as if it went exactly how your highest self would've lived it. Imagine yourself making bold moves, hearing yes, hitting the goals, feeling clear, grounded, focused, and powerful. Did you say something you wish you hadn't? Rewrite it. Did you hold back on something? Picture yourself going for it instead. Your brain can't tell the difference, so give it the version you actually want.

Your brain can't tell the difference between real and vividly imagined experiences. Neuroscience shows it fires the same way either way. Brain scans show that the same areas light up whether you're doing the thing or imagining it. It also doesn't process negatives well. So if you say, 'I hate debt,' or 'I have so much debt,' your brain zeroes in on the word debt and reinforces that image.

This is why it's so important to picture and phrase what you do want, not what you don't.

Replay it all—how you walked, how you spoke, what results came in. Feel the emotion of that ideal day in your body. Then carry that into sleep. That version of your day becomes the blueprint your mind holds onto through the night.

This isn't pretending things didn't happen. It's overriding what you don't want to keep replaying. The world already replays your limitations every time you open your phone or scroll social media. This is about shifting the story back in your favor. Take that five-minute window before bed and own it. Your future is shaped by what your mind rehearses. Train it wisely.

This practice lets you build muscle memory for your highest self. Night by night. Thought by thought. It matters. Especially when the rest of the world wants you stuck in fear, guilt, or regret. You're not here to sleep on who you are. You're here to make it real.

Mirror Embodiment Work

This one's uncomfortable for most at first, but it's powerful. Stand in front of a mirror. Look yourself in the eyes. Not at your hair or your skin or the things you wish were different. Eyes. The window to your truth.

Now speak. Not like a robot. Speak like you mean it—with energy, emotion, and certainty. Tell yourself who you are. Who you're becoming. What you're calling in. Say it until your voice matches the vision. Say it until your body believes it. Even if your brain resists, keep going.

Say things like:

- "I've got this."
- "I make shit happen."
- "Money flows to me."
- "I'm not backing down."
- "I'm stronger than my excuses."
- "I trust myself."
- "I win."

- "I move with confidence."
- "I keep going."
- "I create results."
- "I'm already the version of me I'm stepping into."

This isn't about convincing yourself. It's about claiming it. Most people speak more truth to strangers than they do to themselves, but this changes that. When your subconscious hears you say it out loud with belief behind it, it registers it as real. You're rewiring the program, rewriting the script, and replacing the old junk with a new direction.

Try this for two minutes a day. Set a timer if you need to. Morning is great, but any time works. You don't need to feel "on" or supercharged; you just need to show up. Your voice carries power, and when you turn that power inward, that's when you start leading your life instead of just reacting to it.

Power Anchor

Choose one physical object to represent your future self. A bracelet, a necklace, a rock, a keychain—anything you'll see or touch often. The point isn't what it is. It's what it reminds you of.

Just like Pavlov's dogs, who were trained to salivate at the sound of a bell by associating it with food, you too can condition your body to react to certain cues with the right kind of energy. Pavlov proved that repeated association can trigger automatic responses. The same principle applies to you. If you consistently associate an object, like a bracelet or a keychain, with feelings of wealth, success, and power, your mind and body will begin to automatically link that object with the feeling of having it all. Just like the dogs salivating at the bell, your body will start to respond to that object, anchoring you to the identity you're creating for yourself. This is how you build new habits and create lasting changes in how you show up in the world.

Songs, smells, and sights anchor you all the time. A song comes on the radio and suddenly you're back at your wedding or your first love. The smell of cookies can pull you into your mom's kitchen, and an old truck might remind you of your grandpa.

That's anchoring. Your brain links an outside cue to a memory or feeling so strong that it instantly pulls you there.

Anchor a specific emotion or identity to it. Every time you see it or touch it, you take five seconds to drop into that version of you. The wealthy you. The healthy you. The confident you. Use this object with intention, on purpose.

This is your trigger. It snaps you back into alignment when you're off. You can charge it up by holding it during your visualizations or during your five-minute embodiment practice. The more you associate it with the desired feeling, the stronger the connection becomes. Over time, your brain wires that object to that identity. That's called anchoring. And it works. If a song can trigger tears or a smell can bring back a memory, then yes, a physical object can bring you back to power. Let this object ground you in the identity you're building every single day. Let it be your reminder, your anchor, your nudge back into who you really are.

CHAPTER 19
Divine Desires

SOME DESIRES ARE not random, and they don't appear out of nowhere to distract you. They are planted deep within you, and they stay there because they are meant for you. These desires carry weight, they feel sacred, and no matter how hard you try to silence them, they continue to tug at you.

I'm not talking about surface-level wants or ego-driven goals. I mean the kind of desire that lights you up from the inside, the one that won't back down no matter how long you try to push it away. It's the pull you feel in your gut, the vision that comes alive in your daydreams, and the truth that whispers in those quiet moments when you finally let yourself admit it—you want more.

Some desires don't pass through quickly like random thoughts or ideas. They stay with you. They pull at you when no one's around, almost like they've been waiting all along for you to notice. That isn't an accident. That's direction. They're here to grab your attention, and the moment you stop brushing them off or waiting for perfect timing is the moment you finally start moving with intention.

Desire isn't just about what you want. It's also about what's been holding you back. Be honest, do you even know what's been keeping you stuck? This chapter is about facing the desire that won't leave you alone—the one that, when you finally say yes to it, has the power to shift everything else.

We're going to zoom in on the reality you're living versus the one you know deep down is possible for you. Not the Pinterest-perfect version or some polished highlight reel. The life that actually feels like yours. It's about closing the gap between what you say you want and how you actually live.

You'll get clear on what energizes you, what you're naturally built for, and what it takes to live in alignment with that, not the filtered version, but the real you. If you need a reset or a reminder of where you're headed, flip back to the Calibrate Your Compass chapter because that's where you got honest about what really matters and how aligned or off-course things feel right now.

This chapter, the Divine Desires chapter, takes that even deeper. Now we're getting real about the life you keep imagining, the one that won't stop pulling at you.

Divine Desires aren't about dreaming. It's about actually living the damn dream, feeling it, breathing it in, letting it shape you. Even the messy, unplanned parts of life have something to show you. Back then, I had three kids at home. Daryll was working out of town for weeks at a time, and I was always with the kids. My mom lived nearby, so bingo became our thing. My dad or a sitter would watch the kids, and for a few hours on a Tuesday night, I got to just be with her. That's where bingo nights came in. They weren't just something to do. They were our mid-week reset, our sponta-neous little thrill. No agenda, no pressure, just us chasing luck and laughing at whatever came next. That's where I first learned what risk felt like. How fun, chance, and unpredictability could live side by side. And that maybe, just maybe, the things that look small end up teaching you the most.

Bingo was loud, a little chaotic, and full of laughter, and that was the lesson. Life doesn't come in quiet, perfect packages. It hits hard, moves fast, and rarely sticks to the plan. Life is always going to throw curveballs. But sometimes, those moments are exactly where the lesson is hiding. Bingo halls weren't just noise and numbers. They taught me risk and reward. Seeing your number on the caller's screen, sitting at the edge of your seat, hoping it's the next one called, while my mom's shaking her head at me, smiling as I anticipate dabbing my card with my bright pink dabber on the next number on the screen, then hearing someone else shout bingo right before you. Story of my life! And let me tell you, that stings. You're pissed, hoping they mis-dabbed a number, praying the caller shuts them down so you can swoop in with the win. Then you take a breath, shake it off, and move on to the next game. Every number brought a mix of hope and anticipation. Every win felt electric. Every loss was just part of the game. That loud, chaotic room full of strangers taught me to take chances, roll with what comes, and trust that life can surprise you when you least expect it.

I don't really go to bingo anymore. After my mom passed, I stopped, but once a year over Christmas break, I'll take my kids. It's not just about the game. It's about keeping the memory alive, laughing together, and soaking up a night out with my adult kids. That's wealth too.

Those moments taught me that life isn't just about chance, it's about choosing what matters and daring to want more. And that's exactly what Divine Desires are here to show you.

If you've already locked in a one-year goal using the Seven Step Sorcery System in Chapter 11, that could be your Divine Desire. It's not just some random wish; it's the thing pulling at you with the most energy right now. The one that feels big, personal, and meant for you. The same way bingo pulled me in for more than the game, your Divine Desires pull you in for more than the goal. They're here to guide you.

I know this because I lived it. I learned firsthand that when I stopped chasing money and started following what actually felt right, everything shifted. Let me write it out for you, how I personally lived that truth.

I decided to live differently, not chasing money like it was everything, but choosing what actually felt good. That's how we ended up back in Ontario, trading hustle for slow mornings, cozy routines, and family-first living. Then came a lakeside wedding that felt like a movie. In the middle of that joy, I realized how much of life we had been missing by always preparing for the worst. Trying to stockpile for 'just in case' was making us miserable. That moment woke me up. The more I tried to avoid the bad, the less space I left for the good. Fear was stealing the joy of living.

Years after our big day, we finally went on our honeymoon to Mexico. It felt overdue, like life had pressed pause and then finally hit play again. Warm sun on our skin. Drinks in hand. Laughing like teenagers. For a minute, it felt like life gave us a second shot at something real. The moment we touched Canadian soil, reality smacked us back — we walked into a flooded basement the day we got home. It was a total mess. It was the reminder I didn't want but needed. No matter how perfect something seems, things can flip fast. You can plan all you want, but sometimes things just don't go the way you thought it would.

Eminem once said: *"If you had one shot, or one opportunity, to seize everything you ever wanted... would you capture it, or just let it slip?"* He was asking the same question life throws at all of us. If the moment is there, will you go for it, even though you don't know what comes after?

I chose to stop chasing money and move back to Ontario. I chose to take my honeymoon and live that experience fully. And then life hit—our basement flooded, and not long after, my mom passed away.

So, the question becomes: *If I knew the hard stuff was around the corner, would I still choose the joy?*

If I had known about the flood, or about losing my mom, would I still have captured those moments of joy? Absolutely. Because that's the point. You never know what's coming, but you still choose to live.

Because life doesn't wait for convenient timing. Divine Desires aren't just about the highs; it's about how you handle the lows. It's not about chasing money, but building real wealth from the inside out through real moments, real choices, and choosing joy even when things fall apart. My story changed when I focused on what mattered: my life, my family, and building something real. Not chasing money or status. After eight years together, we got married how we wanted, at a quiet lodge by the lake. No pressure, no fuss, just us and the people we love.

That's what this is really about. Not the dollar amount or ticking off boxes, but the kind of life you're building when no one's watching. The kind that feels rich in a way numbers can't explain.

Your Divine Desire might be a feeling you can't shake, a vision of how life should feel—calm, aligned, real. Not something you chase for the sake of it, but something that feels like home when you let it in. And it shows up in everything: those bingo nights with my mom, the long-overdue honeymoon, the flooded basement, and every curveball in between. It's not just about chasing big dreams, but how you carry yourself while you're in it, living, adjusting, and showing up through it all.

We dig into the hidden fears and unspoken desires that mess with us and hold us back. Because wealth isn't just cash, it's the guts, the memories, and how you live your life. Now that you know where I'm coming from, let's turn the focus back to you.

The reason I shared those stories is to show you that life will never line up perfectly. Joy and chaos live side by side. But your Divine Desires are the pull that carry you through both. Now it's your turn to look at your own life with the same honesty — to see where you are right now, and where you know you're meant to be.

Back in Chapter 13: *Blurring the Lines Between Spending Reality vs Spending Fantasy*, you mapped out your financial reflection—your current spending versus your ideal. Now we're zooming out. This isn't about money, it's about energy, lifestyle, alignment. It's about comparing the life you're living with the life you know you're meant for. Let's map it out.

CURRENT REALITY VS DESIRED REALITY

Answer the following as honestly as you can:

Go through these questions and write your current reality in the left column, and then go back through and write your desired reality (aka if anything were possible, and you were living your best version of life) in the right column.

What is the first thing you do when you wake up in the morning?

Current Reality	Desired Reality

What does your morning ritual/routine look like?

Current Reality	Desired Reality

What do you wear at home, and how do you feel in those clothes?

Current Reality	Desired Reality

What do you wear when you go out with friends, and how do you feel in those clothes?

Current Reality	Desired Reality

What kinds of food do you eat, and how do they make you feel?

Current Reality	Desired Reality

Where do you usually eat your meals? At your desk, kitchen table, or couch? Or are meals one of those things you forget exist half the time?

Current Reality	Desired Reality

What type of exercise (if any) do you do, and how does it make you feel?

Current Reality	Desired Reality

How do you usually spend your free time?

Current Reality	Desired Reality

What does your home look like?

Current Reality	Desired Reality

How does your home environment feel like?

Current Reality	Desired Reality

How do you practice self-care, and how often?

Current Reality	Desired Reality

What role does spirituality play in your everyday life?

Current Reality	Desired Reality

What support systems do you have in your life?

Current Reality	Desired Reality

Look at your "Current Reality" vs. your "Desired Reality" and answer the following questions:
- How close are they? Are they almost aligned, or miles apart?
- What do you feel is standing in the way of your dream life?
- What's one small step you can take for each area that moves you closer to that desired life?

Create an Action Plan

An action plan breaks your big goals into short-term steps that move you closer to what you want. The smaller tasks add up and lead you to the bigger outcome.

Ask yourself:
- What will I do between now and next week?
- How will I finish the task at hand?
- What's the final step I need to reach this goal? (Work backwards.)

- What do I need to do differently this time to actually get results?
- What don't I want to do but know I must?

Let's get real about Divine Desires. This isn't some soft concept. It's built from the gritty, beautiful moments that shape who we are. Those bingo nights with my mom weren't just games. They were lessons in chance, courage, and rolling with whatever life threw our way. That same energy showed up years later when we stopped chasing numbers and started building a life around what actually mattered. Family, laughter, connection, and choosing what felt right, even when it didn't make sense on paper.

This chapter ties everything together—the fun moments and the hard ones that hit without warning. The surprises you never planned for. Wealth isn't only about reaching goals, it's about how you live while moving toward them. It's about what you learn through risks, setbacks, and the decision to keep going even when everything feels off track. As you finish this chapter, remember this: Divine Desires are not just goals. They're signals. They show you what you care about, what matters most, and how strong life becomes when you stop holding back and start living for real.

When your desires are strong enough, you will appear to possess superhuman powers to achieve

— Napoleon Hill ♡

CHAPTER 20
Turning Doubts Into Fuel

You start with big dreams, building an online business, opening a local shop, going back to school, moving to a new city, or finally getting healthy. Then doubts hit. Questions like *Where do I even start? Am I cut out for this? Does anyone care about my vision?* Suddenly, your dream feels shaky, like it might slip away. This chapter is about cutting through those doubts and dead ends and figuring out how to make your ideas happen. We'll break down the four D's: dreams, desires, doubts, and dead ends, and turn them into steps you can take to move forward.

You have the dream and the spark that lights you up, but then the doubts creep in. They cloud your vision, tighten your chest, and make you second-guess yourself. You stall, momentum fades, and before you know it, you've convinced yourself to wait. This is where most people stop. The doubts get louder, the vision slips further away, and before long you're standing at a dead end where dreams deflate and desires dim.

The four D's are Dreams, Desires, Doubts, and Dead Ends. They shape everything. You'll learn to catch the doubts before they spiral and flip the dead ends into redirections.

This is where your dreams and desires stop being ideas and start becoming real. Let's break them down with real examples and the kind of fire that comes from building the life you actually want.

Dreams

Dreams are where it all starts. They're the visions that light you up and refuse to let you settle. They're not some far-off fantasy — they're the version of life that feels real and possible for you. Dreams show up as that nudge that whispers, "This isn't it yet, but it could be." They're bold, personal, and loud enough that ignoring them only makes them come back stronger. Think about quitting the job you hate to finally start the business you can't stop imagining. Or buying a house that actually feels like yours.

Desires

Desires are what light a fire under your dreams. They're the deep pull, the emotional charge, the thing that makes you say, "I need this." It's not just about what you want. It's about what you feel called to go after. Desire is what turns a daydream into a non-negotiable. It's what pushes you to move, to act, to keep going even when it doesn't make sense on paper.

Think about how you keep circling back to the idea of going back to school, even though life's already busy. Or when you look at your kids and know deep down you want to build something better, not just for you, but for them.

Doubts

Doubts show up right when you're starting to get serious. They're the questions that creep in and shake your confidence. Am I too late? What if I fail? What if I look stupid? They're sneaky. They don't come in yelling; they whisper, and if you don't catch them, they grow. But doubts aren't always bad. Sometimes they're just asking you to be honest. To look at what you believe, and decide if it's actually helping you. Picture yourself about to post that first video online for your business, and your brain chimes in, 'Who do you think you are?' That's a doubt. And it's your cue to answer back. The goal isn't to never have doubts. The goal is to see them, question them, and keep going anyway.

Dead Ends

Dead ends aren't stop signs. They're the moments that force you to pivot. You thought things would go one way, but they didn't. That doesn't mean it's over. It means it's time to look in a new direction. Think about pouring months into launching something, only to have barely anyone show up. That stings. But maybe it wasn't the thing, or maybe it just wasn't the timing. That's a dead end, trying to point you somewhere better.

These moments are uncomfortable, but they're useful. They make you reassess, realign, and get clearer on what actually matters. Dead ends don't mean stop. They mean shift.

4D Exercise
Spot Your Dreams

Start by getting really clear on your bigger vision. Write down all the details of what you want—your dreams and desires. As you do this, notice any "yeah, but" thoughts that sneak in. Write those doubts down too.

Example: "I want to own my own home." Then the doubt shows up: "But I don't know if I can afford it." Write it down.

Catch the Doubts

Say your dreams and desires out loud, one by one. Pay attention to any negative thoughts that rise up. Write those down.

Example: "I save money every month." Then your brain chimes in: "It won't be enough." Or, "I don't deserve this." Or, "I'm not capable."

Flip the Dead Ends

Look at the doubts you wrote. Where did they come from? When did you start believing them? Are they actually true? Challenge them. Question them. Decide if they've earned a place in your life—or if they're just blocking your way forward.

Return to Your Desires

Circle back to what you really want. Say out loud what you're choosing to believe now. Put your eyes on where you're going, not the doubts you've already exposed.

This road through dreams, desires, doubts, and dead ends is anything but smooth. It can feel wild, uncertain, and like everything is working against you. But those moments when you're questioning it all are not signs you're failing. They're the exact moments that grow you. Face those doubts head-on. Turn the dead ends into new paths. Every time you stumble, remember it's just part of the process. The breakthrough comes after the breakdown. And the payoff is massive.

And speaking of doubts and dead ends, let me tell you about the time I killed not one, not two, but three money trees. It sounds ridiculous, but that story showed me more about wealth, neglect, and growth than any business book ever could.

The Tale of a Money Tree Murder

Once upon a time, I decided to invest in a money tree. You know, one of those plants that's supposed to bring good fortune and financial prosperity? Well, let me tell you, if killing a money tree was a lucrative business, I'd be a billionaire by now. They say it only takes one ice cube a week to keep these trees thriving, a simple task, right? Yet somehow, I managed to transform this easy-peasy routine into a botanical disaster. Not once, not twice, but three times. This is the tale of a money tree massacre.

There I was, standing with an ice cube in hand, acting like I was performing some sacred ritual. I place the ice cube in the soil, nodding to myself, convinced I'm on the fast track to wealth. Fast forward a few weeks, and my money tree looks more like a twig from a horror movie set. Leaves? What leaves? They decided to abandon ship faster than my dreams of financial abundance.

This tragic tale of my money tree is more than just a plant fail. It was a mirror for how I was unknowingly pushing wealth away. Every time that plant dropped a leaf, it felt like my money was saying, "Not today." I was giving it the same half-hearted effort I was giving my finances, and the results showed.

So, what's the lesson here? It's not about the ice cubes or the watering schedule. It's about the care, consistency, and environment we create. That money tree taught me that wealth isn't built on random, one-off actions. It grows when you give it steady attention, the right conditions, and stop leaving it up to chance.

Now that we've laid my poor money tree to rest, let's move into something lighter and more intentional. This isn't about taking on a massive challenge. It's about making small, playful shifts in your everyday life to start aligning in the energy of abundance.

Wealth isn't built on random, one-off actions. It grows through consistency, nurture, and the right conditions for expansion.

So let's step into something more uplifting and actionable.

Injecting Fun and Wealth into Everyday Life

Trying to remember to feed a plant frozen water wasn't my definition of fun, but transforming the mundane into avenues of abundance can be as simple as changing the notifications on our phones. Imagine each sound: a cash register's cha-ching, a slot machine's jackpot jingle, or even a catchy tune about money reminding you of the wealth flowing your way.

Want to take it further? Change your passwords. Seriously. If you're typing "1234" or your cat's name, we've got work to do. Switch it up to something that actually aligns with what you want. Try names like "AbundanceNow," "WealthFlow," or "RichBitch2025." Every time you log in, it's like a little reminder to your brain: "Hey, we're calling in money over here!"

While you're at it, keep it playful. Notice when you see repeating numbers like 111, 444, or 888. Repeating numbers are a signal of alignment, reminding you that wealth flows faster when your thoughts, actions, and energy are in sync with abundance. Those aren't random—they're little nudges that you're in flow. Rename your bank accounts. Why stick with mundane labels like "checking" and "savings"? Rename them to reflect your desires and goals. Think 'Freedom Fund' for savings or 'Adventure Account' for your travel budget. If you're aiming for a specific financial milestone, like 'Manifesting $5000', create an account just for that goal! Naming your accounts creatively not only clarifies your financial targets but also infuses joy and purpose into everyday banking.

You can also, declutter your wallet. Just like the time I realized my old, cluttered wallet was a symbol of my disorganized financial past, take a moment to clean yours out. Discard outdated receipts and unused loyalty cards, arrange your bills neatly, and give it a good wipe down. Maybe even smudge it with some sage to clear out the old vibes and welcome in fresh prosperity. You could even do a wallet upgrade. If your wallet feels like a relic from your teenage years, perhaps it's time for a new one. I remember the shift in my mindset when I switched to a wallet that wasn't just functional but also made me feel prosperous and organized. It doesn't have to break the bank; find something that speaks to your style and financial aspirations.

The more fun you make it, the more magnetic you become. So set that ringtone, type in that power password, and start carrying yourself like the abundance you want is already here.

Remember my money tree? It wasn't the ice cubes that killed it, it was the lack of steady care. Wealth works the same way. When you treat it with fun, attention, and consistency, it grows. When you neglect it, it withers. The difference is that you get to choose which way it goes.

Here's what I want you to do—just like I did:

- Change your alert tones to sound like money.
- Switch up your passwords so they're little mantras in disguise.
- Keep your eyes peeled for repeating numbers—111, 444, 888.
- Rename your bank accounts so they match your goals. Call it "Freedom Fund," "Adventure Account," or "WealthyAF!."
- Give your wallet a makeover. Your wallet should feel like a space wealth would want to live in.

The truth is, we make money hard. We overthink it, stress over it, obsess about how it's going to come. But when we ease into the idea that money is everywhere, that it's trying to show up for us in big and small ways—we shift. Our mindset shifts. Our energy shifts. And suddenly, we're open. Let this be your starting point. Make this fun. Let it be easy. Because money doesn't just come when we hustle—it comes when we align.

Now that you've flirted with your finances, changed your passwords to power affirmations, and given your wallet a well-deserved makeover, take a moment to acknowledge the shift in your relationship with money. These activities are more than just tasks; they are rituals that invite prosperity and mindfulness into your daily life. By engaging with your money in these intentional ways, you're not only tidying up your financial space but also aligning your energy with abundance and success. Reflect on how these changes make you feel and consider the new possibilities that may unfold as you continue this journey of financial empowerment and personal growth

The truth is, my money tree wasn't just about a watering schedule and wilted leaves, it was a reflection of the 4 Ds in real life. I had the dream of wealth, the desire to grow it, the doubts that crept in every time a leaf dropped, and the dead ends that forced me to rethink how I was showing up. The same way that tree needed consistent care and the right environment, so do your dreams. Doubts and dead ends aren't signs to quit; they're reminders to pay attention, adjust, and keep going until growth takes root.

Doubts might test you, but they're only there to remind you that momentum is waiting on the other side.

CHAPTER 21
Momentum

IN THE EYES of the typical societal norm, I did life backwards. While the usual path goes school, marriage, house, then baby, my path was reversed. I got pregnant first, got married next, and then bought a house. And I did it all while earning a diploma and raising two kids. Why does this matter in a conversation about wealth? Because it's all about momentum. It's about grabbing life as it comes and moving forward anyway. It's what keeps you going through the good, the hard, and the unexpected. It's what turns your backwards steps into forward movement.

Momentum isn't just a trendy word; it's the thing that makes life feel alive. It's what keeps you building, creating, shifting, and leveling up. Not just in your bank account, but in your energy, your choices, and how you move through the world. When you've got momentum, even the messy parts start working for you.

Momentum is proof that you're living life on your terms. I'm talking about wealth that resonates from the inside out, wealth that doesn't care about societal norms or the order of operations. It's about creating a life that keeps moving forward, gathering experiences, and growing richer in every sense of the word.

Momentum shows up when you stop worrying about doing things in the "right" order and just keep moving. It's about choosing your own path and staying in motion. Wealth isn't a checklist. It's how you live, act, and carry yourself every day, no matter the sequence.

Chasing anything from a place of panic never works. The more you grip, the faster it slips away. Real progress happens when you stop trying to control everything and start trusting yourself.

You put in the work. You show up for your life, your people, your goals. And then you breathe. You stop forcing results and let things unfold because they always do when you're grounded and consistent. That's where momentum actually lives — in the mix of effort and trust.

Momentum isn't only about action, it's also about how you see yourself along the way.

It's time to drop the old story that says you're not enough. Money is just paper and digits. It's not the measuring stick for your value or the depth of who you are. You are not your bank account. You're not your income, your bills, or your credit score. You're a whole human with real strengths, real wins, and a life that means something. Stop letting money tell you what you're worth. It doesn't get that power.

When you really get this, your world doesn't just shift, it changes everything. It's like realizing you've had the power all along. Now you're ready to own it, use it, and actually enjoy your life. That's the moment where action and trust finally meet. Where your value isn't tied to your bank account, but to how you actually live.

You keep that fire alive by celebrating the small wins. Every day you show up, you're building something real. Even the quiet moments count. Just because it looks still doesn't mean it isn't working.

Money does not define your worth. If you're stuck on the failures or the missed goals, remember life isn't just about winning. Sometimes not getting what you want leads to something better. Money doesn't decide your value. What matters is the meaning you attach to what you live through and what you have.

How to keep momentum alive when it feels like nothing's happening (yet):

- Trust that it's a journey, not a sprint.
- Remember your why.
- Feel the certainty in your body that this is your purpose and it will work.
- Trust that whatever happens is part of the process.
- Celebrate yourself for taking action and acknowledge how far you've come.
- Truly believe there's no failure, only feedback.

Momentum isn't a one-time burst. It's a decision you make daily. To show up, to move forward, and to trust the process. Even when it feels slow, even when no one's watching.

I want you to write down 3 small wins from this past week, no matter how minor. It could be finishing something you'd been putting off, showing up for yourself when you didn't feel like it, or taking one uncomfortable step forward. Small wins build big momentum.

Momentum is your advantage. It doesn't demand perfection, it craves persistence. Every step you take keeps the energy moving. Keep showing up, keep trusting, and keep building. The results are already unfolding, even if you can't see them yet.

CHAPTER 22
Gratitude Seals The Deal

THE NIGHT MY world crumbled was the night I lost my mom. Anger became my shadow. It wasn't just grief—it felt like betrayal by every doctor who couldn't save her, and by life itself for being so unfair. I wasn't just heartbroken, I was furious. Bitter. Pissed off at everything and everyone. For months, I carried that rage like armor, snapping at life and shutting down, convinced the world owed me for what it had taken.

It was New Year's Eve the year my mom died, and while everyone else was counting down and pretending to be excited, I was just sitting there angry. Pissed off at life. Numb. Negative. Snappy. I didn't care about anything anymore, and not in a powerful way, in a shut-down, don't-talk-to-me kind of way. But something hit me that night. This isn't what she'd want. She wouldn't want her death to turn me into someone bitter. Me being pissed off at the world. That night, I vowed to purge the toxic negativity sucking the life out of me. I left my job. I cut off my friends, I cut people off who drained me. I distanced myself from family. Any energy vampires or negativity in my life, gone. That night, I decided something had to change. That year broke me, but it also woke me up.

It was the hardest yet most transformative year of my life, not because of the sorrow following her death, but because I chose to start living from gratitude instead of grief.

Out of necessity, I made a New Year's resolution to cut the negativity that had taken root in my life. And if you've ever actually stuck to one, you know—it's one of the hardest things to do, but also the most rewarding.

This chapter isn't about grief. It's about choosing gratitude even when life kicks the shit out of you. That shift is what changed everything. At its core, this is about choosing gratitude when life gives you every reason not to, in your hardest moments and even when it hurts. This isn't about pretending you're fine or sugar-coating the pain. It's about telling the truth, even the ugly parts, and deciding to shift anyway. It's about finally getting honest with yourself and realizing that holding onto pain doesn't keep you connected to them; it just keeps you stuck.

You want to honor the people you've lost? Live like they mattered. Live in a way that means something. That's what this is about. Don't get it twisted. I'm not thankful my mom is gone, but choosing gratitude is what helped me survive it. Choosing gratitude didn't just help me survive the grief. It reshaped how I saw everything, even the everyday stuff I used to complain about.

Take everyday bills, for example. Being grateful for bills might sound like thanking the monster under your bed for scaring you—ridiculous, right? But each bill represents something in your life that's pretty incredible.

Let's get specific. Take your cell phone bill, for example. Sure, it sucks to fork out that cash every month, but what does it really represent? Connection. It's how you check in on your kids, stay in touch with your friends, or send a "just thinking of you" text at midnight. It's how you scroll Reels, binge TikTok, Snapchat your bestie, run your business, sell your digital products, connect with customers, stalk your ex (don't lie), book your Airbnb, grab concert tickets, and FaceTime your cousin who moved out west. You swipe right on Tinder, order Uber Eats when you're starving, and yeah, you've even got 9-1-1 in your pocket. You've got a doctor, a nurse, a whole damn universe in your hand.

That bill is more than just numbers—it's freedom, connection, opportunity, and your entire world on demand.

And then there's the internet bill. Another one that makes you groan, but think about it—it's what keeps you plugged in. Social media, emails, late-night YouTube rabbit holes, online courses, random Google searches, the memes that make you laugh when you're having a day, the cat videos you pretend you're too cool to watch.

This isn't just the internet—it's your global connection, your business hub, your entertainment, your education, and for a lot of people, their entire income stream.

We complain about the bills, but the truth is, most of them support a damn good life. Before you roll your eyes at the next payment, pause and realize—these bills mean you've got a life worth paying for. So yeah, let's talk about the gas, the hydro, the roof over your head.

Whether it's fueling your car or heating your home, it's about movement and comfort. It gets you to your favorite people and places, and keeps you cozy on those bone-chilling nights. It's not just gas.

Hydro bills light up your life, literally. Every flick of a switch banishes the darkness, illuminating your home, allowing you to cook, read, or binge-watch your favorite shows. It's easy to overlook and take for granted, but without it, everything stops. That current is a possibility and fundamental to our daily comfort and convenience.

Next time you catch yourself grumbling while paying a bill, stop and ask what it actually represents.

These aren't just expenses, they're signs of a life that's working. A connected, supported, comfortable life. You're not throwing money into the void. You're investing in your freedom, your convenience, your connection to the people and things that matter. Being grateful for these bills doesn't mean you love the cost. It means you see the value. You get what they make possible. That's the shift. You stop resenting what you have to pay for and start appreciating what it gives you access to.

Gratitude isn't just some fly-by-night thing you say to sound positive, or spiritual word vomit. It's a choice you make when life's a mess and you're trying to find your footing again. When you get in the habit of appreciating the little things, the coffee in your hand, the sun on your face, the way your playlist hits just right, you're training your brain to look for what's working. That frequency pulls in more of what you want. Gratitude sharpens your attention and keeps your energy locked on your vision, even when the results haven't shown up yet.

Gratitude isn't just a feel-good trend. It's the real fuel behind the way you move, the way you think, and how you show up for your life. When you choose to live in gratitude, you stop sleep-walking through the days and start noticing what's good. You value what you've built, who you've become, and the connections that matter.

It's not about pretending everything's perfect. It's about seeing the full picture and choosing to focus on what's working. Even those bills we just talked about prove this. They aren't just payments, they're proof of connection, comfort, and a life that's supported. When you shift how you see them, gratitude stops being abstract and becomes something you live every day.

Let's get clear on what gratitude actually means. Merriam-Webster defines it as "the state of being grateful; thankfulness." But gratitude is more than a polite thank you. It's a choice. It's noticing the good even when life feels heavy and choosing to center on what's working instead of spiraling about what's not.

People who live with real wealth understand this. They're not hoarding money or treating success like a secret club. They give, they share, they help. Because they know abundance isn't limited. There's more than enough to go around when you stop acting like you're in competition with everyone else.

Their real edge is that they had that mindset long before their bank account showed it. They gave their time, their energy, and they lifted people up without needing anything in return. Because they knew the energy you put out always circles back, and it usually comes back bigger than you imagined. That kind of mindset? It's powerful, but let's be real, it's not always easy when the numbers in your bank account aren't matching your vision.

It's one thing to believe in abundance when things are flowing, but what about when it feels tight? When your bills are stacking and your income is already spent before it hits your account? That's where most people tap out. But this is exactly where the shift starts to matter most. I know this might sound like bullshit when you're behind on bills and dodging phone calls. I've been there. I've blocked the debt collectors. I've sat there wondering how the hell I was going to make it work. This isn't about pretending everything's sunshine, lollipops and rainbows. This is about choosing a new way of thinking when it feels like everything's crashing down. I'm not blind to how real it is. Some people aren't living paycheck to paycheck—they're living paycheck to next day. That's why this shift matters. Because in the middle of all that chaos, you still have gratitude.

Gratitude works best when it's expressed. Send the text. Make the call. Write the letter. Say what you've been holding back. Let people know they matter.

Say it clearly and don't water it down. Gratitude has power. It shifts your energy fast and raises your frequency, whether you're having a good day or not. What you focus on multiplies. When you start leading with appreciation, life responds with more to appreciate. But if you brush it off or stop noticing the good, don't be shocked when it dries up. Gratitude is simple, but its ripple effect is massive.

Now it's your turn to move. Choose one act of generosity that means something to you. Not for show. Not for a gold star or a smelly sticker. Do it because it feels right and reflects who you are. That kind of giving sends a loud signal to the universe. It says you're in. You trust there's enough. And you're ready for more.

Gratitude is something you live, not something you fake.

You know that feeling when you've got the perfect gift for someone? You can't sit still, hopping around with excitement, practically counting down the seconds until they open it. "Come on, open it up!" you say, practically bursting with anticipation. And when they finally do, it's like you're more excited than they are! Giving just has this magical way of filling you with happiness, sometimes even more than the person receiving it. It's pretty incredible how much joy you can get from making someone else smile and not needing anything in return.

If you're ready to shift into gratitude, start now. Notice what's right in front of you. Let gratitude be the first thought when your eyes open and the last one before you fall asleep. Carry it into everything you do. Let it show up in how you speak, how you move, and how you live.

Gratitude is not just about saying thanks. This isn't about pretending to be positive or slapping on a fake smile. That's like being nice to someone's face while trashing them behind their back. Real gratitude is like real kindness. It's consistent, grounded, and it shows up whether someone's watching or not.

So why does gratitude matter so much? Because it shifts your state fast. It moves you out of lack and into abundance, turning you into a magnet for more of the good. This isn't about pretending the hard stuff doesn't exist. It's about putting your focus on what's working so that the rest loses its grip. When you live from that place, you don't just survive—you expand. You start noticing the beauty in moments you used to miss.

Let's lighten it up for a second with something fun. Ever catch 11:11 on the clock and get that weird little rush? Like it means something? You're not alone. Many people view it as a sign that they're aligned, in flow, or on the right path. Some call it an angel number. Others say it's the universe's version of a head nod. Whatever you believe, 11:11 tends to pop up when you're dialed in and energetically clear.

Here's where it connects to gratitude. Gratitude raises your frequency. It lifts you out of the noise and anchors you in the now. That's the same state that makes you more likely to notice signs like 11:11. Not because they just started showing up, but because *you* started paying attention. You're present. And when your energy is open like that, the synchronicities start stacking. Some people even use 11:11 as a personal check-in. When they see it, they stop and ask, "Where's my energy right now?" or "What can I be grateful for in this moment?" And then there's the classic, "Make a wish"—because hey, even that lighthearted ritual has its roots in hope and belief. It's like a little cosmic reset. A tap on the shoulder that says, "Hey, don't spiral. Align."

So no, 11:11 isn't directly about gratitude—but gratitude puts you in the exact state where moments like 11:11 happen more often. And when they do, take the hint. Pause. Breathe. Smile. Say thank you. It's a small moment that can shift everything if you let it.

I want you to make a list of 25 things you're grateful for right now. Sit down, breathe deep, and actually feel it. Start with the everyday stuff you overlook—your breath, your body, the roof over your head, the food in your kitchen.

Then stretch it. Be grateful for the smell of fresh coffee, the sound of crickets at night, the sidewalk that carries you home, the way music shifts your mood, even the smell of rain on pavement. Random or obvious, big or small—it all counts.

Here's a simple way to play with it:

- Write down 5 things you can see right now.
- Write down 5 things you can hear.
- Write down 5 things you can touch or feel.
- Write down 5 things you can smell or taste.
- Write down 5 people, memories, or opportunities that make your life better.

By the time you get halfway, you'll notice the shift. Your energy, your focus, even your mood starts to change. That's the power of actually feeling it, not just writing it down. I remember one night, sitting on the couch with a pen and zero motivation, and by the time I hit number 17, everything flipped. My energy, my focus, even my mood lifted.

When I look back, gratitude was the fuel that kept me moving forward. It's been the quiet driver behind every shift. Every struggle, every breakthrough, every moment that felt like too much ended up shaping the story. Gratitude helped me see the meaning in all of it.

This isn't surface-level thankfulness. It's real. It's the kind of gratitude that changes how you see everything. Wealth stops being just about money. It shows up in your growth, in the way you bounce back, in the people around you, and in the fact that you're still standing. Gratitude isn't about feeling good for the sake of it. It's about recognizing what's already solid in your life and building from there.

Don't just practice gratitude when things are going well. Make it part of who you are. Let it shape how you move, how you lead, how you love. Gratitude opens the door to more than just success, it opens the door to a life you actually want to live. It didn't just shift my mindset; it rebuilt my life. I'm grateful for the five extra years I had with my mom—time we were given because of a stranger we'll never meet. Someone who lived without ever knowing us and passed without ever seeing the impact they made. They gifted not just more time, but a ripple of memories that touched an entire family tree. That kind of unseen generosity? That's the power of gratitude. And if you let it, it'll do the same for you.

CHAPTER 23
The Frequency Of Money

I PRACTICALLY REPELLED money. I've danced with a million dollars over my lifetime, but let's face it, with bills, groceries, kids, and life's endless carousel of expenses, money seems to have wings, flying away before I can say "savings."

Not everyone's dream is a seven-figure bank balance. Some people just want what money makes possible — freedom, fun, time with family, and more laughter in their days. You don't need millions to live rich. Real wealth isn't only about what's in your account. It's about how you feel, how you show up, and the life you're creating. You don't need to be a millionaire to feel like a million bucks.

Looking back on my childhood, a kind of wealth no amount of money could ever buy surrounded me. Our neighborhood was pure magic. We turned backyards into kingdoms, baseball fields into battle zones, and every street corner held a brand-new adventure. Hide and seek was an all-out mission. We climbed rooftops like little daredevils and tucked ourselves into treetops like pros.

The streetlights were our signal to wrap it up, the universe's way of saying, "Alright, kids, you've had your fun."

Back then, there were no cell phones or fancy toys. What we did have was freedom, and our imaginations ran wild. We stuck together—and that was the real wealth. It was everything. We built campfires by the lake in front of our house, camping out all night. In the winter, we'd slide down this giant hill behind our home we called Bum Rock—a rock shaped like a bum, crack and all—crashing into trees at the bottom to stop ourselves, our laughter echoing through the open spaces.

Just five doors down, the convenience store was our treasure trove of penny candies and 5-cent goodie bags, a sweet reward after a full day of play. Nearby, the basketball court and baseball field were the backdrop for endless rounds of catch with my brothers, and games of marbles, hackie sac, and my favorite, double-dutch with the neighborhood kids.

In a world without cell phones or digital distractions, our connections were real. My house was the go-to hangout, buzzing with kids, laughter, and the kind of energy only childhood can create. My brother's older friends lived across the street, my best friend was next door, and the rest of the neighborhood kids filled in the crew. We weren't just neighbors. We were a little tribe, a constellation of kids who made magic out of nothing.

My richest moments weren't tied to money. They came from freedom, joy, and wild play in a neighborhood where imagination was the real currency. We hit the movies on Fridays, bush parties on Saturdays, and laced up for hockey on Sundays. Life wasn't measured in dollars. It was measured in moments. That's what real wealth looked like.

So why bring all this up in a money chapter? Because, by now you should know that wealth isn't just about your bank account. It's the emotional and mental abundance you allow yourself to feel. Think about how easy it was to switch from school mode to play mode as a kid. Shifting into a wealthy state of mind works the same way. The numbers don't get the final say. So how do you tap into that feeling of wealth, even when the money isn't quite there yet? You shift your state. One of my favorite NLP exercises does exactly that. It's designed to pull up a vivid, empowering emotional state that changes everything.

Can you remember a time when you felt totally_____?
1. "Can you remember a specific time?"
2. "As you go back to that time now, float down into your

body and see what you saw, hear what you heard, and really feel the feelings of feeling totally _____."

That exercise is powerful because it shifts your state fast. And shifting your state is exactly what changes your relationship with money. Let's get real for a second. Money isn't just paper and coins. Life's expenses have this annoying way of making it feel like money grows wings and disappears.

Now here's where science comes in. Dr. Joe Dispenza, author and neuroscientist, shows us how our thoughts and emotions shape our reality. When you think a new thought, new neurons fire. When you back that thought with emotion, the brain wires those patterns in deeper. Keep practicing wealthy thoughts and feeling them in your body like they're already true, thats how you become that version of you.

Your brain doesn't know the difference between something vividly imagined and something real. So when you picture a wealthier version of yourself, living it and feeling it, your brain and body start responding as if it's happening now. That's when you begin attracting things that match that energy. Your biology shifts. That's the frequency of money.

Most people repeat the same thoughts every day, which creates the same emotions, which trigger the same actions, and BOOM, the same bank balance. Same fear. Same limits. Over and over. But when you change your inner state, your thoughts, your energy, your emotions, you send out a new signal. And that signal is what magnetizes results.

Dr. Joe calls it "moving from cause and effect... to causing an effect." You're not waiting for the money to show up so you can feel secure. You feel secure now, and then the money starts showing up. You become the effect. Your job is to rehearse mentally who you want to be. That's what athletes, CEOs, and the most successful people do. You practice being wealthy, not someday, but now. *Think wealth, speak money, be rich.*

I'm not just giving you tools. I'm helping you change your chemistry. The version of you that stressed about money? That was just a biological pattern. The new version is rewiring the subconscious and firing up abundance circuits like a boss. Dispenza's research even shows shifts in gene expression. You can literally become the kind of person who makes, holds, and multiplies money, not just by changing your job or income, but by changing your internal frequency. So, while some people still think "money mindset" is fluffy nonsense, science is saying otherwise.

Thoughts are electric and emotions are magnetic, and together they create the energetic field you carry with you every single day. When you lock into wealth vibes, you start pulling in wealth results because your energy is already tuned to that outcome. You don't need permission to get rich, and you don't need random luck to change your situation. You're not out here hoping money finds you. You are the frequency that money responds to. Think of your mind like an old-school radio. You've got to find the exact station where wealth plays loud and clear. It might sound a little out there, but it's not. Your beliefs, emotions, and daily habits around money are the signal you're broadcasting. And that signal decides what shows up.

Our thoughts and emotions are like bouncers, deciding who gets in and who's left out in the cold. This isn't about a trend or some surface-level mindset hack. It's about shifting into the energy that matches the life you're building. Abundance doesn't come from hoping—it comes from aligning. Your thoughts and emotions set the tone. They decide what stays and what slips away. And I learned that the hard way back in my early work days, in a cramped, dimly lit bar, the one I touched on at the beginning of this book.

In the depths of downtown's nightlife, I was the waitress at a bar where the vibe was as intoxicating as the drinks we served. The air was thick with anticipation and the scent of stale dreams. Yep, pretty much sums up the bars I worked in during my early twenties. The place was packed wall-to-wall with people, the music pounding with a cover band playing ACDC. Every shift started with a hundred-dollar float. That float was supposed to hold me down for the night. A promise of structure in the chaos. But one night, something felt off. I was too trusting back then.

Naive, really. I should've counted it at the start, but the owner told me it was good and to just jump into my shift. So, I did. By the end of the night, when I finally checked, I knew I'd been screwed.

The numbers didn't add up. My float was short before I even had a chance to protect it. I had no idea what I actually started with, but I ended the night with seven dollars in my pocket. Seven dollars after hours of pouring drinks, serving tables, and hustling tips.

That night wasn't just about money. It was about trust, boundaries, and the line I would no longer cross. That was the night I stopped tolerating bullshit. The night I chose energy over income. And I've never gone back.

The icy walk home that night, with a heart heavier than my empty pockets, tears streaming the entire hour through blistering snow up to my knees, and icicles forming on my eyelashes, that was my brutal initiation into the world of financial trust, or the lack of it. I was this close to swearing off business types forever, labeling them all as sleazy con artists. That night wasn't just some screw-up with money. It was my first real lesson in the energy of wealth, trust, and paying attention. The city was quiet, but I was wide awake, walking home and done with all of it.

I was in a city I barely knew. Every step home, the cold bit harder, but it was nothing compared to the heat of my rage. I was fuming. Betrayed, pissed off, and walking straight into the reality of how fast trust can cost you. That walk wasn't just physical. It was a punch in the gut. A wake-up call. I didn't sleep at all that night. I replayed every second, still trying to wrap my head around what had just happened.

At 18, the weight of it all hit me like a storm. Anger burned hot because I knew I'd been cheated. Shock and betrayal sat heavy because someone in authority took advantage of my trust. Embarrassment sank in as I stared at the few dollars left in my pocket after hours of hustling. Fear crept up too, knowing I had to walk home broke, young, and vulnerable through the freezing streets.

Tears came, not just from frustration but from humiliation. Yet underneath it all, I was pissed. Furious. It wasn't just about the missing money. It was about being disrespected, dismissed, and expected to swallow it because I was young and inexperienced. That night cracked something open in me—I wasn't just broke, I was done being treated like I didn't matter.

And then came the nausea. It twisted in my gut, rising with every step, until I couldn't tell if it was from anger, exhaustion, or something else entirely. Sick to my stomach over the mess, not realizing it was more than just stress.

That night forced me to see something clearly—you can't drag the old version of you into the next chapter. That version doesn't get the upgrade. The old you is the price of admission, and if you want to tune into the energy of wealth, you have to leave them behind.

The next morning, I found out I was pregnant. I was only 18. That moment hit harder than the cold night before. Suddenly, it wasn't just about the missing money or that douchebag bar owner. It was about the future. About creating real stability. Real security. I had a baby to think about now. And just like that, everything shifted. Me quitting my job the night before, my boyfriend busting tires during the day, and me half-assing a soul-sucking call center gig twice a week? That wasn't going to cut it. Not even close.

The bar incident was more than just a night gone wrong. Cramped space, clinking glasses, stale beer, and the thick stench of cigarette smoke mixed with the false hope of fast tips. It wasn't just about being shorted money. It was a lesson in trust, value, and the harsh realities of money handling that shape your wealth philosophy. That bitter cold walk home, with tears of frustration freezing on my cheeks, was my brutal wake-up call. It showed me what happens when you trust the wrong people and ignore your gut. It was the moment I realized personal accountability isn't optional if you want to build real wealth.

This isn't just some story about early money mistakes or toxic people trying to drag you down. It's a real look at how your emotions and your financial reality are tied together, shaping each other, whether you realize it or not. For a lot of us, money's been a battle since day one. We were losing before we even knew we were playing. Money has its own energy. If you're not aligned with it, you'll miss it. But once you sync up, things shift fast. Think of wealth like your favorite radio station—you only hear the music when you're tuned to the right frequency. It's not about turning up the volume. It's about locking into the vibration, the frequency.

So how do you get on the wealth frequency? It starts with how you think and how you carry yourself. Think back to being a kid, fearless, bold, convinced you could do anything. That's the energy you bring to money. Wealth isn't just about earning; it's about becoming a magnet for it. Picture yourself walking down the street with certainty, like money already belongs in your life. You don't sit around waiting for it to show up. You move as if it's already yours. You claim it by the way you carry yourself, act with that belief, and back it up with bold action. That's the state of attracting wealth.

Your energy works like a magnet. It pulls in experiences that match the thoughts and feelings you carry the strongest. Just like a tuning fork locks onto a specific pitch, your vibe attracts whatever aligns with it. When you focus on gratitude, visualize success, and speak affirmations that feel true, you raise your energy and make it easier for money to find you. The frequency of money is a reflection of how closely your thoughts, emotions, and actions line up. When you shift how you see and relate to money, your whole financial reality changes. When you lead with gratitude, generosity, and a belief in more than enough, you don't just open the door for your own wealth—you unlock it for others too.

Aligning with the Frequency of Money
Step 1: Reflect and Write

Take a few minutes to reflect on your current money beliefs. What do you honestly believe about money right now? Write them down. List both the positive and the negative, even the ones that feel small or silly. If you need a refresher, go back to the chapter on beliefs and pull from there.

Step 2: Evaluate and Challenge

Look at each belief and ask yourself, "Is this helping me attract wealth, or is it holding me back?" For the negative ones, dig deeper. Ask, "Where did this come from? Is it even mine, or did I pick it up from someone else?"

Step 3: Transform and Affirm

Take every limiting belief and flip it into one that supports the wealthy life you are building.

Example: "Money is hard to come by" becomes "Money flows to me easily and often."

Step 4: Imagine Abundance

Close your eyes and play the wealth movie in your mind. See your bank account rising. Watch your debts get wiped out. Imagine opportunities showing up like clockwork. Feel the emotions of that version of you—joy, safety, gratitude—and lock them in. That is the frequency.

Step 5: Lock in a Money Mindset

Pick one strong affirmation and make it yours.

Example: "I am a magnet for financial abundance and aligned opportunities."

Say it every morning, every night, and anytime your thoughts start spiraling. Then write down three money wins from your day, no matter how small. It could be saving five dollars, receiving a discount, or landing a new client. This trains your brain to focus on what's working and keeps you tuned to the frequency of wealth.

Wealth starts inside, but it doesn't stay locked in there. The energy you carry spills into your relationships, your opportunities, and your influence. That's where social currency comes in. Sometimes it matters just as much as money, and sometimes even more.

CHAPTER 24
Social Currency

YOU'VE PROBABLY HEARD the term "social currency" before. It's not just some phrase social media throws around. This isn't about counting your Instagram followers, Facebook likes, or TikTok shares. It's not about working the room, fake conversations, or collecting names. It's about real connections that move you forward. Your vibe attracts your tribe, and your network? That's your net worth. Social currency is the value you carry in your relationships and reputation, how well people know you, trust you, and back you.

Marketing professor Jonah Berger lays this out in his book *Contagious: Why Things Catch On*. He calls social currency one of the main reasons people talk about certain ideas, brands, or people. If sharing something makes them look smart, connected, or ahead of the game, they're way more likely to spread it. That's how influence works. When you're someone others want to be associated with, your social currency skyrockets, and that energy attracts opportunity. People naturally talk about what makes them look confident and in the know. Whether it's tagging a big brand, quoting someone respected, or sharing something that feels personal and exclusive, it's all a trade. Every post, comment, or share builds status. The goal isn't just to be seen. It's to be talked about in the right circles, by the right people, for the right reasons.

Think of social currency as your backstage pass to success. It gets your name in the right ears, opens doors most people don't even see, and turns your goals from "someday" into "right now." It shifts the question from "Who's that?" to "Where have you been?" Your connections, your circle, and your online presence? That's the fuel behind your next level. But let's be real—you don't need to master every single lesson in this book to create wealth. This is a framework, not a checklist. Social currency is one piece of it. Use it if it serves you, set it aside if it doesn't. Think of it like building a playlist. You don't need every track, just the ones that make you sing your heart out.

Social currency is the value people get from sharing ideas, connections, or experiences that raise their status. It's how we trade attention, trust, and influence. You've heard the quote from Jim Rohn: "You are the average of the five people you spend the most time with." That means your mindset, habits, and results reflect your circle. That's social currency in motion.

In the digital world, it builds empires. Look at any strong personal brand or online business that's thriving. They're not just selling. They're sparking conversations, building movements, and pulling people in. People share because something connects, the same way you recommend a restaurant with great service or a movie that blew you away. If the food is bad or the film is forgettable, you don't rave about it, you move on. But when the experience is memorable, you talk about it, sometimes you even tag it. That's how social currency works. It spreads when the experience is worth passing on. When people want to be connected to you, your presence becomes your power source. Your network is your net worth, but it's not about knowing everyone. It's about being known by the right people, in the right way, with the right energy. You don't need a crowd. You need alignment.

When your presence shifts a room, lights up a post, or amplifies a platform, you turn magnetic. That's the kind of currency that pays in trust, opportunity, and aligned wealth.

Social currency is about the power of your people, your network, your relationships, your crew. That's what launches you into a success that once felt out of reach. It's not about flexing or performing. It's the real connection that cracks doors wide open. When we talk about social currency, we're talking about how your presence, online and in real life, builds your reputation. It's the gold you can't deposit but sure as hell can cash in. It's what makes people curious about you, want to work with you, and genuinely root for you.

So why care? Because it's what makes you stand out in the scroll, in the room, or in the crowd. It's not just about being liked. It's about being remembered, respected, and trusted. To build real social currency, focus on genuine connections. Forget chasing followers. Go for engagement that actually matters. Start real conversations and build relationships, online and off. The goal is to be the one they remember, not just another face in the feed.

How do you start? You begin by being unapologetically yourself. Share what you know with confidence and honesty. Listen fully when it actually counts. Celebrate other people and their wins. Show up even when life is messy and imperfect. This isn't about chasing quick wins that fade fast. It's about building a reputation that lasts and sticks. Don't show up like an AI robot either. AI is here to stay, but copying and pasting what a program tells you isn't authenticity. It's not wealth. Real wealth is showing up as yourself, messy and human, not a script. In the big picture, social currency might be one of your most powerful assets. In today's digital world, your online footprint carries just as much weight as your real-life presence. Social currency is built through connection, through showing up as the real one in a sea of filters, where your value is measured in your energy, your voice, words, and the way you make people feel.

Want to raise your social currency? Start by being unapologetically you. Share your story in your own words, speak your truth with confidence, and bring something genuine to the table. Skip the surface-level likes and focus on deeper conversations that actually matter. The more you show up real, the more people will feel drawn to you. Every honest moment and every meaningful share adds to your value in ways money never could. Social currency in the real world is built on trust and influence, not on showing off or chasing attention. It's about building relationships that move your life and work forward, opening doors you couldn't reach on your own. When you invest in genuine connections, the return touches every part of your life, fueling your business, your growth, and the wealth that lasts.

Having strong social currency means you're a key player in your community and your network. That kind of value brings partnerships, collaborations, and doors that normally stay shut. It's a form of capital that unlocks new ventures, offers fresh insight, and builds a support system you can actually count on. When it comes to wealth, social currency speeds up your success by connecting you to people, knowledge, and resources that move the needle.

It's the quality of your connections and the impact you make that turns relationships into real-world wealth. That becomes your foundation for long-term growth, stability, and aligned success. Social currency is your reputation in motion, showing up in what people say and feel about you, even when you're not in the room.

Now let's put this into practice with a quick audit to see where your social currency stands today.

Social Currency Audit

Purpose: Gauge your current social currency and find ways to boost your wealth in relationships and connections.

Instructions:

1. **List Your Networks**
   Write down all your social and professional networks—online (LinkedIn, Instagram, Facebook, TikTok) and in-person (clubs, groups, communities).
2. **Evaluate Your Engagement**

   Rate your activity in each network from 1 (low) to 10 (high). Think about the value you give and the value you get from these groups/platforms.
3. **Identify Key Relationships**

   Pick out key people who impact your social currency—mentors, peers, influencers. *Note why these relationships matter and how they add to your wealth.*

4. **Action Plan**

   Choose at least two networks or relationships to engage with more.
   Set clear goals like starting a project, offering help, or sharing resources.

5. **Reflection**

   At the end of the month, check in with yourself. Notice any new opportunities, connections, or insights that came from showing up more.

   This will give you a clear view of your social currency and steps to grow it, boosting your overall wealth. Every interaction adds value. Social currency takes time, but it builds fast when you're consistent. Nurture it, grow it, and let it do the heavy lifting. In this world, who you know and how you show up can be just as powerful as what you know. And once you understand the strength of your social currency, you'll see how those connections amplify your impact. That is where we're headed next, into the ripple effect of wealth and the direct impact it has on everyone around you.

CHAPTER 25
Direct Impact

WEALTH DOESN'T SIT quietly in your bank account. It spills into everything and everyone connected to you. When you win, the people closest to you feel it too. Your partner gets to breathe easier and finally chase the dream they've been shelving for years. Your parents no longer have to count pennies or settle for "just enough" because their golden years can actually feel golden. No more budget vacations, we're talking luxury cruises with names hard to pronounce. Your siblings might finally pay off debt, finish school, or have the freedom to chase what lights them up because your success gave them room to breathe. The ripple of your success doesn't stop at your front door. It moves through your circle, reshaping lives, lifting burdens, and creating a new standard of what's possible.

In my twenties, wealth wasn't even in the conversation. Survival was the only thing on the table. I had two little ones in diapers and a third on the way, bills stacked high on the kitchen table, and a boyfriend who worked out of town more than he was home.

Most days I felt more like a single parent than anything else. Some days it was two little ones pulling at my legs, other days it was three voices all needing something at once while I tried to stretch money that was already gone. It wasn't about vacations or dream homes back then. It was about food, rent, and somehow holding it all together. I numbed a lot of it with drinking, trying to fill the hole of an identity crisis I didn't know how to climb out of. Looking back, that stage of life wasn't about chasing dreams, it was about barely holding on. And that's exactly why direct impact matters—because when wealth finally shifts, it doesn't just change your options, it changes the entire atmosphere your family grows up in.

Some people might roll their eyes and think wealth creating ripples is just motivational word vomit. But it's not. I've lived the struggle, and I've seen what happens when survival runs the show. That's why stories of real people using their wealth to create change hit so hard for me.

Listen, this isn't just some woo-woo concept I pulled out of thin air. This is real. Just look at people like LeBron James. He didn't just rise to the top and hoard his success. He went back to his roots and built an actual school in his hometown, giving at-risk kids free tuition, bikes, meals, and even guaranteed college scholarships. That's direct impact. That's showing up with your wealth and using it as a tool to rewrite other people's stories. And Sara Blakely? The badass founder of Spanx? When she sold her company, she didn't just pop champagne and call it a day. She gave every employee two first-class plane tickets and $10,000, just because she could, because she wanted to. Because she understood the ripple effect. That's what I'm talking about. Wealth isn't about collecting more. It's about how different life feels when the pressure is off.

And while wealth can create freedom and ease, it can also expose the truth about people. Money has a way of showing who's really in your corner and who just wants a piece of the pie. And the ugliest side of it always shows its face when money is on the line in families.

It's no different than the inheritance fights that happen at funerals. Wills also have a way of dragging people out of the woodwork fast, crawling out the second money's on the line, acting like they're owed a piece. The truth is, you're the only one who decides where your impact goes, and no one else gets to direct it for you. Your impact is yours to direct, not theirs to claim.

This chapter isn't here to pump you up with feel-good lines.

It's here to get you clear on what wealth really does once it shows up. Real wealth isn't just about bigger houses or shinier cars. It's about the way it shifts the ground under your family's feet, how it changes daily choices, and how it upgrades the lives of the people closest to you. When you can see that clearly enough, your mind and body start moving toward it automatically. The point isn't to dream about "someday." The point is to recognize the direct, tangible changes your success creates and to own the responsibility that comes with it. Direct impact means understanding that your wins lift everyone in your circle, and how you use that power is what sets the tone for the life you're building.

Identity Shifting: The 2.0 Switch

Identity shifting is about leveling up into the 2.0 version of yourself. It's not willpower tricks or quick hacks. It's rewiring who you believe you are at the core. Your qualities, your characteristics, your habits, your standards—all of it. You're not replacing who you are, you're amplifying the real you that's always been there, the version that knows how to rise when given the chance.

If you carry the story "I'm someone who can't hold on to money," your choices will quietly prove you right every time. But when your identity flips to "I'm someone who makes money, keeps money, and multiplies money," your decisions shift automatically. You don't have to fight for every change. You act different because you are different.

This is what makes identity shifting the real game-changer for wealth. You stop playing from your old limitations and start pulling from the traits of your next-level self: discipline, confidence, generosity, self-trust, resourcefulness. The more you practice those qualities, the faster your brain and nervous system accept them as your new baseline. That's when life starts lining up to match the upgraded version of you.

Identity shifting is what I call the 2.0 Switch. It's about lining up with the wealthy framework you've been building through this book. Instead of forcing willpower or chasing hacks, you reset the standards that drive your choices. That's why it belongs inside the W.E.A.L.T.H. Sequence—because the way you see yourself is the engine behind everything else. Once the switch flips, your actions don't feel like effort anymore. They're just the natural expression of who you've decided you are.

That's the power of the 2.0 Switch. Wealth isn't just about building numbers in a bank account. It's about stepping into the honest, ambitious, and driven version of you who naturally makes better moves. The more you embody those qualities, the faster your brain and body accept them as your new normal. And when that happens, your outer world follows.

Step 1: Spot the Old Self: Write down the qualities of your current identity that no longer work for you.

Example: "I'm inconsistent. I doubt myself. I avoid responsibility. I'm passive when it comes to opportunities."

Step 2: Claim Your 2.0 Qualities: Choose three to five qualities your next-level self embodies fully.

Example: "I am disciplined. I am reliable. I am resourceful. I am ambitious. I am confident with money."

Step 3: Anchor It Physically: Close your eyes, breathe deep, and imagine yourself stepping into a room where your 2.0 self already lives. Notice how they walk, how they hold themselves, and what they're wearing. Do they look polished, relaxed, powerful? Picture their posture, their expression, their energy. Feel the confidence, calm, or excitement they carry. Step into that version of you in your mind, take a breath, and lock it in.

Step 4: Act It Out Today: Pick one small action your 2.0 self would do today and actually do it. Maybe it's checking your account without fear. Maybe it's finally making that phone call you've been putting off. Maybe it's choosing a healthier meal instead of defaulting to old habits. Every action reinforces the switch.

Step 5: Repeat and Reinforce: Every morning ask yourself, "Am I acting from my old self or my 2.0 self?" Keep choosing 2.0. Over time, it becomes automatic.

When you make the 2.0 Switch, the people around you feel it too. Your upgraded self shows up differently in every relationship, every opportunity, and every decision. That is direct impact in action—the shift inside you reshaping the world around you.

Back in Chapter 2, I asked you to picture who in your life would be directly impacted by your wealth — your partner, your parents, your kids, your friends, even your employees. You've already made that list. Now I want you to take it further. This isn't about imagining anymore, this is about seeing the ripple effect in real time, about understanding that your wealth doesn't just stop with you. It multiplies into the lives around you. That's the effect of your wealth in motion.

Direct impact and identity shifting are not separate ideas. They're two parts of the same whole, and they sit inside the W.E.A.L.T.H. Sequence, which was built to show you how wealth moves from the inside out. This is where it all comes together. When you shift your identity into the 2.0 version of yourself, you don't just change how you think, you change how you show up. And when you show up differently, the people around you feel it. That's the bridge between identity shifting and direct impact. One rewires who you are, the other multiplies what that new version of you can create in the world.

When you bring identity shifting into the W.E.A.L.T.H. framework, everything connects. The 2.0 Switch upgrades who you are on the inside, and direct impact shows how that upgrade multiplies on the outside. Together, they're the accelerator. One is about rewiring your qualities and characteristics so you step into a higher standard. The other is about watching those shifts spill into your relationships, your opportunities, and the people who count on you. This is where the framework clicks into place—the inner and outer alignment of wealth working side by side.

Now let's take this from idea into practice. It's one thing to understand how identity shifting and direct impact connect, but it's another to see how it plays out in your world.

This exercise will help you see how your wealth can make life different for the people around you.

Direct Impact Exercise

1. **Revisit Your List**

Pull out the list you wrote earlier of people who would be directly impacted by your wealth.

2. **Add Details**

    Don't just write "my parents" or "my kids." Write what would actually change. Would your parents travel more? Would your kids have more opportunities? Would your employees feel more secure? Spell it out.

3. **Expand the Ripple**

    Think beyond the obvious. Who else gets lifted when you rise? A neighbor? A community? A cause?

4. **Visualize the Shift**

    Close your eyes and walk through the scenarios. Picture your success unfolding in real time. What does it look like? What does it feel like?

5. **Anchor the Emotion**

    Notice the gratitude, relief, joy, and pride that ripple through these moments. Lock those emotions in. That feeling is fuel.

Now it's time to go beyond the list and see what it looks like when those changes are real. Don't just think about who benefits, imagine the scenes playing out as if they're happening right now. Take the list you just made and translate it into real moments that could happen within the next year. Write three specific scenes your wealth would create, like your parents booking a trip without checking prices, your sibling clearing college debt that has hung over them, or your friend finally launching that business they've always wanted with your support. Note who benefits, how their day changes, and what you would do to make it real. Choose one scene and name the first action you will take this week, whether that means making a call, setting a transfer, introducing a connection, or putting a date on the calendar. Treat that single step as your green light and start creating it now.

When you rise, you lift people with you, and that is the kind of impact money was always meant to create. Wealth is the goal, but legacy comes from what you choose to build with it, and that building begins inside your mind long before it shows up in your account. Throughout some of my stories, you've seen the real meaning of attraction and it's not only about money flowing in, it's about the people, the energy, and the opportunities that appear when you line yourself up with the life you want. Aligning with the right people, energy, and opportunities bring you closer to the wealth that matters. From pouring drinks at the bar to bingo nights with my mom, from a flooded honeymoon to a New Year that flipped everything, every moment proved that attraction isn't luck. It's a way of life. This entire A-Attract section has been about teaching you to use attraction as your wealth tool. You set your focus so clearly on what you want that it cannot help but find you. It happens not because you are waiting for it, but because you are already living it. The stronger your vision and the deeper your emotion, the faster life reshapes itself to meet you exactly where you stand.

All of this builds up to a truth that might stop you in your tracks. Here's the part that will make you question everything you though was solid.

Purpose Over Pain

Humans can endure almost anything if they find meaning in it. It's about purpose being stronger than suffering and how your mindset shapes survival and fulfillment. From cavemen carving symbols into stone to us scrolling endlessly today, our minds have always built stories to live inside. Money, religion, culture, even human rights — none of them are absolute. They exist because as a collective we agreed upon them, just like as a whole country we agreed upon money, which I showed you earlier in this book. That agreement makes them feel solid but strip it away and you're left asking what is real and what is constructed. And when the noise in your head tries to convince you that it defines you, remember this: you are not only your thoughts. You are the awareness noticing them and choosing which ones to fuel and which ones to release.

Purpose over pain is what carries you further than fear ever could. It's the reason you can endure the impossible and still rise stronger. The world you live in is a story, and you have the power to write a new one. The question is, are you ready to pick up the pen?

We started this section with imagination, because if you can't see it on the inside, you'll never see it on the outside. Divine Desires gave you the permission to own what you want without guilt, and the 4 D's pushed you to break the old patterns that held you back. Momentum showed you how to move forward without second-guessing yourself, and, of course, the Gratitude chapter sealed the feeling of already having, even when doubt showed up.

You are no longer trying to attract wealth. You are wealth. You walk in it, think from it, and speak as it. You live from a place of certainty instead of hope. This section wasn't about becoming someone new. It was about returning to who you've always been before the world made you question it.

This isn't surface-level mindset work. This is full identity rewiring.

You're not "trying" to attract wealth anymore.

You *are* wealth.

Now act like it.

L
LANGUAGE

WHAT YOU SPEAK SHAPES WHAT YOU LIVE

Wealth is not his that has it, but his that enjoys it
-Benjamin Franklin

YOU WANT TO know the fastest way to change your reality? Change the words coming out of your mouth. No, I'm not talking about swapping out swear words for fairy dust. I love a good F-bomb when the conversation calls for it. I'm talking about the language that runs your life—the way you talk to yourself when no one's listening, the stories you keep repeating like a broken record, the words that either push you forward or keep you stuck exactly where you are.

This section isn't about mantras or one-size-fits-all affirmations that make you feel better for five seconds. We're not here to play nice. We're here to rip the lies out of your head, strip down the limiting beliefs that have been running the show, and rebuild the way you talk to yourself so your words actually push you forward instead of holding you back.

By the time you're done with Section L, you won't just think differently, you'll speak from your future self's energy. Every word will carry intention. Every sentence will shape your next level aka the 2.0 version of you. This is where your language starts working for you—loud, clear, and fully aligned.

CHAPTER 26
Limiting Beliefs: The Lies Keeping You Stuck

OPENING YOUR MIND to what's possible is like cracking open a door to a life you didn't even know existed. You're probably wondering what's been jamming that door shut? I'll tell you straight, it's your own thoughts. Yep, those sneaky little voices called limiting beliefs. They're invisible, loud, and feel like background noise you didn't even notice until you finally turned it the hell off.

I hit a point where I was done. Done with settling and done caring about what other people think. People who drained me had to go. I was done shrinking myself to fit into jobs I only ever took to get by, and I was sick of the same old story running the show. That loop of 'I'm not good enough' had been playing on repeat, and I finally tuned it out.

Even back when I was a teenager, I was grinding. Paying my own bills, balancing school, a job, and a long-distance relationship. If I had that kind of grit then, I sure as hell have it now. So I cut the noise, cleared the clutter, and made room for the version of me I actually wanted to be. The shift came fast, exactly what I needed to snap out of the story that had been keeping me stuck. I stopped lying to myself and tearing myself down. We all do it, most of the time without even noticing. It becomes second nature to talk bad about ourselves, like it's the default setting we never questioned.

WHAT ARE LIMITING BELIEFS?

Limiting beliefs are those quiet thoughts that sneak in and tell you your dreams are too big, too bold, or too far out of reach. They plant fear and doubt so subtly, you don't even notice it's happening. Just enough to keep you stuck. Just enough to hold you back. They build walls around your potential, steering you away from the life you want. And your brain clings to them because it craves comfort. It wants autopilot. It clings to old stories, even when those stories are straight-up trash. The scripts start playing: You'll never have money. You're not good enough. You don't deserve more. Who do you think you are? And right when you're about to make a move, they hit you with hesitation. They make you second-guess yourself and shrink when you should rise.

Limiting beliefs are the subconscious thoughts that tell us we can't.

Can't be wealthy.
Can't be successful.
Can't have a healthy relationship.
Can't lose weight.
Can't change.

They stay buried deep but run the show like background noise you don't even realize is playing. Always whispering, "Stay small. Stay safe. Don't bother trying." They disguise themselves as logic. They pretend to protect you. But what they really do is keep you stuck. Most of them got wired in when you were too young to question them. Passed down from parents, shaped by old wounds, or built from moments you've forgotten. Yet they still run your life. They shape how you see yourself, your money, your relationships, and your future. And the second things start going right, those old beliefs kick in. You sabotage it before it sticks. That's how they work. That's their job. But it's time to fire them.

And they are sneaky in how they work. On the outside it might look like you have everything under control, working hard, checking the boxes, holding it together. But inside, old beliefs are still running the show like a thermostat that is rigged. The heat stays just low enough to stop you from rising higher. They never scream at you, they whisper quietly instead. The worst part is that the voice eventually starts to sound like your own. You might say you want more money, more joy, more freedom, but if your internal setting is locked on "barely getting by," then that is where you will stay. The moment things begin heating up and you finally start to get ahead, your subconscious resets the thermostat and pulls you back into familiar territory. You are not broken or flawed, your life simply programmed those settings long ago, and nobody ever gave you the manual to change them.

Until now.

Our brains are wired to be lazy. Seriously. They're designed to take the path of least resistance and cling to the familiar. That's not weakness, it's survival. But in today's world, that "comfort zone" becomes a trap, and limiting beliefs thrive in that trap. They cozy up, whispering, "It's safer here," every time you try to do something bold, something different, something game-changing.

When doubt starts running the show, you end up shrinking yourself without even realizing it. You hold back. You downplay what you want. That's how self-sabotage shows up—settling for less because some outdated belief convinced you that's all you get. That ends here.

FIVE COMMON LIMITING BELIEFS (AND WHY THEY SUCK)

"I'm just not cut out for wealth."

How many times have you told yourself you're just not made for wealth? It's meant for other people but not for you? That's a lie. Wealth doesn't choose people. It responds to mindset, to consistency, to how serious you are about not quitting. You don't need anyone's approval. You're already built for it.

"Success is just luck."

People believe this because it gives them an out. If success is all luck, then they don't have to try, risk failure, or face their own excuses. But that's not how it works. Success comes from what you do consistently, not what shows up randomly. It's built, not gifted. Sure, timing matters—but only if you're already doing the work. Sitting around hoping to get lucky keeps you stuck. Taking action is what moves things. Decide you're already in. Then prove it up with effort.

"I don't deserve happiness or success."

This one runs deep. It doesn't come from truth—it comes from old pain. Maybe someone made you feel small growing up. Maybe life kept knocking you down until you started thinking good things just weren't meant for you so you started knocking yourself down. That's where this belief gets planted. It's not about what you've done, how hard you've worked, or how perfect you've been. It's about knowing you're already enough. Thinking you don't deserve happiness or success is just another way of saying you think you're not valuable. You are valuable right now, exactly as you are. You don't need to earn peace or hustle for joy, because those things already belong to you. You get to have good things because you're human—and that's enough.

"I have to work hard to make money."

This one's baked into almost everyone. It comes from generations of struggle—parents, grandparents, even school systems drilling in the idea that hustle equals worth.

The reality is that effort matters, but suffering doesn't. Making money isn't about how hard you push; it's about how aligned you are. You don't get paid more just because you're exhausted. You get paid when your value, your energy, and your actions line up with what you're creating. Money doesn't demand sacrifice. It responds to freedom, clarity, and the courage to choose ease.

"I'm not good enough."

This belief hits hard because it doesn't just stick to one area—it spreads. It shows up when you go for the job, when you set a boundary, when you think about asking for a raise, or even when someone compliments you and you brush it off. It isn't the truth, it's conditioning you picked up along the way. Somewhere in your past, you learned to question your value, maybe from a parent, a teacher, or from life handing you one challenge after another. You were never the problem. The belief was, and it's time to call it out because you are good enough. You always were!

WHY THIS MATTERS

Limiting beliefs don't just mess with your bank account. They affect every part of your life. They show up in your work, your body, your relationships, and your confidence. When you carry beliefs like "I'm not good enough" or "I suck with money," you're not only blocking more income, you're also holding yourself back from the love, the energy, and the freedom you want. These beliefs sneak into how you spend, how you ask for support, how you treat yourself when you make mistakes, and how you talk to yourself when no one is around. That is why this work matters. It is not just about money. It is about who you get to be.

Top 5 Signs You're Operating from a Limiting Belief:

- You hesitate on opportunities you actually want
- You downplay your wins or brush off compliments
- You keep sabotaging progress just when things start going well
- You repeat the same patterns with money, love, or health
- Your inner voice is a full-time hater, not a coach

Also Words like:
"I always attract the wrong people."
"I'll never lose the weight."
"I'm not smart enough to succeed."
"I'm just not cut out for more."

Those aren't facts. They're just old scripts your brain keeps recycling. And the brain? It's wired to prove you right. Tell yourself you're bad with money, and it'll show you missed payments, avoided statements, and empty accounts. Think love never works out? You'll keep choosing the same mess in a different body. But when you finally get honest about the beliefs running the show, that's when things start to shift.

Everyone has greatness within them. The second you believe you deserve better, everything changes. The moment you believe different, you make different choices. Those choices build momentum, and momentum creates the confidence and clarity to break the cycle for good. Limiting beliefs are nothing more than repeated thoughts, and you have the power to replace them. The process starts by catching the lies you have been telling yourself, calling them out, and choosing thoughts that are true and support you. Your brain rewires itself based on what you think and repeat, and that is the power of neuroplasticity. If "I'm not enough" has been playing on a loop, your brain will build it in as the default, but you can flip it by choosing a new thought and locking it in every single day.

IDENTIFY. QUESTION. REWRITE.

Your beliefs are just thoughts you've repeated so many times they feel like facts, but they're not. They're learned patterns, and you have the power to change them.

1. **Spot the behavior that keeps looping,** like overspending, procrastinating, or ghosting your own goals.
2. **Identify the belief driving it.** For example: "I'm not smart enough" or "People like me don't succeed."
3. **Trace it back.** Where did you pick it up — childhood, a breakup, an old job?
4. **Question it.** Is this even true? Is it your truth, or something you inherited?
5. **Replace it.** Choose a belief that actually supports you. Say it. Own it. Live it.

When your actions don't line up with your beliefs, your brain feels the tension. That's called cognitive dissonance. Most people shrink their actions to fit old beliefs, even when those beliefs are lies. Flip that around. Shift the belief first, and your actions will naturally rise to match it.

Instead of treating failure like the boogeyman hiding under the bed or in the closet, pull it out, grab its tail, and face it.

That gnarly beast of unworthiness whispering that you don't deserve real love or happiness? That one's been lying to you. It's the same belief that fuels sabotage, keeps you stuck, and blocks everything real. Time to cut the crap. You are absolutely worthy — and it's about time you acted like it.

Be brutally honest with yourself. When excuses or self-doubt creep in, pause and ask, "Is this true or just old bullshit on repeat?" If you catch yourself thinking, "That's just how I am" or "I can't change," shake that lie up like a strong cocktail — no guilt, just truth. There are no quick fixes here. Hunt those beliefs down, call them out, and replace them with ones that move you forward.

You've seen how these lies run the show, and you've got the tools to shut them down. No more hiding. No more shrinking. Life isn't happening to you anymore, it's happening for you, and you're the one holding the reins. Playing it safe only keeps you stuck. So ask yourself: *What would I regret not doing?* Let that answer pull you forward, louder, bolder, braver. Because you're not stuck with old beliefs. You get to choose new ones, and that choice changes everything.

CHAPTER 27
Rewire Your Wallet

THE WAY YOU think about money is shaping every decision you make, even the ones you don't realize you're making. Money beliefs are sneaky, and if you want more wealth, then stop treating money like it's the enemy or some prize you've got to beg for. If you grew up hearing, "We can't afford that" or "Money doesn't grow on trees," your brain didn't just hear those words, it built a blueprint. Those words built patterns in your mind of scarcity, guilt, and lack. Now when money shows up, your body tenses, and when it leaves, you tell yourself "See? It never stays."

The subconscious mind takes in about 2.3 million pieces of information per second, while the conscious mind only handles around 126. That means most of your choices, reactions, and patterns are happening below the surface. Old beliefs run on autopilot until you choose something different. If your internal setting is locked on survival, it will not matter how hard you work. You will always find ways to stay stuck in just getting by. That voice in your head shapes everything you do: your choices, your confidence, and your results. If the thoughts in your mind are filled with fear, shame, or doubt, your life will reflect it. Not because something is wrong with you, but because your brain believes what it hears on repeat. Pay attention to those thoughts, question them, and replace them with ones that move you forward. "I'm bad with money" becomes "I'm learning to manage money with confidence."

"I always pick the wrong partners" shifts to "I choose relationships that support and respect me."

"I can't change" turns into "I'm already changing, one decision at a time."

Money isn't good or bad. It's not who you are or what you're worth. It's a tool, nothing more. What gives it weight is everything you've been taught to believe about it. Guilt, fear, shame, struggle, that's the baggage, not the money. Most people don't even realize they're carrying it. But the way you think about money? That's what decides how it shows up, how it moves, and whether it stays. Change the way you think about money, and you change how it shows up for you.

When you start challenging the beliefs tied to money, worth, and success, you take your power back. You stop shrinking to fit old rules and you stop playing small. By age seven, your subconscious has already soaked in most of what it believes. It doesn't filter; it just absorbs. Those early messages build your default settings. Just because it got wired in early doesn't mean it has to stay. You can rewire it. You get to pick new thoughts, new beliefs, and a new reality.

Up to 99% of your thoughts and actions are driven by your subconscious. Only a sliver, about 1 to 5%, is actually conscious. Real change happens when what you want lines up with what you believe underneath. That is when momentum kicks in and success gets easier. Your beliefs shape everything: your decisions, your emotions, and your results.

Want a different life? Then start with the story underneath. Dig up the old beliefs, question them, and call out the ones that no longer fit. "Thoughts become things" sounds cute, but let's be real. It takes more than thinking; it takes rewiring. As an NLP trainer, I know that's the work that actually shifts the outcome. Wanting beliefs to disappear is not enough. Awareness is just the first step, but action is what transforms your reality. You already have the tools. What actually matters is using them consistently. No belief is permanent or locked in place. You are not stuck.

By the age of seven, you have already built a story about who you are. That story came from what you lived through, what was missing, and what you decided all of it meant. The truth is that story is not who you are. It is only a script, and like any script, it can be rewritten. That rewriting begins right now. Your stories are nothing more than memories, perceptions, and thoughts repeated so often that they begin to feel like facts. They are not facts, and they do not define you or control what comes next. You have the power to rewrite your narrative whenever you decide.

Old money beliefs are outdated and ineffective. Let them go already. You are the one holding the pen, so write something that works. You want wealth, freedom, choices, early retirement, and the full life that comes with it. But then that voice creeps in, saying rich people are greedy, wealth is selfish, and wanting more makes you a bad person. That voice is lying to you. Those beliefs are outdated and designed to keep you small. You cannot build what you secretly resent. That is not growth. That is sabotage. If you are watching a show you do not like, or a song comes on the radio you cannot stand, you change the channel. The same goes for the stories you keep on repeat in your mind. If they do not serve you, change the channel.

Limiting beliefs do more than block your income. They block your momentum and the moves that could change your life. A belief is nothing more than a thought repeated so often it feels true. Change the thought and you change the outcome. Find the lie, call it out, and replace it with truth until the new belief takes hold. That is how real shifts happen.

Now pause and take a hard look at what you actually believe about money. Most of it came from your family, your upbringing, or things you absorbed without even realizing it. Write some of them down and see what has been driving your choices.

Think about beliefs like:

- Wealthy people are bad or dishonest
- There's never enough money
- I spend money as soon as I get it
- Other people seem to have money, but I never do
- I'm not good with money or I can't be trusted to manage it
- If I have money, people will just want something from me

The list goes on.

When you drag these beliefs into the open, it becomes easier to see how much they have been steering your life. No wonder money feels out of reach when your choices are tied to fear, lack, or shame. The good news is that once you see the pattern, you can change it. Do not overthink it. Shift one belief, then another, and let the momentum build. Old stories lose their grip when you stop repeating them. New ones take over the moment you decide to own them. That is where change begins.

And while we are at it, what are your strengths? If you cannot name them, it is time to reconnect. You cannot rise fully if you forget what makes you unstoppable. To become who you want now, you need to get clear on what you actually want. Not what you should want or what others say you want. Focus on what excites you, not what you are trying to avoid. Stop saying, "I do not want debt" or "I do not want problems." Ask yourself what you really want.

Personal growth is not easy. It forces you to face your fears and desires, and it will feel uncomfortable. But once you figure out what truly drives you, nothing can stop you. Stop comparing yourself to others and nail down your real reason, your core why. That is your compass, and without it, you will quit when things get hard. Most people's why is weak. "I want more money" sounds good, but it will not carry you through the tough moments. Your why needs to be strong enough to keep you going when everything feels like it's gone to shit.

Limiting beliefs are nothing more than lies you have repeated to yourself for far too long.

Choose a new thought and build a belief that fuels your 2.0 self. Your subconscious doesn't care if something is imagined or physical. If you believe it, it responds. That new belief becomes your new reality fast.

Squash Any Limiting Belief

What's one limiting belief you're ready to let go of today? Here's how to shift it, especially around money:

1. **Identify the behavior.** What keeps showing up? Are you procrastinating, overspending, or ghosting your own goals?
2. **Pinpoint the belief.** What thought or assumption is feeding that behavior? What belief keeps giving it permission to exist?
3. **Trace it back to the root.** Where did it start? Childhood, a breakup, a job, or something you were told?
4. **Ask why you've held onto it.** What role has it played? Did it protect you or give you certainty?
5. **Name what it costs you.** What has this belief taken from you? How much emotionally, financially, or in your growth? What is the real price of keeping it?
6. **Question the truth.** Is it fact, or just a story you have repeated too many times?
7. **Create a new belief.** Choose one that supports who you are becoming.
8. **Anchor it daily.** Act like it is already true. Your subconscious does not care if it is imagined or real, it will respond either way.

It all starts with what you believe is possible. So, what do you want to believe from this point forward? You get to decide. Right here. Right now.

THE MONEY ANGLE

Money is neutral. But your beliefs about it? Those are loaded. They come from childhood, media, religion, culture, and trauma. And they can block your wealth more than anything else.

Ask yourself:

- What did I hear about money growing up?
- What did I see my caregivers do with money?
- How do I talk about money now?

Are you saying things like:

- "Money doesn't grow on trees."
- "We can't afford that."
- "People with money are selfish."
- "I'm not good with money."

Those aren't facts. They're beliefs. And they're shaping your financial reality right now.

To shift them:

- Start talking about money in a positive way.
- Practice gratitude for what you have.
- Visualize wealth as safe, expansive, and aligned.
- Learn to manage money with joy, not dread.

Your net worth will rarely grow beyond your self-worth. That isn't just a nice phrase, it's the foundation.

It's not limited to money either. It shows up in your friendships, your health, your parenting, and even in how you see yourself. Believing you have to do everything alone stops you from asking for help. Believing you have to earn love makes you overextend. Believing you can't change keeps you stuck.

Stop waiting for perfection, permission, or proof. Ditch the scripts you didn't write. Start telling stories that fit who you're becoming. You were never meant to live in a box someone else built. You were made for more.

It's time to start believing it.

CHAPTER 28
The Brick Road

My love story started on April Fool's Day over 25 years ago, and the joke's still going strong. I spent more than half of my relationship in a different province, him out west, and me back home juggling life. Every day, a handwritten letter showed up in the mailbox. I've kept every one. Those letters became our bridge, connecting two lives that refused to drift apart. While I was pregnant with my firstborn, still living with my parents, the distance hit harder. Phone calls became our lifeline. Every night, we'd talk until bed. But as the phone bills piled up, so did my mom's complaints, even though my part time job was footing those bills. I was juggling being a pregnant teen, work, and hormones, all while learning to stretch every dollar I had, learning how far a dollar could stretch and how fast it could disappear.

Back then, money was just numbers on a calculator. Budgeting felt like basic math, but learning the real value of money was a whole different lesson. That lesson didn't fully sink in until my thirties, when I had to face how much unlearning it actually takes to handle money differently.

This isn't just a trip down memory lane. It's about the beliefs we built before we even knew we were building them—money, love, worth, struggle. They formed young and were rarely questioned, but now is the time to examine them. We dismantle, inspect, and rebuild. We peel back the layers of our financial story to see how it shaped us and rewrite it with clarity. Beliefs shape your reality, deciding whether you rise or stall. If your identity doesn't match what you want, it's time to dig deeper into the foundation. The subconscious is your personal truth-seeker, literal and loyal with no bullshit. It will hunt down proof of what you believe. Think you'll never earn more than 50K? It will make sure you're right.

It will find the evidence. It will nudge you into self-sabotage. It keeps your life capped like a thermostat locked on low. If your internal setting says, "I'm an 80K earner," then hitting 90 or 100K triggers panic. It feels unfamiliar and doesn't match who you believe you are. So you overspend. An unexpected bill shows up. You ghost your own progress. Suddenly, you are right back at 80. That is not bad luck. That is identity. The same thing works in reverse. Drop to 60K and suddenly you are fired up. You stay late, push harder, and do what it takes. Not because someone told you to, but because your subconscious is scrambling to pull you back to your set point of 80K.

That's your financial thermostat. And it lives at the identity level. So if you want new results, more money, more peace, more alignment, you don't fight the symptoms. You reset the temperature.

LAYERS OF BELIEF

Everything you believe has layers, like onions. Or ogres. (Shrek was onto something.) These layers form over time from what we've heard, seen, absorbed, or assumed. They start as comments from parents, teachers, friends, and society. Then experiences reinforce them. And soon, those layers start to feel like facts.

But under all those layers? Your core. The part of you untouched by trauma, opinions, or false conditioning. That's your true self. That's where your truth lives.

Underneath all the layers is our core. Our core is where our magic and potent power exist. It is what makes up our true self, aka our Wealthy Self.

The Disney classic, Shrek, talks quickly about layers:
Shrek: "Ogres are like onions."
Donkey: "They stink?"

Shrek: "Yes. No."
Donkey: "Oh, they make you cry?"
Shrek: "No."
Donkey: "Oh, you leave em out in the sun, they get all brown, start sproutin' little white hairs."
Shrek: "NO! Layers. Onions have layers. Ogres have layers. Onions have layers. You get it? We all have layers."

We all have layers.

When we peel back the layers and rebuild, we reach our core. The goal is to move past the surface noise and get to the root. That's where the healing happens.

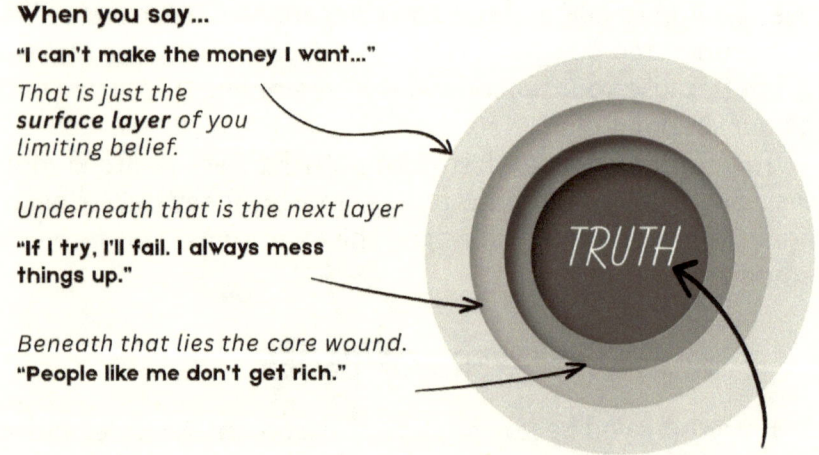

THE TRUTH = "I create wealth because I'm meant for more."

Beliefs don't just show up out of nowhere. They're built, brick by brick, from repetition and emotional intensity. Maybe your family always struggled. Maybe you watched your parents fight over money. Maybe you heard, "Money doesn't grow on trees," so often it got tattooed on your nervous system. You decided something, and then you found evidence to support it. Again and again and again. Until that became your truth, it became who you thought you were. Beliefs aren't set in stone though, they're patterns, and patterns can be changed.

Thoughts turn into words. Words shape beliefs, beliefs guide actions, actions become habits, and habits create your reality. It's a straight line from what you think to how you live. You've heard the rotten fruit story. Picking off the bad fruit doesn't fix the tree. It keeps growing back. The real problem is in the roots. Same with your beliefs. You've got to get to the core—the moment you decided things had to be that way. That's where real change starts. This book digs into those buried beliefs running the show. You don't need to spend years in therapy. Sometimes just seeing it clearly is enough to shake something loose. Awareness opens the door. The work starts there.

Start with the surface belief, peel back the next layers, then land at the core:

- What's the belief on the surface?
- What's underneath that?
- Is there another layer?
- What's the foundational root belief that, when shifted, changes the rest?

The Brick Road of Beliefs

You don't just snap your fingers and believe something new. It doesn't work like that. Your brain will reject anything that feels too far from what it already knows. If your inner voice is stuck on "I'm broken" or "I'll never get ahead," trying to jump to "I'm thriving" is going to feel fake. That's why we build it brick by brick.

Making your beliefs click with your conscious mind is like building the Brick Road of Beliefs. Ease into it. You can't just jump from one extreme to the other. Instead, you lay down the path brick by brick, crafting a bridge your mind can cross without freaking out. This way, you gently nudge yourself closer to the belief you want without your brain hitting panic mode and clinging to old, unhelpful patterns.

Each belief has to land in your mind, and each new thought has to feel possible. You're not bypassing your doubts—you're shifting them. You move from "I'm stuck" to "I'm figuring it out" to "I know what I want" to "I'm already living it." This is how you build a new default. Not through force. Not through pretending. But by showing your mind a better path, one believable step at a time.

Make Your Beliefs Believable to Your Conscious Mind with Belief Bridging

Your conscious mind has one job—to protect what it already believes. The conscious mind acts as a shield. It won't accept anything it doesn't believe or trust. If you deeply believe, "I'm terrible with money," jumping straight to 'I'm a financial genius" won't work. Your conscious mind will raise alarms: "WARNING! WRONG. NO. NOT TRUE."

That's why, when working with the conscious mind, make new beliefs believable. New beliefs have to feel possible, not like fantasy. You start with something your mind can actually accept, and you build from there.

Belief Bridging: Rewiring What You Believe

Belief change starts by making your new belief believable. Your conscious mind won't accept what it doesn't trust. So, jumping from "I'm broke" to "I'm a millionaire" will trigger your brain to call bullshit. That's why we bridge.

Example for self-worth: I never feel like enough
→ I wish I could believe I am enough
→ I'm willing to explore what enough feels like
→ I'm starting to recognize where I do feel enough
→ I see proof that I already am
→ I am enough, exactly as I am

For money: Money always slips through my fingers
→ I want to believe I can hold on to money
→ I'm open to learning how
→ I imagine becoming good with money
→ I notice I'm improving
→ I take care of my money

We walk ourselves across the bridge one plank at a time.

Instead of leaping from one extreme to the other, you lay it down slowly. That's how your mind buys in. No resistance or rejection. Just one solid step after the next until you're grounded in the belief you actually want.

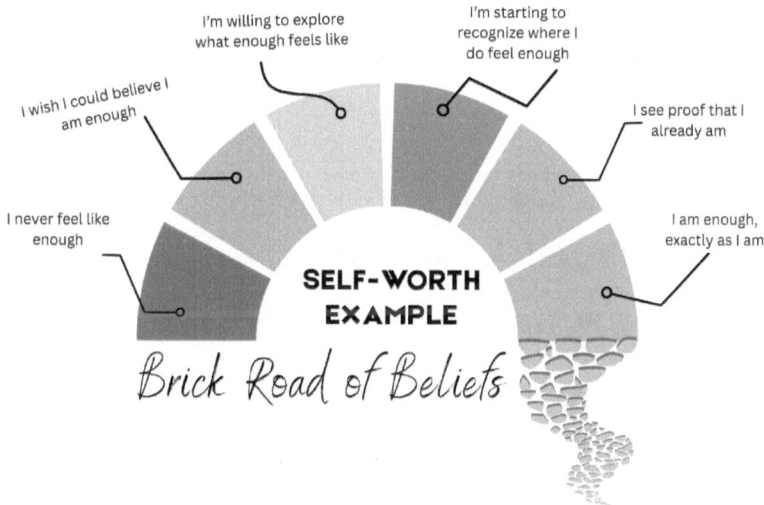

Start with your Brick Road of Beliefs. Write them out step by step:
1. What's the belief you're carrying right now that weighs you down? (Brick 1)
2. What's the belief you actually want to hold — the truth your Wealthy Self has always known? (Brick 6)
3. What's your Belief Bridge — the steps in between that feel believable enough to move you closer, one brick at a time? (Bricks 2–5)

The Sequence to Aligned Wealth

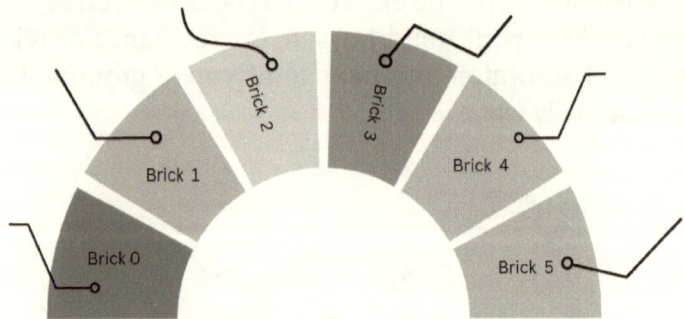

Use this space around each block to jot down your shifting beliefs, or recreate your own Brick Road on a separate piece of paper.

Stuck? Use this Brick 1-6 checklist

1. **Brick 1:** Name the current belief holding you back.
2. **Brick 2:** I want to believe _____.
3. **Brick 3:** I am open to _____.
4. **Brick 4:** I can imagine myself believing _____.
5. **Brick 5:** I can find proof I am starting to live _____.
6. **Brick 6:** New truth I choose now: _____.

Each brick you lay down is a new rule. If you believe money only comes from nonstop hustle, then that's the life you'll live. If you believe you'll always struggle, you'll keep finding ways to prove it true. If you think success means doing everything yourself, you'll stay buried and exhausted. If you've decided wealth only happens for certain kinds of people, you've already built the box you're stuck in.

Your beliefs set the tone. They shape your results. They write the rules of your reality. So, stop and ask — are those rules working for you or keeping you stuck? You get to change them. You're in charge here. No one else.

What do you want to be true? What would feel good, even if it sounds like a stretch right now? Try these:

- The more I enjoy my life, the more money flows in
- Opportunities show up for me in surprising ways
- Money comes to me in both expected and unexpected streams

- The more I trust myself, the more abundance grows
- Rest, fun, and joy fuel my wealth

These are your rules now. Make them real and speak them out loud. Believe them and live by them.

You're building a world with no limits. None of the old rules apply. Not the ones from your childhood, school, or the industry you work in. Wipe out the old programming (family rules, school rules, society's rules) and sit in a clear moment, right now, where you choose fresh beliefs for yourself. This isn't temporary. It's about deciding, in this moment, free from the past and outside noise, what you want to make true. What beliefs actually feel good? What do you want to be true in the world you're creating?

You're not just shifting a belief. You're building a new foundation. One aligned truth at a time.

This chapter opened with my story because that's how beliefs are built, subconsciously, emotionally, and on repeat. I was young, under pressure, juggling money, survival, and self-worth. That story was the start of so many beliefs around struggle, love, and value. Everything you just read? It's the exact work I had to do to rewrite it all. That story set the stage. The tools you just got are how I changed it. Proof that beliefs can shift, identity can evolve, and alignment is built—not born.

CHAPTER 29
Scripted Spells

HAVE YOU EVER heard the phrase "words are wands"? It's not just cute witchy talk, it's the truth. What you say, think, sing, type, and repeat in your head becomes the foundation of your reality. Your words literally shape your world. With money, success, and self-worth, the words you use matter. Like a lot. Saying things like "I'm broke" or "I'm so tired" on repeat? You're not just venting. You're training your subconscious to believe that version of you is your default. Your brain hears it, feels it, sees it, and then turns it into your reality.

Your subconscious speaks in pictures. So even if I say, 'Don't think of a blue tree,' your brain still has to picture it. That's the power your words hold. Experts estimate we think between 60,000 and 80,000 thoughts a day. That's about 2,500 to 3,300 an hour, or 41 to 55 every minute. A thought repeated over and over becomes a belief. And about 95% of our thoughts are on repeat.

Neuro-Linguistic Programming (NLP) shows that language isn't just talking. It programs your subconscious. Created by Richard Bandler and John Grinder, NLP shows that words carry energy, not just meaning. Every "I am" statement shapes who you are. Say something often enough, and your brain builds neural patterns that lock it in. This isn't woo—it's how your brain wires reality. Change your language, change your results. The words you speak shape your life. So pay attention.

Every single word that comes out of your mouth is painting a picture in your mind. That's why when it comes to money, success, and your future, your words need to match your energy. If you're constantly saying you're tired, broke, or behind, your brain builds that version of you. It doesn't argue. It listens, it accepts, and then it makes that your truth. To shift your energy, start by changing how you speak. Instead of saying 'I'm tired,' say 'I'm ready for more energy.' It sets the tone for how you want to feel and live.

If you want different results, it starts with what you say to yourself. Change the script, change the story. This is the work you do while driving, folding laundry, standing in line, or walking to the mailbox. Your language is always on. So every moment becomes a chance to shift.

Here's a simple exercise to start catching and shifting your everyday thoughts.

1. **Become aware of your thoughts.**
   Notice what keeps coming up during the day.
2. **Record your thoughts.**

   Write down what's running through your mind, the good and the bad.
3. **Evaluate your thoughts.**

   Ask yourself if each thought brings you closer to or farther from your goals. If it brings you closer, keep it. If not, move to the next step.
4. **Shift to empowering thoughts.**

   Rewrite the negative ones into stronger statements.
   Examples:
   - "In the past, I used to believe _____. Now I'm learning how to _____."
   - "The truth is _____."
   - "I'm open to the idea that _____ is possible."
   - "I can see how _____ could become my reality."
   - If you're wrestling with feelings of inadequacy, like "I don't know enough," flip it to something more constructive:? wsa

     "I've been soaking up knowledge through books, resources,

and courses for 3 years. I know a lot and I'm learning to rewire my brain for success."

5. **Track and notice.**

   Notice the ones that keep showing up. Those repeats are your patterns, and once you see them, you can change them.

   Writing this out might feel like work, but it gets easier the more you practice. Soon you'll be swapping thoughts on the fly without even trying. Do it for a week and it starts to feel automatic. The results make it worth it.

   Your subconscious mind captures the images your words create. Saying things like "I'm tired" or "I'm exhausted" reinforces those feelings. To change this, switch your words. Say, "I'm excited to feel more energized" or "I'm looking forward to waking up refreshed." This isn't just blind optimism—it's strategic. You're guiding your subconscious to build a new reality. Your language is shaping your thoughts, and your thoughts are shaping your life.

   Stop replaying the setbacks. Put your focus on the outcome you want. Picture the connection, the calm, the win. Let that image become your new normal. When you focus on what you want instead of what you fear, your subconscious gets on board. Your words aren't background noise, they're the fuel of your life. Every sentence you speak and every thought you repeat is either building the future you want or chaining you to the past. Words are tools. Use them with intent. Speak what you want into existence. You're not just talking. You're building your life.

CHAPTER 30
Money Incantations

Hustling at Dairy Queen for $4.75 an hour, I got a real taste of how money, or the lack of it, plays a starring role in the everyday choices we make. It wasn't just about scooping ice cream; it was a crash course in economic reality. Choosing between that badass leather jacket or the thrift store jean jacket and settling for the cheaper option wasn't just a matter of taste; it was about what my bank account said I could afford.

Every time I opened a menu, my eyes involuntarily darted to the right-hand side, scanning the prices. I didn't look at the meals first—I looked at the cost. That chicken cordon bleu or filet mignon didn't stand a chance if the number beside it was too high. Price made the decision. Hunger came second. I still remember choosing the cheapest thing on the menu, skipping the good stuff, and thinking, "I'll have the house salad… and a side of water, thanks." Money always had the final say.

That pattern doesn't magically go away as we grow up. A lot of us still let money call the shots, even now. But what if that power was never about the numbers in your account, and always about the language in your head? That's where incantations come in. We're not just talking positive vibes here. We're talking about rewiring your identity with words that actually shift your wealth frequency. And no, this doesn't mean we're veering into witchy territory. This book is grounded in mindset, science, NLP, and energetic alignment—not potions and crystals. This is the only time I'll use this kind of language, and it's only because it lands. It makes you feel it. That's the point.

Navigating the financial maze from my Dairy Queen days to now, I've learned just how powerful words really are. They're not just sounds, they shape everything. That's why I've traded basic mantras for something with more edge: incantations. It's not about repeating words to feel better. It's about rewiring your identity and shifting your frequency. So why settle for ordinary language when you can speak in a way that changes things? Let's get into it and call in the wealth that's always been yours.

Affirmations are statements we repeat to anchor in who we're becoming. They're not just words; they're a way to train your brain to believe in the identity you're stepping into. Say it enough times, and it sinks into your subconscious. It starts running the show. That's how you shift how you think, feel, and act. Over time, these new thoughts override the old limiting ones and build new mental pathways that back the life you want.

Affirmations aren't magic spells that drop money in your lap. Research shows they can lower stress, improve performance under pressure, and help you see yourself in a new light. But they only work when they're backed by action. Saying "I'm a millionaire" without changing habits won't change your bank balance. Pairing affirmations with aligned choices and consistent behavior? That's where they become a real tool instead of empty words.

Incantations, or what you might call affirmations and mantras, are those personal declarations we repeat with intention. They're the words we choose to reinforce our identity and goals, spoken again and again, until they become a part of our internal dialogue.

They Used It. Look Who's Proof.

1. **Louise Hay** – A pioneer in the affirmation world, she built her legacy and healed her life through daily positive statements.
2. **Oprah Winfrey** – She learned affirmations as a kid growing up poor, and credits them for helping shift her identity on her way out of struggle.
3. **Jim Carrey** – Before he was famous, he literally wrote himself a

check for $10 million and carried it in his wallet for years—all while repeating the act as a rehearsal for what was to come. A bold example of belief backed by action.

These aren't abstract stories. They're proof that words—when backed by aligned action—can serve as a launchpad to real transformation.

Let's break it down further to get clear on what affirmations really are and how to use them, especially when it comes to building wealth. An incantation is essentially an affirmation, but with more edge and energy. I call them incantations because it makes the practice feel stronger and more intentional. Your words carry weight. They're what turn thoughts into identity. Whether you say them out loud, whisper them under your breath, scream them into a pillow, or write them down, they're meant to reinforce and claim who you are and who you're becoming. Around here, we use the word incantations because we're not just repeating words, we're rewiring identity.

So, what exactly are affirmations, and how do they work? At the core, they're repetitive phrases we tell ourselves to plant specific beliefs deep in the subconscious. When you repeat positive, empowering statements consistently, you begin to shift your thoughts, and over time, your reality starts to shift with them.

People often choose affirmations that reflect success, worth, and abundance. Things like "I am a magnet for wealth" or "Abundance flows to me effortlessly." The key is daily repetition with real belief behind it. That's what makes it stick.

Here's how to make affirmations work. Pick words that actually mean something to you, something that reflects the wealth and abundance you want to live. Say them daily, at the same time if you can. That consistency wires them deeper into your mind. But don't just say them flat. Feel them. Let the words hit. Let them land. Embody what they mean. And don't expect magic in a day. Stick with it. You're not just repeating words. You're building a new financial identity from the inside out.

Here are some sample money incantations for you to consider.

You're encouraged to tailor them to your liking or create your own.

- I effortlessly achieve every goal I set.
- I feel powerful, smart, and courageous.
- Wealth and abundance fill my life.
- Abundance is my natural state.
- Money flows to me easily, frequently, and abundantly.
- I am worthy of wealth and abundance.
- I am open to receiving more money and success.
- Creative ideas for wealth and success flow from me.
- I see abundance and opportunity everywhere.
- My income is constantly increasing.
- Money flows quickly to me from unexpected sources.
- I attract financial prosperity into every aspect of my life.
- I am unstoppable, courageous, and powerful.
- I always have enough money for anything I want.
- The more money I have, the more I can help others.
- I give myself permission to live a wealthy life.
- I love money, and money loves me.
- I release all doubts, fears, and negative beliefs about money.
- I am unlimited in my ability to succeed.
- I am open and ready to receive unlimited wealth.
- I am worthy of having millions of dollars.
- People love to pay me.
- I'm grateful for all the good I do with money.
- Money is effortless and flows to me with ease.
- I trust myself with my wealth.

Every time you say one, you're retraining your mind to expect wealth, not just wishing for it. Let them run through your head like your favorite playlist. Say them in the mirror, shout them in your car, write them in your journal. Your brain listens. Say it like you mean it. Say it like your rich self already knows it.

CHAPTER 31
Life Is A Game And There Are Rules…Or Should I Say 12 Laws To Be Exact

I started asking a better question… What if we stopped pretending there's only one way to do things? The real power comes from blending it all, pulling from everywhere to create what actually works. We're not here for cookie-cutter solutions or a one-size-fits-all approach. This isn't just strategy or mindset or spirituality, it's all of it. Mental, emotional, energetic, spiritual. When it all aligns, that's when shit changes. For real. For you, and for the people you're here to impact.

Horror Movie Turned Money Rules Moment

Featuring the legendary monologue from Randy Meeks in the classic 1996 film Scream… followed by my own legendary twist.

Randy Meeks, Scream (1996):

"There are certain RULES that one must abide by in order to survive a horror movie successfully.

Number one: you can never have sex.

Number two: you can never drink or do drugs.

And number three: never, ever, ever under any circumstances say, 'I'll be right back'—'cause you won't be back."

Why the Scream reference? Because just like horror movies

have survival rules, building wealth has its own set—and breaking them costs more than a jump scare.

Christina Ostroski, Wealth Rules... (Present Day):

"There are certain RULES that one must abide by in order to successfully build wealth.

Number one: you can never play small.

Number two: you can never ignore your energy or your beliefs.

And number three: never, ever, ever under any circumstances say 'I'll start tomorrow'—because you won't."

Wealth, like horror movies, have rules. Break them, and the cost is real. The good news? You don't need to guess what the rules are. This chapter is about pulling apart the myths and showing you the rules that actually run the game. And just so we're clear, I'm not a movie buff or a horror fanatic, but I was a teen in the 90s era. If you grew up then too, you know those movies were everywhere—Ghostface, Jason, Freddy, Michael Myers. The rules always mattered, and so do these. That's why this chapter isn't about wishful thinking or waiting for luck to strike. It's about using manifestation in a way that actually works. Not later. Not someday. Now.

Your beliefs guide your thoughts, fuel your emotions, and set the tone for every action. Your brain doesn't question you—it follows orders. Decide that money is hard to make or that wealth isn't for you, and it will keep proving you right. That's your Reticular Activating System (RAS) at work, filtering out anything that doesn't match your story and highlighting everything that does. If lack is your story, lack is what you'll keep finding. So how do you change the story?

That's where manifestation comes in. It isn't about setting a goal and waiting for something magical to happen. It's about shifting the way you think, the way you feel, and the way you experience life.

Manifestation is alignment in action—rewiring your subconscious, dropping the blocks, and stepping into the version of you who already lives the life you want. Stay with me here. You've already started shifting—maybe it's been loud and obvious, maybe it's been quiet and subtle. Either way, you can feel it. The way you think is different. The way you see yourself is changing. That's proof this work is landing. Most people never get this far. You're not most people.

If manifestation is new to you, welcome. This isn't wishful thinking. It is about choosing how you show up every single day. Your thoughts shape your emotions, fuel your actions, and build the reality you experience.

Manifestation itself (as in "think it and it magically appears") is not backed by science. What is backed are the mechanisms behind it: how thoughts, beliefs, emotions, and actions shape perception, decision-making, and outcomes.

Manifestation, in scientific terms, is focus + belief + emotion + repeated thought + aligned action. What most people call the "law of attraction" is really just spiritual language for what psychology and neuroscience already prove works.

Your mind functions like a magnet. The energy you send out circles back. If you broadcast high energy, more of it finds you. When you remain in a low vibe, you receive more of that same heaviness. The fundamental principle remains simple: like attracts like. That is the game the universe is playing, and like any game, it comes with rules. You have heard about the Law of Attraction, yet the real power player is the Law of Assumption, a principle most people still manage to overlook entirely.

I decided to bring the most powerful universal laws into this book because they're too important to skip. These laws don't care about background, status, or opinion. They just run the show every second of the day. Gravity pulls on everyone the same. Fire burns whatever it touches, no exceptions. The planet spins on its axis nonstop. Your heart beats thousands of times each day. These laws are working every second, whether you pay attention or not. Think about it—Jason always comes back, Freddy haunts your dreams, Michael Myers never stops walking, and Ghostface loves a good twist. Just like universal laws, they show up whether you believe in them or not. Ignore them, and you're in trouble. Pay attention, and you know how the game is played.

We already live within physical laws. The Law of Vibration says everything is always moving, always humming with energy, even the stuff that looks solid. The Law of Universal Gravitation keeps every one of us grounded, pulling on everyone the same. And Newton's Law of Motion reminds us that momentum is real—once you're moving, you stay moving, and once you stop, it takes effort to get going again. These laws aren't opinions or trends.

This is where co-creation starts. Every thought, belief, and emotion you carry gives off a frequency. High energy lifts you up. Low energy drags you down. You've felt it before, that heavy weight when you're stuck in fear or that spark when you're lit up with possibility. Your dream life is already sitting at a higher frequency, and the more you match it, the faster it comes into view. Protect your energy. Feed your mind what expands you. That's how you pull in what you're asking for.

Energy doesn't lie. When you focus on fear, it keeps circling back. When you focus on possibility, more of it shows up. Life reflects what you bring to it. These rules are always running, whether you notice them or not. Ignore them, and they'll still shape your reality. Pay attention, and you can use them to your advantage. The rules don't bend for anyone, and now you're about to see exactly what they are.

Manifestation: *The phenomenon that occurs when something that was originally a part of your imagination becomes actualized into your physical reality.*

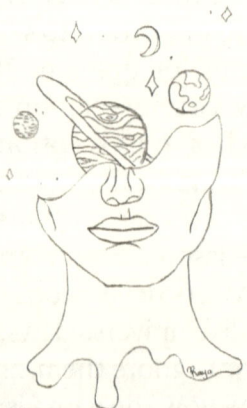

My daughter was 12-years-old when she came home from school and said:
"Mom, I don't know if anyone's ever taken a picture of the mind, so I drew one for you."
Children are always listening, absorbing information, consciously and unconsciously!

12 Universal Laws You've Probably Never Been Taught

Most people only ever hear about the Law of Attraction, then wonder why nothing's lining up. The problem isn't that you're doing it wrong, it's that you've been playing with one piece of the puzzle. The universe runs on way more than one law. These are the rules that keep everything balanced and moving. My big lightbulb moment was realizing the Law of Attraction is just a fraction of it. If wealth or success feels out of reach, this is usually why—you've been trying to play the game without knowing all the rules. Learn the others, and everything starts moving quicker. Life isn't practice. You get one shot, so why wouldn't you use all the power that's available to you?

Everything you want is possible. You just need the right tools and understanding of how life actually works. When you understand how the laws behind it all operate, you stop guessing and start creating results.

1. THE LAW OF ONENESS

Everything in the universe is connected. There's no true separation between you, me, the planet, or the energy around us. Every though, action, belief, or emotion you put out affects the whole, and what others put out ripples back to you. It's all linked. If you're tearing someone down, that energy circles right back to you. If you're celebrating someone else's win, you're showing yourself what's possible. Oneness reminds you that there's no separation here. The energy you give is the energy you live in.

2. THE LAW OF VIBRATION

Nothing stands still. Not you, not your thoughts, not the universe. Life runs on frequency, and the way you think and feel is broadcasting right now. Energy is always moving, never sitting still, and you are part of that flow. Your thoughts, emotions, and beliefs all send out a signal, and that signal sets the tone for what comes back. When your energy lines up with the life you want, things move faster and feel lighter. When it doesn't, everything feels heavy, blocked, and hard. People pick up your vibe before you ever speak a word. It shows in how you think, how you treat yourself, and how you carry yourself through the day. Clean up your energy, raise it, and hold it steady, because that's when you stop pushing and start attracting.

3. THE LAW OF ACTION

This one gets skipped by a lot of spiritual teachers, but let's be real, manifestation doesn't work without movement. You can meditate, journal, visualize, and raise your vibe all day long, but if you're not taking real steps, nothing in your life will change. The Law of Action says your physical steps activate the energy you're putting out. This isn't about random hustling or busy work that drains you. It's about inspired action that feels aligned and comes straight from your intuition. When you stop overthinking and start moving with clear intention, momentum builds fast. You're showing the universe you're serious, and that's when opportunities open and results start showing up.

4. THE LAW OF CORRESPONDENCE

Your inner world creates your outer world. Whatever is happening inside will always show up outside. If you want to change what you see in your life, you have to shift what is happening within you first. Forcing change on the outside without doing the inner work is wasted effort. This law is the mirror. It reflects your beliefs, emotions, and thoughts right back at you, whether you realize it or not.

5. THE LAW OF CAUSE AND EFFECT

This is basically karma, because what you put out always comes back around eventually. Life does not play favorites, it treats everyone the exact same way. It doesn't care what kind of seeds you decide to plant, it just grows them without judgment. There is no emotion involved, no opinion added, only pure results showing up for you. If you are not loving what is showing up in your life, it is time to check what you have been putting in. Are you planting seeds of confidence, joy, peace, and growth in your daily life? Or are you planting fear, jealousy, resentment, anger, or unnecessary drama that weighs you down? What you think, what you say, and what you do are all seeds that grow. If you want better outcomes in your life, start planting better seeds right now. People often say, "karma's a bitch," because it's a blunt reminder, almost sarcastic way of warning that negative actions eventually circle back, but at its core it is just cause and effect, you reap what you sow.

6. THE LAW OF ATTRACTION

This one gets all the attention, and for good reason. Like attracts like. What you put out is what you get back. It isn't about being worthy, it's about the energy you're sending out everyday. The universe doesn't care if it's positive or negative, it just mirrors it straight back to you. If your life is full of things you didn't exactly order, don't take it personally. Ask yourself what kind of energy you've been putting out. Your thoughts, your words, and your actions are pulling things toward you all the time. Whatever is showing up is proof of what you've been attracting.

7. THE LAW OF PERPETUAL TRANSMUTATION OF ENERGY

This might sound like a mouthful, but it's simple: energy is always moving, shifting, and changing form. Nothing stays the same. The second you decide to change your energy, you begin changing your life. The energy you carry today is not locked in place; you can shift it at any moment. You are never stuck, because energy is never stuck. Every thought, every action, every choice has the ability to change the frequency of your life.

8. THE LAW OF COMPENSATION

Compensation is simple. What you give will always circle back. When you put out time, energy, service, or love, the universe balances it by sending something in return. That return might look like money, opportunities, support, or growth, but it always matches the energy you put in. If you give with strings attached, resentment, or guilt, you block the very flow you are trying to create. When you give freely and stay open to receiving, life responds in powerful ways. Giving and receiving are two sides of the same coin, and this law makes sure the balance always plays out.

9. THE LAW OF RELATIVITY

Nothing in life has meaning until you give it one. Every situation just is — until you decide what it means to you. Challenges only feel big when you measure them against someone else's story or your old expectations. This law reminds you to zoom out. See things for what they are, not how they look in comparison. The moment you shift perspective, you shift your power.

10. THE LAW OF POLARITY

Everything in life has an opposite. You cannot have light without dark, joy without pain, happiness without sadness, up without down, or success without setbacks. Every challenge, frustration, or disappointment helps refine your vision and points you toward alignment. Polarity is like yin without yang, one cannot exist without the other. It is the reminder that every low carries a high andevery ending carries a beginning.

11. THE LAW OF GENDER

Everything in creation has masculine and feminine energy working together. It has nothing to do with male or female as people think about it, but with balance. Masculine energy is about action, structure, logic, and giving. Feminine energy is about intuition, flow, creativity, and receiving. Both are always present, and both are needed. Too much of one without the other creates imbalance. When you're pushing nonstop without space to receive, you burn out. When you're only waiting to receive without taking action, nothing moves. Mastering this law means blending the two, using structure and flow, logic and intuition, and giving and receiving. When you balance both energies, you allow flow, and that's when real results show up.

12. THE LAW OF RHYTHM

Everything moves in cycles. Just like the seasons, the tides, or your own energy, there's a natural rhythm to it all. Life ebbs and flows...Nothing stays the same forever, and nothing lasts forever. When you hit a slow season, it doesn't mean you're done, it just means you're in a reset or buildup phase. When things pick up, ride the wave. When they slow down, don't panic, rest and recalibrate. The rhythm of life is always moving, and when you work with it instead of against it, you stop burning out and start building momentum.

Intentions mean nothing without action. That is where the real shift happens. You are not doing this alone, you are co-creating with the universe. You show up with the "what" and the "why," and the universe handles the "how," "when," and "who." It always responds to your focus with a clear yes. Be specific about what you are asking for. Manifestation is simple: what begins in your imagination can become your reality when you are aligned and taking action. That is the power of universal laws like the Law of Attraction. This is not mystical or woo. Energy follows thought. Focused energy becomes form. The Law of Attraction has always been here. It works for anyone, anywhere, and anytime. Whatever you focus on, you attract. Negative thinking attracts more negativity. Clear and intentional thinking attracts more clarity and opportunity. When you align that with action, your life starts shifting fast.

Like it or not, we're all walking magnets; whatever energy we put out, we pull right back in.

Own It With 'I Am'

Let's talk about the most powerful phrase you'll ever speak.

The most powerful words in the English language combined is **I AM**. Whatever comes after it? That's your identity. That's your direction. The "I am" statement is no joke—it's the blueprint your subconscious builds from.

Who do you need to become to live the life you know is yours?
Speak it into existence:
I am powerful.
I am confident.
I am magnetic.
I am a beam of light.
I am intelligent.
I am a force of good.
I am creative.
I am valuable.
I am successful.
I am beautiful.
I am loved.
These aren't just words. This is identity work.
Now it's your turn. Write it. Repeat it. Feel it.
I am...
I am...
I am...
I am...
I am...

Put it on Post-it notes. In your affirmations app. On your lock screen. On a card in your wallet. Keep it in your face, in your energy, in your subconscious. *Write it out.*

To manifest anything, you have to become the version of you who already has it. Embody that version now. Tap into the emotions that match the life you are calling in. When you feel as if it is already real, you speed up the timeline. Your emotions act like a magnet, pulling in everything that aligns. They show you how close you are to the frequency of your dream. The closer you get to that feeling, the quicker it starts to materialize. This does not mean you sit back and wait. It means you take action from alignment, not from fear. When your energy is clear, the next step usually reveals itself. You do not need to chase it or overthink it.

The right people show up, the right ideas land, and the momentum builds naturally.

If you are still stressing over the how, pause. That is not your job. The universe handles the delivery. Your role is to hold the energy of "it's already mine" and stay grounded in that. Letting go of control isn't quitting. It's alignment, and that's where your power begins. Manifestation is not about begging or about chasing; it is about trusting. The universe always says yes. Stay grounded in your vision. Get clear on what you want. Take aligned action. Then let it breathe. You've already placed the order. Now trust it's on the way.

I want you to picture yourself one year from now, fully living your ideal reality. This isn't just about visualizing it. It's about defining the version of you who already has what you want and making decisions from that place right now.

Reflect & Apply the Universal Laws

1. Which universal law hits home for you the most?
2. How can you see yourself using this law in your daily life right now?
3. What shifted in the way you look at wealth, success, or alignment after reading this chapter?
4. When you think about your next big move, which law do you want guiding you?
5. What does living in alignment with the universal laws mean to you personally?

Use this to anchor what you've learned. Don't just read the laws, decide how you'll live them.

When life feels messy, you face it. It is not about pretending things are fine or forcing fake positivity. It is about trusting that challenges have purpose. Hard moments are not here to break you. They are here to teach you and build you stronger. The Law of Polarity and the Law of Relativity prove nothing is one-sided. When something feels off, it is a signal to realign. It may feel uncomfortable, but it is never pointless.

People will doubt you, and that is normal. They will judge, gossip, and misunderstand you. It is not your responsibility to convince them. The Law of Perpetual Transmutation reminds you that energy is never fixed. You can always shift it into something new. You do not need to prove your growth to anyone. Stay focused and keep moving forward. The right people will recognize it at the right time. You do not need to drag everyone with you. Some will fall away, and that is part of progress.

Life runs on a system that always responds. These laws are active whether you see them or not. Once you understand that, your approach changes. You stop forcing and start aligning. That does not mean sit still. It means you learn when to act and when to trust. It means you know when to push and when to pause. Everything is energy, and learning to read it is a core skill.

Laws at a Glance Cheat Sheet

Quick, badass one-liners for each law:

- **Law of Oneness:** We're all connected.
- **Law of Vibration:** Match the mood of what you want.
- **Law of Action:** Manifestation needs movement. Get off your butt.
- **Law of Correspondence:** Inner world = outer world.
- **Law of Cause and Effect:** You reap what you plant. Karma, baby.
- **Law of Attraction:** Like attracts like.
- **Law of Transmutation:** High vibe eats low vibe for breakfast. Shift energy. Alchemize it.
- **Law of Compensation:** Give + receive. Period.
- **Law of Relativity:** Your problems aren't permanent.
- **Law of Polarity:** Contrast creates clarity.
- **Law of Gender:** Balance your hustle with flow.
- **Law of Rhythm:** Everything moves in cycles. Find your flow.

Remember when I mentioned the Scream movie at the beginning of this chapter? The whole point of those films was that survival came down to knowing the rules. Break them and the cost was real. Sure, being a rule breaker sounds badass, but when the rules are universal, breaking them only hurts you. The Universal Laws work the same way. They're not suggestions, and they're not optional. You can ignore them, but you'll feel the consequences every time. The difference is, this isn't about horror, it's about your life. When you know the rules and live by them, you stop getting blindsided and start creating outcomes on purpose. So if you've ever watched Scream, you know the rules decide who makes it to the end. And when the villain chases someone and instead of running out the front door they run upstairs, you're sitting there yelling at the screen because the rule is obvious: don't trap yourself. The Universal Laws work the same way. If you ignore them, you trap yourself in cycles that could have been avoided. They're always running in the background, and if you pretend they're not, you'll keep repeating the same mistakes. The difference is, you don't have to play the victim here. You've got the rules now, and when you use them, life stops feeling like a horror show and starts working in your favor.

Take a breath. You've just moved through some serious inner recalibration, and this section was not light. This was the part where most people quit or stay stuck, but you didn't. You showed up. You looked straight at the beliefs that were holding you back and decided they don't get to run the show anymore. You reclaimed your voice, rewired your mind, and upgraded your identity from the inside out. You didn't just learn about limiting beliefs, you dismantled them piece by piece. You took affirmations further, turning them into incantations that shift energy. You built the Belief Bridge between where you've been and where you're headed, and you started walking across it like the future version of you is already in charge—because they are.

We cracked open the truth about this wild thing called life. It's a game, and there are rules, real rules and the Universal Laws are always in play whether you know them or not. But now you know them, and you've got the rules. You're no longer trying to manifest from vibes alone. You have the strategy, science, and soul backing you. That combo is unstoppable. If you feel different right now, it's because you are. You've activated something.

The Sequence to Aligned Wealth

You've upgraded how you think, how you speak, how you believe, and how you play. And that new version of you is about to step fully into their wealth era. You've done the deep inner work, and now it's time to move into the next part. This is where you'll learn how to catch your thoughts before they spiral and how to keep your brain locked on the future you're creating. This next section is where it gets exciting.

T
THOUGHT-CATCHING

EVICT THE THOUGHTS THAT ARE LIVING RENT-FREE

> *I have not failed, I've just found 10,000 ways that won't work*
>
> *- Thomas A. Edison*

"Oh, you're from a small town. People like you don't make it big."

"You're not meant for more."

"Keep your head down. Be realistic. Don't rock the boat."

I grew up with that small-town mentality, and it's no joke. It's this unspoken belief system passed down like a family recipe, but instead of cookies, it feeds you doubt, fear, and dreams that stay stuck inside your head. In a town where everyone knows your name, and nothing stays private, opinions fly fast, and your business never stayed yours for long. And success? That was for other people, city people. Definitely not girls like me, who knew every crowd in town and could name every person on her street.

The biggest dream most people had was moving two hours away to work in the mines or staying still and working at the local construction company. And if you had bigger goals? You were "too much." Or worse, "not realistic."

That's the problem with growing up around those thoughts. They start to feel like the truth. It becomes easy to believe your postal code sets your limit. Before you know it, you're playing small without even realizing it.

Thoughts are just recycled stories your brain keeps repeating because no one ever taught you to question them. They're not facts. They're old programming. And that's what Thought Catching is about—getting honest about the mental noise that's been running your life so you can rewire it for who you are now. Not who you were at 16 when someone told you to play small. This is where you learn to spot the junk, challenge the lies, and replace them with truth. You can absolutely become the confident, wealthy version of you, but you have to think like them first. You've been conditioned to forget your power. Time to wake up and take it back.

CHAPTER 32
Rewriting Reality: Dodging Mental Mayhem

EVER STOP TO think about how many thoughts run through your mind every single day? Thousands of them are just recycled noise from yesterday. The more they repeat, the more they harden into beliefs, and those beliefs quietly shape your reality. Your subconscious is always listening and building your world around what you've accepted as true. That's why thought-catching matters. The longer you let the old junk run unfiltered, the more it writes your story for you.

Let's get into language, because your words shape your entire world. If you keep saying things like "I'm exhausted" or "I'm broke," your subconscious takes that as truth and builds your reality around it. Flip it and say, "I've got energy" or "I'm figuring out how to bring in more money," and everything starts to shift. You're rewiring your brain to expect better, and your results begin to match. Perception is everything. It's the lens you're looking through. Focus on what's missing and you'll only multiply the lack. You'll miss the opportunities right in front of you. That's why catching your thoughts is a game-changer. Every time you flip a negative thought, you shift the lens you're seeing life through. That's how you rewrite reality.

Ask yourself the real questions, like are you doing things you don't even care about? Are you hanging out with people who drain you? Are you saying yes to things that make you want to scream no? Are you holding back from the life you actually want? Audit all of it. Then look around and notice if the people you love are doing the same thing. Call it out. You might end up saving them years of struggle.

I'll never forget one of my lowest moments. It wasn't about business, but it taught me everything about self-trust. I was standing at the checkout, toddler screaming, debit card declining. My cart wasn't full of food, just bananas and diapers. When that red-faced wave of shame hit, I wanted to disappear into the cereal aisle.

I had two choices at that moment. I could spiral into "I suck at life," or I could breathe and catch the thought before it swallowed me. I took a breath and reminded myself, "This doesn't define me. This is temporary." That moment shifted everything. Not because money suddenly showed up, but because I backed myself right there in the mess. That's what self-trust looks like. That's what wealth consciousness actually is. And I didn't even know it yet.

You need to know where you're going. But first, you need to get brutally honest about where you are right now. Most people skip that part. They avoid the mirror.

But if you don't own your current reality, you'll struggle to shift it. The farther you are from your truth, the harder it is to create a life that actually fits. If you're moving without a real why, you'll end up in a life that feels off.

Your time is currency, so spend it on things that light you up or teach you something new. That's how you create a life that excites you every single day. Most people stay stuck in the same place until something painful forces them to move. You don't need to wait for the breakdown before you take action. Move now, stretch into the next level, and then push yourself to stretch again. That is what real leadership looks like. You lead by showing the way, not by only talking about it. You walk through fear first so others see it can be done and follow after you.

You're here reading this book, so I already know you said yes to yourself. But saying yes is not the finish line, it is only the beginning. Wanting change is never the same as actually doing the work.

You have to show up fully, and you have to keep moving forward. Comfort zones are prisons built by old habits that trick you into staying small. Your subconscious is powerful, so use it wisely and train it with intention. Point it toward what you want, not what you fear or avoid. Humans are wired to stay safe and fit in, but that survival instinct makes you fear judgment and rejection. That fear keeps you small, makes you play nice, and convinces you to stay safe. But safety is not where growth lives, and it never will be. You grow the moment you break the pattern and choose differently on purpose.

Most of what we believe is backwards. We think the outside world shapes us, but it's actually the opposite. Everything in life is neutral until you give it meaning. That means you can change anything—by shifting what it means to you. Even at the uncon-scious level, meaning is the root. Look at someone like Bill Gates. He has the same twenty-four hours as you. But he built an empire, protected his health, and gave back on a massive scale. Time was never the problem. He just made better decisions with it. You don't need more hours in the day. You need to choose better from the ones you already have.

Have you ever caught yourself saying, part of me wants to go out dancing, but part of me wants to stay home and binge Netflix? Or maybe part of you wants to go for a walk, but another part wants to crash on the couch. Sometimes you even hear yourself say, part of me wants this, but part of me wants that. Those moments matter, because they show you the different parts inside you, each pulling in its own direction.

Parts are internal voices or identities that form from lived experiences, especially emotional ones. Ever said, "Part of me wants to go for it, but another part is scared"? That's a parts conflict. Each part has its own agenda.

It's trying to protect you, even if it doesn't feel that way. Most parts are born from unprocessed emotions or trauma that never got fully resolved. When something painful happens, especially in childhood, your nervous system doesn't always know how to handle it. So, your mind creates a part to carry the weight.

That part might show up as the strong one, the avoidant one, or the overachiever. It stepped in to help you survive when you needed it most. Back then it may have served a purpose, but now it can be the very thing holding you back. It tells you never to let your guard down, it pushes you to stay busy so you never stop to feel, and it quietly runs the show until you finally catch it.

You've already met these "parts." They're pieces of your identity created to protect you. Recognizing and integrating them is how you stop fighting yourself and finally align with what you want.

One of my favorite metaphors for this comes from *The Matrix*. In the movie, humans live inside a massive virtual simulation—what they think is reality is really just code. The Oracle is part of that code. She's designed with a specific role inside the system. But over time, she starts making her own decisions.

She still exists in the Matrix, but she's not following the original rules anymore. She's not fully controlled by the program. That's exactly how it works with your mind.

Your unconscious creates a part to help you survive something hard—usually trauma or intense emotion. That part has one job and that is to protect you. But eventually, it starts operating independently. It makes choices without checking in with who you are now. Just like the Oracle, it's still inside you, but it's running on old code.

And sometimes, it works against what you consciously want. That's why part of you might want to succeed, and another part keeps sabotaging it.

Conflict shows up because most parts come in pairs. One wants one thing. The other wants the opposite. But when you zoom out and look at what they're both trying to protect, you'll usually find they're actually fighting for the same higher value, something like love, freedom, or purpose. That's where parts integration comes in. It's about helping those conflicting parts find common ground.

Let's say one part wants to make a ton of money. Another part wants to serve and stay humble. Those seem like opposites, but they're not. They're both trying to protect your integrity. They just need to be updated and aligned. Once they are, things flow again.

We can all read the same page and see the same words, yet every single person will walk away with a completely different story. Your mind filters everything through your past, your beliefs, and your programming. That is why catching your thoughts and learning to rewrite them is so powerful. NLP calls this your "model of the world." Every second, your brain is flooded with over 2.3 million bits of information, but it only lets in about 126 of them. What gets filtered depends on your mood, your memories, the time of day, your values, your location, and even the language you speak. Two people can listen to the same podcast and have opposite reactions, one feeling inspired while the other couldn't stand it. At the same concert, one person might be crying while another is scrolling on their phone. Even something as small as asking someone for coffee feels completely different at two in the afternoon compared to two in the morning. Your filters are running behind the scenes all the time, shaping how you see and experience reality.

That's how perception works. And that's why learning to catch and shift your thoughts isn't a nice-to-have. It's non-negotiable. You're not seeing life as it is. You're seeing it through the lens your filters allow.

Your brain is constantly filtering and organizing information. When you split your focus between past regrets, future worries, and endless noise, everything gets messy fast. The way forward is simple. Be here now. Stay present. Even if we're all in the same room watching the same show, each of us walks away with a different version of what happened. We each filter life through our own lens. Same "Matrix," but different programming. Even when we're reading the same page, we're creating totally different stories, shaped by our beliefs, experiences, and whatever part of us is running the show. Most people live like they're stuck in circumstances they can't control. They say things like, "I can't make money because my parents were broke," or "I'll never find love because everyone in my family is a mess." Society wires that in from the start. We're taught early on that other people's opinions, especially those of anyone who's in "authority", matter more than our own. And it starts young. I remember being in elementary school, thinking I had crushed my art project. A+ effort, all the way. I was proud of that project because I gave it everything. Same with my tests, I studied, I focused, and I was proud. And then boom. The teacher slapped a C-minus on my work like it was garbage. I sat there thinking, "What the hell? I tried. I showed up. And now you're telling me it's not good enough?"

That's the kind of stuff that sticks. You start wondering if what you think even matters. You begin doubting your own judgment and looking to everyone else for approval. And that's the trap. That's how we're trained to shrink. But you're not here for that anymore; we don't have to play by those rules.

This is how parts keep running the show in the background. They feed you old rules, old limits, and you accept them as truth without realizing it. But your brain doesn't work in words, it works in images. And that's why what you focus on matters.

How Your Brain Filters Reality

If I tell you, "Don't think of a blue tree," your brain immediately pictures one. Why? Because we think in images, not words. Around 65 percent of people are visual thinkers, and research shows that our brains process visuals 60,000 times faster than text. That's why focusing on what you don't want still locks in the image and pulls your actions toward it. The simple fix is to shift your focus and start painting a clear mental picture of what you actually want. Your brain will grab that and run with it. Pay attention to the words you use with yourself all day. Watch the mental snapshots your mind keeps replaying. If they don't match the life you want, flip them. Speak with certainty. Focus on what feels aligned and powerful. Keep repeating it until it becomes second nature. And if you really want proof of how this works, just look at kids.

Kids are like sponges in the best and worst ways. Before age seven, they're basically walking subconscious minds. Their conscious brain isn't even fully developed yet. Everything you say and do goes straight in and leaves a mark. That pattern gets hardwired early and stays. Kids are wired to please, to follow instructions. It's baked into their DNA.

Most people do not know that the language they use messes with a kid's programming. You tell a kid, "Don't get your shirt dirty." Five seconds later, they're rolling in mud. You say, "Don't spill the milk"—all they hear is "spill the milk." Then, milk gets spilled everywhere because their brain didn't process the "don't." It zones in on the image. Get dirty. Spill milk. That's what lands. That's what plays on repeat.

Now swap out kids for adults. The same thing applies. Tell yourself, "Don't go broke," and your subconscious only locks onto "broke." It doesn't register the negative. You just gave it a target. Flip it instead. Say, "I'm building wealth." Say, "I handle money with confidence." That hits different. That's the loop your subconscious will run.

You already know how powerful your thoughts are. What matters now is training yourself to catch them in real time. Most of what runs through your head isn't new—it's recycled noise that turns into belief if you let it. Belief becomes your filter, and your filter becomes your reality. The way out of that loop is simple: notice the thought, challenge it, and rewrite it.

Let's flip the script.

1. **Catch your thoughts**
   Pay attention to the chatter in your head. Notice all of it.
2. **Write them down**
   The good, the bad, the annoying. Get it out of your head and onto paper.

3. **Call them out**

   Ask yourself if this thought is helping you move forward or just keeping you stuck.

4. **Rewire it**

   If it's trash, replace it with something that serves you. Use these prompts:

   - "In the past, I used to believe _____. Now, I'm learning to _____."
   - "The truth is _____."
   - "I'm open to the idea that _____ is possible."
   - "I can see how _____ could become real for me."

   Example:
   Instead of saying, "I don't know enough," flip it to, "I've been soaking up personal development for three years. I know a lot, and I'm learning how to turn it into real results."

5. **Track the patterns**

   Tally the thoughts that keep repeating. Spot the loop and call it out.

   Yes, this takes effort. But if you stick with it for even one week, you'll start training your brain to flip thoughts automatically, like muscle memory. The more consistent you are, the easier it gets. You stop reacting on autopilot and start creating on purpose. This isn't about thinking better for the sake of it. It's about building a life that matches what you want.

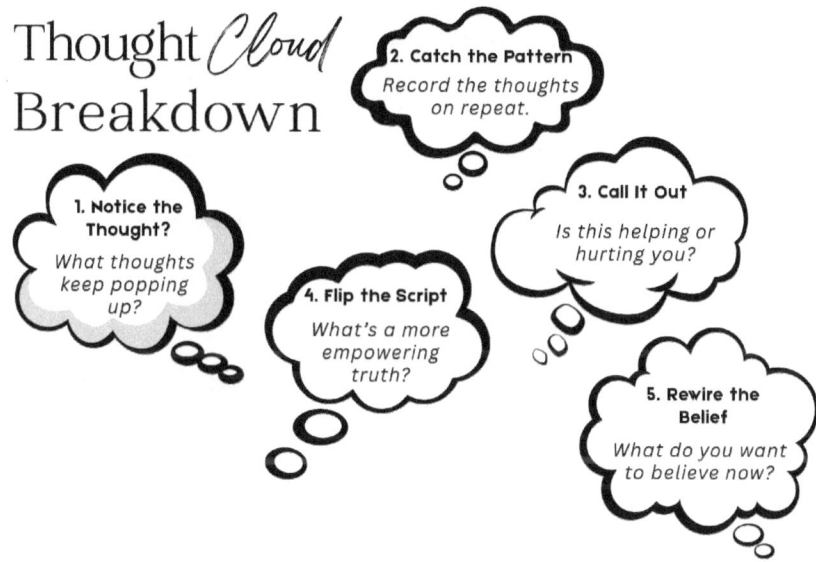

THOUGHT-CATCHING CHEAT SHEET
Your Reality Rewrite Tool

1. **What thoughts keep popping up?**
   Write down three repeating thoughts that are not helping you.
2. **Is this thought helping or hurting?**

   Next to each one, label it as helping or hurting.
3. **What's the truth?**

   Flip the thought into something empowering.
   Example: *"I'll never get out of debt"* becomes *"I'm learning how to manage money and build wealth."*
4. **What do you want to believe instead?**

   Use one of these sentence starters to rewire it:
   - "In the past, I used to believe... now I know..."
   - "The truth is..."
   - "I'm open to the idea that..."
   - "It's possible that..."
   - "I am becoming someone who..."

5. **Track it daily for 7 days**

   Write your thought down each time it shows up. Use tally marks beside it so you can see how often it repeats. Then, right next to it, write a new version that helps you.

Take your favorite new thought and put it on a sticky note where you'll see it every day—like your mirror or fridge—so your environment reminds you of what you believe now.

CHAPTER 33
Money Meter

How often do you feel like you're smashing into the same income ceiling, stuck in a financial loop that never seems to end? You've got an inner money thermostat that keeps toggling between not bad and could be better, no matter how hard you try to break through. You push forward, yet somehow you end up right back where you started. This is about your money meter, your financial thermostat, or whatever name you want to give it. We're pulling back the layers to see what's really running the show and resetting it to match the wealth, success, and freedom you were built for. This work doesn't stop with cash. The shifts you make here ripple into everything—confidence, boundaries, habits, and relationships. It's all connected. You've got an internal gauge that controls how much of all of that you allow yourself to have. Most people don't even realize it's running the show. But once you do, everything changes.

Gay Hendricks cracked this wide open in his book *The Big Leap* with his concept of the Upper Limit Problem. He explains that we all carry a preset internal limit on how much good we'll actually allow ourselves to have. It acts like a thermostat, locked in by past experiences, upbringing, trauma, culture, and family patterns. That limit becomes your default. When things start feeling too good, too aligned, or too abundant, your subconscious hits the alarm. It signals that something must be off, and that's when the sabotage kicks in. A fight gets picked. A deadline gets missed.

The Sequence to Aligned Wealth

Money disappears. You catch a cold. You cancel plans. You pull back from your goals. All because a part of you still believes it isn't safe or possible to hold this new level of success, love, joy, or wealth. That is the Upper Limit Problem. It's not that you cannot succeed. It's that you don't yet know how to stay there without spiraling back. You haven't expanded your capacity to receive and hold what you've worked for.

Hendricks breaks down four zones that most people live and work from.

The Zone of Incompetence is where you struggle. You're doing things you're not good at, and it drains your energy because it never feels natural.

The Zone of Competence is where you can get by. You're capable, but so is everyone else. There's nothing unique about it, and it doesn't light you up.

The Zone of Excellence is where you shine and probably get paid well. It feels good, it looks impressive, and it usually wins applause. But it is also where most people get stuck, because it feels safe. It keeps you comfortable but not fulfilled.

The Zone of Genius is different. This is where your work feels effortless, expansive, and deeply aligned with who you really are. It's the space where your gifts, your truth, and your purpose all collide. Most people never reach it because the safety of excellence keeps them from stepping into the extraordinary. Moving into your zone of genius means tearing down the internal stories that hold you back. The ones that whisper you're not good enough, you'll fail, people will judge you, or success will cost you your freedom, health, time, or relationships. Those thoughts are the real sabotage. The ceiling isn't time, money, or strategy. The ceiling is in your mind.

Owning your Zone of Genius is just the first step. The next is raising your capacity to hold it by catching the patterns that drag you back and resetting the inner thermostat that sets the limit on how good your life gets to feel. Growth isn't about hitting a goal once and slipping back. It's about expanding what you allow and keeping it. The real move isn't reaching the level you want, it's staying there and letting it become your new normal.

Imagine setting your house thermostat to 60 degrees. When the room temperature reaches 64 degrees, the system kicks in and cools it back down. That's what thermostats do. They keep things steady, predictable, and safe. But this isn't just about the air in your living room. It's the same thing with how much love, success, happiness, or money you let in. If your internal thermostat is set too low, the moment life starts getting better, you'll find yourself pulling it back down without even realizing it.

Psychologists call this your happiness setpoint. It's your emotional baseline. No matter how high you rise, you end up returning to what feels normal. I call it your capacity meter, because that's what it really measures. It's linked to your identity and your beliefs about what's safe, what's possible, and what you think you deserve. A lot of new millionaires go broke within a few years. Not because they're bad with money, but because the money didn't match who they believed they were. If someone only sees themselves as a thirty-thousand-a-year earner, and then millions suddenly land in their lap, the brain panics. That level of wealth doesn't feel familiar. So, they blow it, lose it, or give it away—just to get back to what feels normal.

That same pattern doesn't just show up with money. It's everywhere. You push past your limits, then life yanks you back. Maybe it's the same income ceiling, maybe it's your weight bouncing back, or maybe it's relationships hitting the same pitfalls That's your internal setpoint calling the shots. It means there's a deeper setting running the show that needs adjusting. And that's what this section is here for—to figure out where your capacity meter is set and raise it. Once you shift the setting, everything else begins to rise with it.

You've got a capacity meter that sets the tone for everything: money, love, success, even how good life gets to feel. Think of it like your internal thermostat. Go past your set point, and sabotage sneaks in. That pattern isn't random. It's tied to your identity and what you believe you're worthy of. Look at lottery winners. Most lose it all because they never saw themselves as millionaires. Their brain pulled them back to what felt familiar. The same cycle shows up in everyday life too. Your bank account climbs after payday, but somehow it slips back to the same number. You finally start eating better, then fall right back into old habits. Relationships hit the same wall over and over. There's a limit that feels "too much" and another point that kicks you into panic. Between those two edges is where most people live without realizing it. Everyone has a number they circle back to, and that number is what I call the financial "oh no" zone.

For some people, that alarm goes off at ten thousand. For others, it hits when they hit zero. And some don't even flinch until they're five thousand in debt. That number is different for everyone. This is why you need to get honest about your own money comfort zone. Think back to the times you felt solid and on top of things. What was in your account then? What did that feel like? This gives you a clear view of what you've been allowing and what triggers you to hustle or shut down. That's how you start shifting the limit and building a money relationship you can actually trust.

That's not random. That's sabotage. Start noticing how it shows up. That awareness puts you back in control. Think back to the lowest point you've hit financially. What did it look like? What did it feel like? What finally made you say, "That's it. I'm done." And be honest, did you really change after that moment, or did you slip right back into the same loop? Start tracking the highs and lows of your money story. What's the most income you've ever had in a month, or the most you've ever held in your account at one time? And what happened right after? Did you shut down? Spend it fast? Did it trigger panic or guilt? Now go back to the lowest number that forced you to hustle harder. What was going on in your life when that happened? Write it all down—the highs, the lows, how you felt, what actions you took, and what you avoided. That's where your patterns live. And once you see those patterns clearly, you stop letting them run your life.

This Spot Your Setpoint exercise next is about your financial thermostat and how it plays out across every area of your life—not just money. It reveals how your internal capacity has been limiting your results in areas such as money, health, love, success, visibility, and more.

SPOT YOUR SETPOINT
Track your capacity meter across all 8 life areas

MONEY

- What's the highest monthly income you've ever had?
- What happened right after?
- What's the number that usually triggers hustle or panic?

CAREER OR BUSINESS

- What was your boldest move or biggest win?
- When did you start playing small again?
- What patterns keep repeating at the next level?

HEALTH + BODY

- What's your feel-good weight or energy level?
- When do your healthy habits fall off?
- What always pulls you back to your 'normal'?

LOVE + RELATIONSHIPS

- When has a relationship felt next-level?

- What triggered the disconnect or drama after that?
- Do you notice a cap on how good you let love get?

FRIENDSHIPS + COMMUNITY

- When did you feel fully seen and supported?
- Did you pull back or isolate afterward?
- How many close connections do you truly let in?

TIME + FREEDOM

- When did you feel the most free and spacious?
- What made you stop giving yourself that freedom?
- What patterns always steal your time back?

SELF-WORTH + CONFIDENCE

- When were you showing up unapologetically?
- What caused you to shrink again?
- What triggers doubt even when you're winning?

JOY + FUN

- What's the most lit-up you've felt recently?
- When did you stop letting yourself enjoy it?
- Do you feel guilty when life gets too good?

Now look at your setpoint across these areas. What do your high points have in common? And what tends to happen right after things feel really good? Notice if your subconscious is trying to protect you from something. That awareness shows you where the old pattern lives.

Then shift into identity. Who do you need to become to live consistently at your next level? What beliefs, behaviors, and boundaries does that version of you hold? And what are you no longer available for? This is where you raise the bar on what you allow in your life and reset your baseline for good.

You've had moments where everything felt aligned, like life was finally clicking, and then just as quickly it slipped back to normal. That isn't luck or coincidence. That is your capacity meter at work, pulling you toward what feels familiar. Maybe you stopped showing up for yourself, stepped back from the people who lifted you up, or let habits slide right when you were gaining momentum. The pattern might look different each time, but the push back is the same. What changes everything is catching it. The doubt. The second-guessing. The voice that whispers "it will not last." The moment you recognize it as sabotage, you stop letting it run the show. This chapter is not about chasing more. It is about learning to hold more and letting your next level become the new normal.

Like I said earlier, you raise your baseline and begin attracting what matches it. That's how wealth expands in your life. Your financial thermostat sits in your subconscious and sets your default. Let's say you've built your comfort zone around 80K a year. Your thoughts, feelings, and actions all line up with that number. That becomes your normal. Now imagine you bring in an extra 10K. You hit 90K, and before you know it, your system starts to panic. It doesn't feel safe, so the old habits try to pull you back. You slip into the familiar patterns you've always known.

Your subconscious says this is too much, too fast. You start spending, avoiding, or shutting down, whatever it takes to land you back where you're used to. Same thing when you dip below that set point. If you drop to 70K, your mind scrambles to get back on track. You push harder, hustle more, and obsess over making it right. That pattern is not random. It is the thermostat keeping things familiar. Ever notice how your bank account always circles the same number? That's no coincidence. That's your set point pulling you back to what feels normal. I've said it once, I'll say it twice.

The same thing happens with weight. Say your comfort zone is 170lbs. If you creep up to 180, your brain sounds the alarm and pushes you back down. If you dip to 160 or 150, that same alarm kicks in and scrambles to get you back up to 170lbs. It's not just about habits or food choices. It's the same internal thermostat at work, pulling you toward what feels familiar, even if that "familiar" isn't where you want to be.

You've been running on patterns that were set a long time ago, and they have quietly shaped how much you allow yourself to have. The good news is that you are not locked into that story. You can adjust the setting and choose a new baseline that becomes your standard. When you shift who you believe you are, your results begin to line up with that belief. A stronger identity creates a stronger reality.

Think about the times you worked hard, got close, and then it slipped away. That cycle is not proof that you are weak or unmotivated. Those limits were written years ago, often without you even realizing it. You get to decide if you keep following them or if you create a new script.

This is not only about money. It is about what you allow across the board. Your capacity meter has been deciding how much love, joy, health, and success you let in. That old programming does not have to stay in charge. From here, you get to choose. You get to let yourself receive more. You get to let the good last. It is about letting life rise and allowing it to stay that way.

So, the real question is—are you ready to turn it up? Ready to stop playing small, stop pushing good things away, and finally match your life to your potential? This is your reset moment. The patterns, limits, and ceilings don't get to run you anymore. When your thermostat is set low, you'll always find ways to pull yourself back down.

That's how sabotage creeps in. Not because you don't want more, but because your subconscious believes more isn't safe. And that's where your internal capacity meter comes in.

The Sequence to Aligned Wealth

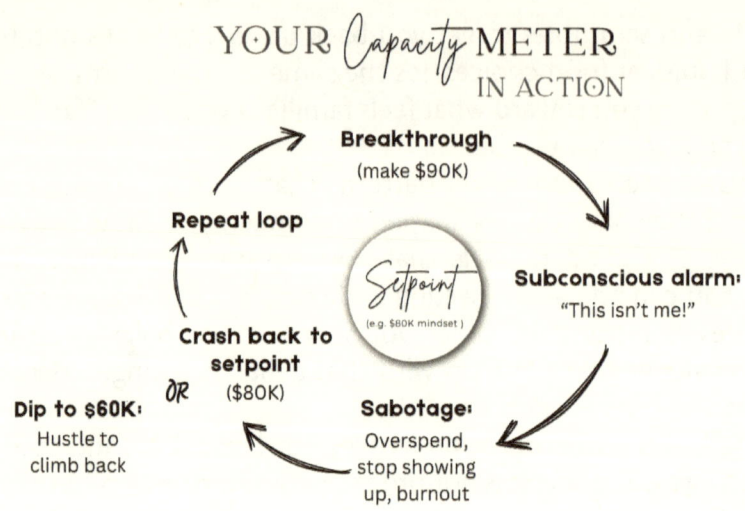

YOUR *Capacity* METER
IN ACTION

REPEAT LOOP - UNLESS IDENTITY SHFITS

Your internal capacity meter is sneaky and powerful, shaped by the identity you've carried over time. It's the quiet voice that whispers, "This is just who I am," and it drives the patterns that keep showing up in your life. Picture it like an old-school thermometer, the kind your parents or grandparents slid under your tongue when you were sick, with the thin red line rising or falling. That line is your visual cue, when that red line rises, it's like your wealth heating up and expanding. When it drops, things start cooling off, showing where your comfort zone kicks back in. That's what your capacity meter looks like. It tracks how much you let yourself hold, and when you drift too far above or below what feels normal, it pulls you back. This pattern doesn't just touch your finances. It threads through how you eat, rest, work, and connect. Some days you're in full flow, and other days it feels like you're dragging through mud. That's not about effort; it's about the settings running your life. Your mind has learned when to press go and when to slam the brakes. Feeling stuck isn't about money or numbers—it's about the identity that keeps replaying the same limits. It's about the story you've been living and the identity you've accepted as normal.

So, let's figure this out:

Capacity Meter Tracker

This is about tracking, logging, and noticing the moment-to-moment swings — not just reflecting on highs and lows like the setpoint exercise from earlier. Think of it as a monitoring tool instead of a reflection tool. Start paying attention to your "thermometer" in real time. Notice when you feel yourself creeping toward your upper or lower limits. Use the prompts below to track it for the next week:

Daily Check-In

- Where's my energy today on a scale from 1–10?
- Where's my money confidence today on a scale from 1–10?
- Did I notice myself holding back, avoiding, or sabotaging?

When Things Felt "Too Good"

- What happened right before I felt the urge to pull back?
- What thoughts showed up? (Example: "This won't last" or "I don't deserve this.")
- How did my body react? (Tension, fatigue, distraction, spending, overeating, etc.)

When Things Felt "Too Low"

- What triggered the drop?
- What behaviors kicked in? (Overworking, people-pleasing, shutting down, overspending, etc.)
- What signal told me I had to hustle harder or snap out of it?

Patterns

- Do I notice the same triggers or habits at both ends of the meter?
- How do I usually bring myself back to "normal"?

- What would it look like to hold steady at a slightly higher baseline?

Both exercise's compliment each other because the Spot Your Setpoint exercise is the wide-angle reflection across all life areas, and the Capacity Meter Tracker is your zoomed-in, daily/weekly monitoring tool.

Your capacity meter is only as strong as the identity behind it, whatever follows "I am" becomes your reality, and if you've been running on old settings, your thermostat has been capping how much money, love, joy, and success you let in. You don't have to crash or burn out to reset it. You can choose to adjust it right now. That choice starts with identity. The version of you who earns more, receives more, and holds more doesn't show up after the win. They show up first, the version of you who lives at the level you're calling in, so decide it's safe to hold more, keep your standard high, and let life rise to meet the identity you refuse to drop.

CHAPTER 34
Mindshift Magic

GROWING UP IN Elliot Lake, a small town where everybody knows everybody, you didn't just know your neighbors, you knew their secrets, their drama, and probably who they hooked up with last night. It was cozy in a way, but it was also a bubble. If you dared to dream beyond bomb fires, pit parties, and cheap beer from someone's older brother, the whispers would start. "Who does she think she is?" wasn't just a phrase—it was a warning. It felt like small-town thinking kept everyone boxed in. That's where the stuck feeling kicks in. Ambition gets side-eyed and dreams feel like trouble. In places like that, people know your business before you even open your mouth, and the second you step outside the mold, the eye rolls start, and the whispers spread. You learn very quickly that there's a ceiling, and it hangs low.

The rule is unspoken but clear: don't stand out too much. You go to hockey games or play in them. You join baseball or soccer, watch fireworks on Canada Day, and maybe sneak off for a smoke behind the arena or the rock, but you do not shine too bright or stand in the spotlight. Then life loops on repeat. You graduate, get a decent job, stay still, settle down, and keep the peace. If you ever talked about leaving or building a different life, people didn't clap. They questioned. They whispered, "She thinks she's better than us." "She'll come crawling back." Small towns don't just keep you close. They hold you in place, shaping your choices and tightening their grip. It didn't just hold your plans hostage, it shaped your identity. It was like a black hole swallowing you whole, keeping you in the dark.

Growing up in a small town felt like we were all stamped with the same silent label: dreams not included. From the start, the script was handed to you: graduate, land a safe job, stay close, and settle early. Big ambition wasn't for us. That kind of reach was reserved for "city people," not kids raised on late nights and bonfires. Anything outside the norm was marked as off-limits, a warning not to want too much.

I remember that heavy, suffocating weight of everyone else's expectations pressing in. "You can't make it big here," they'd say. "This town swallows big dreams whole." For a while, I believed them. But eventually, we made a different move. We packed up, left the whispers behind, and reached for more possibility. That choice cracked everything open and became one of the best decisions I ever made.

When you grow up in a small town, it's easy to shrink and think your dreams take up too much space. But the truth is, your roots don't limit your reach. Where you started doesn't decide where you're going. That town was built on comfort. Everything was close, familiar, and routine. The same streets, the same names, and the same stories repeated. People gave up long-term joy for short-term ease and called it safety. Chasing something bigger felt like rebellion. It felt like screaming into the void and only hearing silence, side-eyes, or doubt. You're allowed to want more, even if you come from a place where dreaming bigger makes people uncomfortable. It doesn't matter if you grew up on a dead-end street or spent weekends at camp with kids you've known since kindergarten. What matters is where you're headed, not where you started. You don't settle just because you grew up in a small town. You don't shrink your dreams because someone else told you to. Settling dims your light. The shift happens when you stop letting your past set the tone and start building a future that actually fits.

Growing up in a place where everyone knows your name also means they think they know your story. They decide who you are before you've had the chance to figure it out for yourself. Every conversation is recycled, and every move you do seems like someone's always watching you. We learn to shrink and play it safe, making choices that keep us from stepping out of line. Big dreams get questioned, and bigger ones get criticized. High school becomes the first ceiling we hit, where standing out feels out of place and blending in feels safer. Leaving town was never just about packing boxes. It was about leaving behind the version of ourselves that played small to make others comfortable. The deeper shift comes when we start realizing our thoughts aren't just passing feelings, they're the blueprint for the walls we keep running into. No one teaches you how to think. What you believe about yourself decides which opportunities you even notice.

Scientific studies in Cognitive-Behavioral Therapy have shown that your automatic thoughts play a direct role in your emotional state, decision-making, and behavior. Dr. Daniel Amen, known for his work in brain imaging, explains that every thought sparks a chemical reaction in the brain. That means your mindset isn't just personal, it's biological. The stories you tell yourself shape your habits and guide what you do. They set the tone for how you feel, the choices you make, and the actions you take. This isn't just about positive thinking, it's about the way your brain is wired. When you interrupt a limiting belief and replace it with something stronger, you are literally shifting the pathways your brain runs on.

The brain learns through repetition and responds to imagery. That's why visualization, identity work, and belief rewrites are so effective. They aren't surface tricks, they're how your subconscious gets reprogrammed. Every time you imagine a new outcome, your mind begins building the path to it. When your conscious goals line up with what you believe deep down, everything starts moving smoother.

Limiting beliefs are sneaky. They whisper garbage that keeps you stuck. They make you second-guess your brilliance and trip over your own momentum. Beliefs can build empires or burn them to the ground. Like Tony Robbins says, it all comes down to the meaning you give it. Your past can fuel you or freeze you. These beliefs are just old scripts. You didn't ask for them, but they got in anyway.

Now they're in the background, shaping every decision, influencing every move—and most of the time, you don't even notice. Our brains are wired for certainty. We cling to routines, relationships, and familiar jobs because they feel safe. But when it's time to reach higher and go after what we want, we freeze. Somewhere deep down, we don't believe we can pull it off. That's the grip of a limiting belief. Beliefs shape how we see the world. Beliefs work like glasses. When they're clean, you see things clearly. When they're smudged, everything looks off. A limiting belief is like walking around with dirty lenses — the world isn't the problem, it's the filter that makes you think you're not enough.

So what is a limiting belief? A limiting belief is any thought that convinces you something isn't possible, even when it is. It's the voice in your head saying, "You can't." "You're not ready." "You don't have what it takes." And those thoughts? They kill your joy, your momentum, and your power faster than anything else. We all carry them. But the good news is that you can ditch them. You can replace the beliefs that drain you with ones that support where you're going. These limiting thoughts aren't facts. They're borrowed and passed down by parents, teachers, religion, culture, small-town mentality, or even someone who once made you question your worth. They slip into your subconscious and hide beneath the surface, running in the background, shaping how you think and what you allow, quietly driving choices you didn't mean to make.

Let's name them for what they are:
"I'm not good enough."
"Money's hard to make."
"I'll never follow through."
"I don't deserve it."
"People like me don't get rich."
"It's better to be safe than sorry."

Sound familiar? These beliefs sneak in quietly but hit hard. Left unchecked, they wreck your momentum and steal your power. They shape what you believe is possible, how you show up, and how much you let yourself receive.

So how do you spot them? Set a bold goal, like making 10K a

month, or if you're an entrepreneur, landing five new clients, and notice what surfaces. What you start thinking and telling yourself, what words pop up in your head. Pay attention to the voice that says, "I'm not ready because..." or "It's too late for me." Those are beliefs blocking you. And let's be real, they're full of shit.

Some beliefs I see come up repeatedly are below

Top 25 Limiting Beliefs That Have Worn Out Their Welcome:

1. I'm not smart enough.
2. I'm not worthy of success.
3. I'm not good with money.
4. I always mess things up.
5. I have to work hard to make money.
6. I'll never get ahead.
7. I don't have what it takes.
8. If I shine too bright, I'll make others uncomfortable.
9. If people really knew me, they wouldn't like me.
10. I'm too old to start over.
11. It's selfish to want more.
12. People like me don't get rich.
13. I have to be perfect to succeed.
14. I don't have the time.
15. I've already missed my chance.
16. It's better to play it safe.
17. If I try, I'll probably fail, anyway.
18. I should just be grateful for what I have.
19. I'm too much.
20. It's too late for me.
21. Nothing I do is good enough.
22. What I have to say doesn't matter.
23. No one else has ever done it, so I can't.
24. Change is hard and takes forever.
25. I've tried before and it didn't work, so why bother?

You just read a handful of limiting beliefs, but the list doesn't stop there. These thoughts keep spinning in people's heads every day, keeping them stuck. The quickest way to catch them is by setting a goal and paying attention to the voice that shows up. That little voice loves to throw garbage at you. Set a goal to make more money, and suddenly it says, "I could never do that. I'm not smart enough."

Limiting beliefs usually hide behind words like *never, can't, or impossible.* They get loud when challenged, but the truth is they're not facts. Everyone has potential and success starts with believing in yourself enough to take action. Action builds proof, and proof strengthens belief. So, next time you catch yourself making excuses or clinging to an old thought, stop and ask: Is this true, or is it just a lie trying to keep you small?

You can harness that power and get your subconscious working with you instead of against you. Real change happens when your goals and your deeper beliefs stop clashing and finally line up. If you feel stuck, start by getting clear. Write down what you don't want and let that point you toward what you do. From there, choose the thoughts and actions that back up the future you want. This is your story, and the next chapter is yours to write.

MINDSHIFT MAGIC RECIPE

Ingredients:

> 1 cup Courage
> 2 tbsp Imagination
> A pinch of Self-Reflection
> A dash of Creativity
> A sprinkle of Dreams

Instructions:

> Light a candle. Get cozy. Breathe deep.
> Ask yourself: *What rules or non-negotiables have you created for your life?* Write every belief that pops up. Do not filter your answers, write the first thing that comes to mind.

Next, picture your ideal day. How do you want to feel? What lights you up? Jot it all down—from sipping your morning coffee to getting ready for bed.

Now tap into what you *really* want to be surrounded by. Love? Freedom? Money? Adventure? Picture what you want around you. Don't water it down and be honest with yourself.

Think about the world you want to create. How do you impact others? What legacy are you leaving? Write that down too.

Visualize another version of you—the one who already has it all. What's their life like? How do they show up? Describe them in detail.

Read it all back and let it sink in. What you just wrote is already planting itself in your subconscious.

Blow out the candle. You've lit something way bigger inside. Keep that energy with you and watch what happens.

Your beliefs might be true or complete bullshit, but if you believe them, you'll act like they're facts. Beliefs turn into habits, and habits start to become second nature. That's self-hypnosis and it is time to snap out of it.

Start right now by picturing yourself back in that small town where doubt echoes from every corner, but beneath the noise, there's a flicker of possibility. Let yourself notice the thoughts that try to pull you back and replace them with ones that push you forward. Hold tight to the small wins that prove you're moving in the right direction. Step into the role of the author of your own story. Let confidence guide you and determination carry you.

Say it out loud:
I am powerful.
I am confident.
I create my own future.

Write those words down. Put them where you'll see them—on your desk, your mirror, or your phone screen. Let them sink in until they feel like second nature. This is how new beliefs start to stick. Wealth is more than money. It's the people you love, the moments that matter, and the fire that keeps you moving forward. Let your "I am" statements land like a final note in a song. No more waiting. No more holding back. This is where you take charge of your thoughts and own your story. You're not the one wondering if you're too much. You're the one who knows you were never meant to play small.

> *Money is only a tool. It will take you wherever you wish, but it will not replace you as the driver.*
> —Ayn Rand ♡

CHAPTER 35
The Daily Thought Audit; Your 5-Minute Wealth Rewire

LET'S BE HONEST with each other, your bank account isn't random, is it? It's a carbon copy of the stories running through your head. If you keep saying "I'm broke," guess what? You are. If you keep saying "I always find a way," guess what? You do. I see it daily. People light candles, chant affirmations, post vision boards all over social media, but their inner thoughts are a mess of doubt, fear, and old stories. They don't notice the tiny patterns until they ruin their results again and again. This audit fixes that. You need to stop hoping and pretending. It's your fast track to rewiring your brain to think and act wealthy automatically.

WHY THIS TINY RITUAL PACKS A MASSIVE PUNCH

Your mind spits out over 60,000 thoughts a day. Most of them are the same ones you had yesterday. So, if yesterday's thoughts were, "Money is hard," "I never have enough," or "Why bother?" — today will be too. Reading this book cracked open your awareness. But daily life will try to slap you back into default mode. This audit is how you fight back and win.

If you ever:
- Panic before checking your bank account
- Apologize when someone mentions money

- Get jealous of other people's wealth
- Obsess over bills at 2 AM
- Feel guilty wanting more money
- Google "how to make money fast" and chase quick fixes that never work

Then you need this. It's a reset for how you think about money. A quick way to clear out the noise and stop old thoughts from running the show.

AUDIT LIKE A WEALTHY PERSON

HOW IT WORKS

When: Morning, before you start your day. Midday, when something tests your patience, or throws you off. Night, so you don't drag your old beliefs into tomorrow.

Where: Your bed, your car, or even the bathroom. Anywhere works. No excuses.

How long: Five minutes max. It can save you years of repeating old patterns.

STEP-BY-STEP WEALTH AUDIT

1. Morning Reset

You wake up with your brain still carrying pieces of yesterday's thoughts. Clean them out before your first coffee.

Do this: Write three honest thoughts about money. Be raw. Circle the worst one.

Then flip it immediately.

Examples: "I can't save," becomes "I trust myself to handle money well, starting today."

"I never get ahead," becomes "Money flows to me in bigger ways now."

Why it works: Your subconscious is a sponge in the morning. What you feed it first sets the tone for the day.

2. Midday Check-in

This is when old patterns sneak in. A coworker brags about a raise. A surprise bill hits. Your mind drifts into doubt while driving.

Do this: Stop and take a slow breath. Ask, "What money thought is running this moment?" Spot the sabotage and flip it immediately.

Examples: *"This bill is killing me"* becomes *"Paying this means I'm safe and provided for." "I don't deserve that,"* becomes *"I get to want big things without guilt."*

Why it works: It stops old wiring from hijacking your day.

3. Nighttime Wrap-up

Before bed, close the loop. Prove to your mind you are already building wealth, even in small ways.

Do this: Write three wealth-aligned things you did today. Did you speak kindly about money? Did you stop a negative thought? Did you invest in something that grows your income?

Why it works: Your brain learns through repetition and evidence. The more proof you give it, the faster it locks in new patterns.

Write your rewrites on sticky notes and place them where you will see them often, like your mirror, fridge, or laptop. You can even download a sticky note app for your phone. You can also set up three phone reminders: one for your morning reset, one for your midday check-in, and one for your nighttime wrap-up. If a notebook makes it feel richer, use that instead. Do this for at least twenty-one days because that is how habits begin to stick. Keep going until wealth-focused thoughts feel automatic. The moment you catch broke thoughts before they even finish, you are free.

Your thoughts set the tone for every dollar you bring in. If you ignore them, you'll stay stuck hustling with the same results. If you check them daily, you'll create momentum that keeps building. This audit isn't nonsense, it's the foundation for a wealthy mindset.

Call the thought out, reframe it, and keep practicing until it sticks.

When you do, fear around money starts to fade and confidence takes its place. Keep this reminder in front of you, tape it up, pin it, print it, or save it on your phone. The version of you who already lives with wealth is waiting.

Alright—deep breath.

You just walked through some heavy (and hella eye-opening) truths about money. The patterns, the silence, the conditioning, the "oh-my-god-why-do-I-do-that-every-payday" kind of stuff. But now? Now you're not in the dark anymore.

You're catching the thoughts, and you're noticing how you show up and how you hold back. That kind of awareness comes from finally seeing the patterns that have been running the show in the background for years. That shift is where real power is.

Here's what I want you to remember:

Money is neutral. It's not good or bad. It's just energy. You're the one giving it meaning, and now you get to decide what that meaning is. Your relationship with money mirrors your relationship with yourself. If you avoid your bank account, chances are you're avoiding other truths too. If you judge yourself every time you spend, notice where else that judgment shows up. These habits are connected. Heal one and you start healing the rest. You don't have to be "good with money" to be worthy of it. Say that again. Slowly. There's no gold star for deprivation. You don't need permission to have wealth. You already have it.

So now what?

You show up. You track your wins. You rewrite your story. You build trust with yourself around money—bit by bit, dollar by dollar, belief by belief.

Don't overcomplicate it.

The Money BFF Audit

- **Talk to your money like it hears you.** Set a regular "money date." Light a candle, pour a beverage of your choice, and

open your accounts without spiraling. That's progress, and it builds trust.
- **Clear the shame.** If you wouldn't say it to a best friend, stop saying it to yourself. Everyone makes money mistakes, but you don't need to live inside them.
- **Celebrate the wins, no matter the size.** Paid off a credit card? Did a check-in? Walked past the clearance rack? Own it, brag about it, let it count.
- **Catch the sneaky thoughts.** Notice the quiet *"I can't afford that,"* the whisper *"people like me don't,"* or the loud *"this is too hard."* Spot it, question it, replace it, and move forward.
- **Stay curious instead of critical.** Ask why you spend the way you do. Ask why saving feels hard, or why success makes you feel guilty. Treat it as information, not judgment.

Healing your money relationship isn't about perfection. It's about partnership and showing up like you're worth it. Because you are.

And each time you do, money responds. It reflects your attitude, matches the energy you give it, and follows your lead into new opportunities.

Start by checking in with your bank account without fear or shame. Look at it the same way you'd look at a friend you actually want around. Noticing your thoughts isn't a trick, it's a skill that changes how you move through your day, and when your thinking clears, your choices get sharper, and your actions follow. That's where your confidence shines. Every time you pause, question the thought, and pick a better one. That's how you build trust with yourself. That's how you prove you are not your past, you are not your fear, and you are definitely not the harsh story you once believed about yourself.

You're the one in charge now.

That's the real magic of this work. It's not about being flashy. It's about being consistent. The people who build lasting wealth and freedom don't let their thoughts run wild. They stay aware, own their choices, and they keep doubt from running the show.

So if you've been wondering why something still feels off,

why success feels close but never quite lands, this is probably the reason. This is where the shift happens. This is where you stop saying, "Why does this always happen to me?" and start saying, "Okay, I see it. Now I choose differently." We've dug deep in this book.

You've done the work. You've cleared the path. And now we step into the final piece of the W.E.A.L.T.H. puzzle: Heal.

Because if you don't release what's underneath—the guilt, the shame, the pressure, the fear—you'll keep building on top of wounds. And you'll keep wondering why success never feels as good as it should. You've done the mindset work. You've shifted your identity. You've taken consistent action. You've shown up when it mattered most. Now it's time to heal.

H
HEAL

CLEAR THE WOUNDS THAT KEEP YOU BROKE

IF YOU LOOK at what you have in life, you'll always have more. If you look at what you don't have in life, you'll never have enough. - **Oprah Winfrey**

If you're here, your relationship with money probably hasn't been the greatest. Maybe it's felt like a toxic situationship, one that ghosts you, then comes back just to drain your energy and your bank account. I've been there more times than I can count. This is where the shame spirals, old patterns, and emotional avoidance stop. It's time to start healing the real roots of your money story. I'm not talking quick-fix mindset jargon. I mean years of "money is hard" programming passed down from family, society, or every time you had to double-check your bank balance before buying groceries. I know that life too well. This isn't about fixing you, because you're not broken. This is about taking your power back and realigning with the truth that money isn't the enemy. It's been waiting for you to treat it like a partner instead of a problem.

Over the years I have followed leaders like Tony Robbins and Mel Robbins (no relation), Bob Proctor, and Dave Ramsey. They may have different approaches, but they all agree on one thing: mindset is the game-changer. These are people I've learned from throughout my years in the personal development world, and their teachings have shaped how I look at money and success. Tony Robbins explains that success is "80 percent psychology and 20 percent skill," meaning mindset is the foundation beneath everything else. Bob Proctor reminds us that money goes where it's invited and stays where it's welcome. Mel Robbins keeps it simple, showing that small steps and self-compassion are how you get good with money. And Dave Ramsey? He's known for straight-up strategies like discipline, debt payoff, and consistent action.

The real challenge isn't your bills or even your paycheck. It's the conversation happening in your head every time money comes up. That little voice that says you'll never get ahead or that you don't deserve more. Those aren't facts. They're old patterns you learned, and they've been steering your choices without you even noticing. You've been told your whole life not to talk about money. Don't ask how much people make, don't tell anyone how much you make, because it makes people uncomfortable. But why? Why can't we talk about money or be proud of what we earn? Somewhere along the way, we were taught that asking about income is rude and that sharing success is showing off. That idea came from generations who were told money talk was impolite because it could make others feel small or insecure. It was a way to keep peace and keep people "in their place." The truth is, money only makes people uncomfortable when it forces them to compare. It's not bragging to be proud of what you've earned. Talking about money helps us learn, grow, and normalize wealth as something to celebrate, not hide.

Healing your money story means going deeper than numbers. It means facing the shame, guilt, or fear that shaped how you've handled money. Most people grew up with tension when bills showed up, or constant pressure to work harder without ever being taught how to manage what they earned. All of that is part of your money story, but it doesn't have to define you.

This is the moment we turn toward self-compassion. The shame and self-blame that kept you circling the same money struggles don't get to run the show anymore. Breaking those cycles is how you finally create space for something different. The process is messy, and it won't be perfect, but that's not the point. Progress is what matters. Power comes from showing up, not from waiting until you feel ready. This is your turning point.

CHAPTER 36
Your Relationship With Money - Purging Your Poverty Mindset

YOUR RELATIONSHIP WITH money is exactly that. A relationship, and for most people, it probably feels like a toxic love affair. You ghost it, resent it, obsess over it, and then complain when it doesn't show up the way you want. You must realize that money will only meet you as deeply as you're willing to meet yourself. This is the moment to change how you handle it, and we are going to begin by healing the wounds that have been holding you back. Release the shame you've been carrying and start showing gratitude in how you treat money, because that shift is where things start to open up. Every relationship in your life runs on energy. Your parents, kids, friends, coworkers, even your pets, how you show up matters. Money is no different. It mirrors your energy and meets you where you are.

Think a bout y our f avorite r elationship r ight now. M aybe it's your partner, your ride-or-die best friend, or the one person who gets you. How do you show up for them? You check in, stay connected, care deeply, and speak about them with love and respect. Money deserves that same energy. Now pause and be honest. Do you show up for money or avoid it?

Picture that same relationship, but now imagine you never talked about them. You kept them hidden, never spoke their name, and felt weird bringing them up. Strange, right? It's the same with money. You have to normalize the conversation. Money has no meaning until you decide what it means for you.

Imagine your best friend drops by. You laugh, connect, enjoy each moment, and when it's time for them to leave, you don't panic. You don't spiral. You trust they'll be back. That is how a healthy relationship works. Now ask yourself, do you react the same way when money leaves? Be real. When you pay a bill or make a purchase, does resentment creep in? If yes, hear this loud and clear. Money is an energetic flow. To call in more, you have to feel good about both the giving and the receiving. Every time you spend, anchor yourself in this truth. There is always more where that came from. And trust me, there is. Money is limitless when you see it clearly.

Let me take you back, not to pageants or teenage years, but to my thirties—when everything really started shifting. I had already lived through the broke beginnings, the early motherhood hustle, and the survival mode years. But my thirties? That's when I stopped tolerating the struggle and got serious about changing the way I handled money. I started doing the real work. I wasn't just dreaming of wealth—I was actively breaking the habits that kept me stuck, healing the shame, and deciding I would never settle for financial chaos again.

By forty, I wasn't playing small anymore. I was done apologizing for wanting more and pretending that positive thinking alone would fix anything. I had to face my patterns head-on. I had to clean up the emotional weight tied to every dollar, every decision, and every time I said, "I can't afford it" or "maybe next time." This is where things got real and now it's your time to face the beliefs that keep you broke, the stories that keep you small, and the habits that were never truly yours to begin with. No more ghosting money, resenting it, or waiting for it to save you. Money reflects how you treat it and if you avoid it or talk about it with fear, it won't feel safe with you. Start treating it like someone you care about. Give it attention, even when it feels uncomfortable, and speak to it with the same respect you'd give a close friend. That's how you build trust, and that's how a solid relationship with money grows.

That's what your money has been waiting for. That same level of care, attention, and respect. That's how you create a sense of safety, bring order to the chaos, and build a lasting relationship with money. If talking about money makes you want to shut down, you're not alone. Most people weren't taught how to face it with power. Most were taught to either chase it, fear it, or pretend not to care about it. But pretending doesn't build wealth. Presence does.

It's time to start talking about money like it's your closest ally. Respect it, appreciate it, and stay connected even when things feel tight. When you do, shame begins to fade, and confidence takes its place. This isn't about perfect budgeting or getting every dollar right, it's about rebuilding trust in yourself and in the energy you bring to your finances. When you treat money like a real relationship, everything shifts. It becomes steady, it becomes supportive, and it reflects your worth instead of your stress. Let's make that your new normal.

Growing up in the eighties, money talk was practically taboo. Maybe you were told not to mention bills at the dinner table. Maybe you learned to keep your paycheck a secret or that asking someone what they earned was considered rude. Money made people uncomfortable, so we stayed quiet. But silence didn't protect us, it disconnected us and kept us stuck. What people think about your money isn't your responsibility, and hiding your story doesn't make you stronger, it only keeps you small. The truth is your relationship with money has never been just about numbers. It has always carried emotion, memory, and meaning. For some of us, money sparked arguments or tension in childhood. For others, there was never enough, so the stress became familiar. And for many, money became tangled with self-worth, status, or control. That early conditioning still echoes today.

This isn't only mindset, it's something wired into your body. Dr. Bessel van der Kolk, author of *The Body Keeps the Score*, explains that trauma stays in the nervous system long after the moment has passed. If your first memories of money carried fear, shame, or scarcity, your body may still tense whenever it comes up. That isn't weakness, it's survival. But now that you can see the pattern, you have the ability to shift it. You can begin teaching your body that money is safe, steady, and no longer something to fear. Your money mindset is made of beliefs and emotions that run under the surface, and it shapes everything about how you deal with money. It influences how you spend, how you save, and how far you allow yourself to go after what you want. When those beliefs are rooted in fear or lack, money feels heavy and hard. When your beliefs move toward abundance and worth, money feels like support instead of something that pulls you down. Most people struggle here because they think money has to be complicated or shameful. That belief isn't yours alone. It came from silence, secrecy, and the confusing messages handed down to you. If your family never talked openly about money, you probably learned to avoid it too, and that silence often turned into stress. The real shift begins when you stop hiding. Imagine what would change if you faced money with curiosity instead of shame. What if it felt like a trusted friend instead of a stranger you avoid? Building a healthy relationship with money starts with breaking the silence and asking the questions you've been avoiding. What do I believe about money? Where did that belief come from? Does it still serve me today? The answers may not be easy, but they will always be worth it. Each time you strip away secrecy, you also strip away fear. That creates space for better habits, clearer decisions, and more freedom. That's when money stops feeling like a fight and begins to feel like support.

    Before we move into the next step, let's connect the dots between the work you've already done and what comes next. You already did the digging back in Chapter 4, and if you skipped the money story exercise, pause here and go back because that exercise matters. You can't rewire what you refuse to face. The beliefs you have already uncovered are powerful, but they don't last unless you turn them into promises. Just like vows in a relationship, your money beliefs carry weight when you treat them as commitments that guide you on how you show up. Vows aren't just words, they lock in the work you have been doing and prove to yourself that the change you're creating is real. Now that you've uncovered the roots, it's time to set your vows and put them into practice. Every

belief you've carried about money has been shaping how it shows up in your life. Some of those beliefs came from family patterns, others from pain, and many from pure survival. But you're not in survival mode anymore, you're building something solid. Now is the time to write new vows with money, ones that match the version of you that's growing. These aren't watered-down affirmations. They are bold, grounded commitments that define the relationship you're choosing with money going forward.

Redefining Your Money Relationship Exercise

This next three-part exercise is where things get practical. First, you'll write your money vows. Then, you'll check in on how your patterns show up. Finally, you'll practice treating money like a real relationship you care about. Take your time with each part. They build on each other, and together they'll reset how you show up with money.

Part 1: Write Your Money Vows:

Write these prompts in your journal or notes so you can come back to them anytime. Say them out loud if that helps also.

- I vow to treat money like a trusted partner, not a burden or a threat.
- I vow to stop avoiding my finances and start showing up, even when it's uncomfortable.
- I vow to speak about money with clarity, respect, and power.
- I vow to forgive myself for past money mistakes and to stop dragging shame around.
- I vow to make decisions that reflect the wealthy version of me—not the scared version of my past.
- I vow to trust that money responds to the energy I give it, and I choose to give it trust, gratitude, and direction.
- I vow to let money support me in building a life I love.

Read them daily and post them where you'll see them. These are your new money vows, declared by the version of you who refuses to play small. You can also add your own vows to this list. Make them personal and specific, so they actually mean something to you. A vow works best when it includes three things: what you choose to stop doing, how you want to show up, and the energy you'll bring to money from now on. When you write yours, think of it like a declaration. You're choosing what ends today and what begins now.

Part 2: The Money Check-In

Use these prompts to see how your money relationship mirrors your other relationships. Answer in full sentences for real clarity.

Relationships

Think about how you show up in your closest relationships.
- What qualities make a relationship healthy and empowering for you?
- Which behaviors have no place in a relationship with you?
- How do you know when a relationship feels draining or toxic?
- Do you notice similarities in how you handle people and how you handle money, like avoiding certain conversations or feeling uncomfortable when it gets serious?

Feelings and thoughts

- When you talk or think about money, how do you actually feel?
- Do you feel confident with money, or do you get unsure sometimes?
- Does your attitude about money change depending on who's around?
- How much mental space does money take up for you, and are those thoughts grateful or stressful?

Body check

- Does money mess with your sleep or your appetite?
- What happens in your body when you open your banking app?
- Describe exactly where you feel it and what it feels like.

Purpose and desires

- Beyond paying the basics, what do you truly want money for right now and later?
- When you picture those wants, what stories or judgments show up?
- How could having more money help you give back or make an impact?
- What legacy do you want your money to build for you, your family, and others?

Vision

- What does your ideal relationship with money look and feel like in your daily life?
- What feels missing right now, and what would have to change to close that gap?
- What is one specific step you can take today to move closer to that vision?

Habits

Review your current money habits with honesty and detail.

- Do you spend fast, save everything, or keep it balanced? What payoff does any of that give you?
- If you save for a rainy day, what good does it do? Does that habit come from freedom or fear? Are you preparing for possibilities or bracing for disaster?
- If you tend to spend quickly, what would shift if you saved more often? How would that feel?

- How does spending honestly make you feel in the moment and how does spending make you feel after?
- What reminders or routines would keep you consistent with money?

Have a Heart-to-Heart with Money

Picture money sitting across from you looking you straight in the eye. Be direct, honest, and specific.

Ask yourself:
- What have you been avoiding when it comes to money, and why do you think that's continued?
- What are you finally ready to release or heal, starting now?
- How can this partnership grow stronger from here on out?
- When has money already had your back in small or major ways?
- What fun or freedom has money already made possible for you this year?
- Which possibilities excite you when you imagine your financial future?
- How do you want to feel about money from this moment forward, in one clear sentence?
- What promises are you ready to keep showing money that you are serious about this relationship?

This is where your relationship with money starts to shift. It's not just about numbers. It's about building trust, being honest with yourself, and showing up consistently. Money is like a relationship that grows stronger the more you show up for it.

Part 3: Make Money Your BFF

Treat money like a close relationship and start showing up for it like you mean it.

Try this:
- Think about your favorite person right now. Your partner,

your best friend, whoever makes you feel seen and supported. How do you show up for that person, that relationship? Are you present? Do you check in? Do you cheer them on?
- How do they show up for you?
- What do you love about how they treat you or how they make you feel?
- Be honest. How do you treat your money right now? Are you ignoring it? Obsessing over it? Avoiding it?
- If money were your best friend, how could you show up differently starting this week? How would you nurture, respect, and trust that relationship?
- Pick one new action you will commit to this week to prove to your money that you are in it for the long haul. Track your spending, check in, celebrate a small win. Anything counts.

How will you keep yourself honest with this work? Will you go and set a reminder on your phone? If you do, pick a consistent time each week to check in with your money. You could even stick a note on your mirror that says Money loves me to keep the energy in front of you. Whatever helps you stay connected, commit to it and follow through. Start small, build the habit, and keep showing up. Show up for your money like it's something you genuinely value, because it is.

You've already done the reflection and made the plan. Now it's time to put it into motion. This work isn't just about willpower or discipline, it's about devotion to the version of you that takes money seriously. You wouldn't ignore someone you love, and you wouldn't leave their messages unanswered or forget their birthday. So don't ghost your finances either, because this relationship deserves attention. Stay close to the connection you're building and check in with it regularly. Celebrate every win you create, even the ones that feel small. Keep looking for ways to make this bond stronger, because the energy you give to money is always the energy that comes back to you.

Stick to what you said you'd do, because abundance shows up when you prove you're ready to hold it.

If money still makes you feel boxed in, anxious, or constantly behind, this is a chapter you'll want to return to again. If you've ever stayed awake at night wondering how you were going to pay for life while everyone else seemed to have it figured out, this part is written for you. I know that place because I've been that girl—pregnant at eighteen, broke, pretending everything was fine in my twenties, and finally doing a complete overhaul in my thirties. I changed that story, and the truth is you can change yours too.

Healing your relationship with money means shifting what you believe, how you feel, and how you behave with money every single day. It means money is no longer viewed as a threat or something to fear. It becomes a trusted partner. That shift happened for me when I decided money wasn't my enemy. I stopped treating it like something that was out to get me, and I started treating it like something that could support me. That single decision changed everything.

Start right now, not someday, and not when things finally feel easier or when you believe you deserve more. Begin while it still feels uncomfortable and move forward even if fear is whispering in your ear. Struggle does not need to be your forever story. It is only a chapter, and you have the power to write the next one. Get clear on where you really stand today and stop turning a blind eye to your numbers. Face the facts of how money feels in your life right now. From that place, set goals that actually reflect who you are and where you're going. Use everything in this chapter to build something better. Treat money like a relationship that matters, not like a fight you are tired of repeating. That is how lasting change begins.

This part of the work is not just about writing nice ideas on paper. It is about facing the real way you treat money and choosing to build something different. Your habits, your stories, and your patterns all leave clues. The way you show up for money tells the truth about the kind of relationship you are creating. If you have been avoiding it, the results will show. If you start treating it with respect, that will show too. The point is simple: money responds to how you engage with it, and the energy you give is the energy that comes back.

Stay the course and keep showing up for yourself. Prove to yourself again and again that you are worth more than survival. Money is not just paper in your wallet. It is energy, it is freedom, and it will rise to meet you when you stop treating it like the enemy. Before you call in more, clear the old weight that has been draining your energy and pulling your money away in the background. This is your reset. The moment you stop treating money like the enemy is the moment everything shifts.

Don't let the fear of losing be greater than the excitement of winning

—Robert Kiyosaki ♡

CHAPTER 37
The Five Emotional Debts: Why Your Wallet Bleeds Dry

MONEY LEAKS DON'T come from your bank app, your accountant, or even your so-called money mistakes. They come from you. If you've ever sat there wondering why you keep getting raises, landing clients, or bringing in more sales, but your bank balance still feels unsteady, it's because you're carrying five emotional debts that no budget or tracker can fix. These debts live rent-free in your mind, your heart, and your spending habits. Each one pulls you backward the moment you try to move forward. Just when you think you've built a cushion, they drain it dry.

These emotional debts will keep running your money until you take back control and tell them their free ride is over. If you don't, they'll empty your bank faster than the worst stock crash or the dumbest get-rich-quick scheme ever could. This isn't just my opinion. It's a cold, hard reality.

Nearly 70% of people who come into sudden money end up broke again within just a few years. Not because they're careless, but because money only ever amplifies what you already have inside. If your capacity to hold wealth is tiny, no jackpot or windfall will make it stay. Look at celebrities who crash after sudden fame, athletes who blow through millions before retirement, or families who lose inherited wealth within a generation. Money magnifies what's already there. Stop pretending this is about cutting lattes or using coupon codes. Start seeing your money leaks for what they really are: emotional sabotage disguised as spending habits. Once you face and clear these five emotional debts, your income finally has a place to land and stay.

Let's crack each one wide open and make sure you never have to feel broke when you're meant to feel wealthy.

Shame

Shame shows up fast with money. It's the voice that tells you that you don't deserve what you've earned. It's the weight that hits when you buy something you've been wanting for months and instead of pride or excitement, you feel wrong for having it. It's the reason you hide shopping bags or avoid opening your bank app. Shame keeps you small. It makes you second-guess every decision and turns simple moments, like paying for groceries, into proof that you can't be trusted with money. It doesn't matter how much you make — if shame is in charge, it will never feel like enough.

This is why you can build a savings account and still blow it the second it feels good. Keeping money means believing you deserve it, and shame will fight you before it lets you own that truth. Shame hides in secrecy and silence, keeping you from facing the truth. It wants you to avoid your bank statements and hope for the best while quietly tearing down any sense of safety you could create for yourself. Let's be clear and call it out for what it really is. Shame is financial self-abuse.

It keeps you playing small, spending recklessly when you feel unworthy, and never trusting yourself enough to plan ahead. Wealth doesn't stand a chance in a wallet run by shame. The truth is simple and unavoidable when you finally face it. Your income will never rise higher than the lowest amount you secretly feel safe holding. You cannot budget shame away. You cannot spreadsheet it out of existence. The real cure is bringing shame into the light, speaking it out loud, and stripping it of its power. Say it with me "I am allowed to have money." "I am allowed to feel secure". "I do not owe my struggle to anyone." The second you drag shame into the open and call it by name, it loses its power. Hold your head high and own the fact that you are not a walking debt. You are worthy, right now, of keeping what you earn. Own this truth like it belongs to you and refuse to give it back. The way to clear shame is simple, name it, speak the opposite truth out loud, and stop hiding.

Guilt

Guilt is the relentless debt collector that shows up the second you get ahead. You feel it like a knot in your chest when you check your bank balance and see more than usual. It pushes you to give it away, spend it fast, or treat everyone around you until you are right back where you started. This is why you tip double when you really can't afford it or why you offer to cover the dinner bill even when you shouldn't. Guilt convinces you that money only counts if you've sweated for it, suffered for it, or nearly broken yourself to earn it. If it comes easily or unexpectedly, your mind rushes to get rid of it before someone points out that you have "too much."

This is exactly how surprise windfalls vanish overnight. That bonus you waited all year for? Gone in a weekend getaway and an impulse shopping spree. That tax refund? Spent before it even hits your account. Your brain runs an old program that says easy money must be dirty money. So, you punish yourself until your balance drops back to what feels "normal." The same thing happens with raises and promotions. Someone finally gets the bump in pay they've dreamed about, but within months they're broke again. Not because they can't manage money, but because guilt won't let the extra stay. Their identity doesn't match the new income, so the money slips away.

True wealth asks you to drop the guilt you've been dragging around with money. You don't need to grind yourself into exhaustion to deserve rest. You don't have to prove your generosity every time cash shows up. You don't need to play the savior, the provider, or the rescuer just to feel okay about your own success. The next time extra money lands in your hands, pause and notice the guilt creeping in and let it rise without doing what it tells you. Sit with that bigger number in your account. Breathe into it. Resist the urge to plot how to spend it away. Let it stay. That's where you prove to yourself that you can hold abundance without bleeding yourself dry to earn approval.

The cure for guilt is proof. Prove to yourself that you can keep what comes to you. Prove that you can sit with abundance without guilt, without panic, without giving it all away. You don't owe your money to anyone. You owe it to yourself to hold it.

Fear

Fear is the weight that turns money from a tool into a threat. It lives in your body, ready to twist every good thing the second it lands in your hands. You know fear is running the show when just thinking about more money makes your stomach turn and your mind jump to the worst outcomes you can imagine.

Fear shows up the moment your balance looks healthy. Instead of feeling safe, you start thinking about what could go wrong. What if I lose my job? What if the market crashes? What if I get a flat tire, a rock in the windshield, the fridge breaks, or one of the kids gets sick? So, you spend faster than you earn, not because you're careless, but because spending feels safer than losing. Fear is why you settle for less pay than you deserve, stay quiet instead of asking for a raise, stay in jobs you've outgrown, or overwork yourself trying to keep everyone else happy.

You tell yourself you want more, but the moment more shows up, your old survival mode kicks in. Too much money feels dangerous because it is unfamiliar. Holding it feels harder than spending it. Even the wealthiest people crumble when fear is behind the wheel. We see it with people who finally build savings, only to drain it at the first sign of trouble. The furnace breaks, the roof leaks, or the basement floods, and fear makes them panic-spend before the money ever feels safe. Before they know it, the account is empty, and the regret feels heavier than the money ever did.

To break fear's grip, you have to stay put when every part of you wants to run. You don't fight fear by spending faster or distracting yourself with noise. You fight it by letting the wave rise and pass while you hold steady. Money is not out to get you. It is neutral. It will stay if you stay calm enough to keep it. So, the next time your paycheck lands, don't run to spend it on things you don't even want. Let it sit and notice the urge to swipe, tap, splurge, and to make it disappear. Breathe through it. Show your body that it is safe to hold money. Each time you do this, your capacity grows stronger. Fear shrinks every time you prove to yourself that more money doesn't mean more danger. It means more freedom. And you can handle that.

Hurt

Hurt is the old wound that eats away at your sense of financial safety, whether you admit it or not. It's the betrayal you never got over — the ex who drained your joint account and walked away without looking back. It's the family fights over money you overheard as a kid, the slammed doors, the nights you fell asleep listening to grown-ups curse each other out over overdue bills. Hurt teaches you that money is not safe. It teaches you that people cannot be trusted when money is on the table. So now, even though you say you want more wealth, a piece of you braces for it to disappear the second you let your guard down. You do not trust money to stay. Worse, you do not trust yourself to keep it safe.

So you push money away or spend it fast, convincing yourself that if you burn through it first, no one else can take it from you. This heartbreak hides behind every wall you've built with money. It's why you don't ask for what you're worth. It's why you avoid investing, partnering, or doing anything that would mean opening your books to someone else's eyes. Hurt makes you guarded, suspicious, and tense. It keeps you settling for less because having more feels unsafe. Healing hurt isn't about pretending nothing happened. It's about forgiving so the past stops running your future. And no, forgiveness doesn't let anyone off the hook. You forgive because dragging old pain into every new dollar only keeps you broke and bitter.

I want you to say this out loud, that money did not hurt you, people did, money is not out to get you. Money is a neutral tool that follows your lead once you stop treating it like an enemy.

Your job now is to stop punishing your future for the mess someone else left in your past. Call the hurt by its name. Let yourself feel it one last time. Then close the door on it and decide that from today forward your money is safe with you. Not because people changed, but because you did. The way you heal hurt is by facing it directly instead of burying it. Speak the truth of what happened without softening it. Allow yourself to feel the weight of it and then release it as something you no longer carry. Each time you do this, you prove to yourself that the past cannot control your future. Your money is safe with you now because you chose to make it that way.

Unworthiness

Unworthiness is the belief sitting underneath every other money struggle you carry. It's the voice that whispers, *I am not good enough, smart enough, or strong enough to hold real wealth.* It cuts into your goals before you even take the first step. No matter how much you earn, your subconscious will find a way to push money out of your hands just to match the low value you secretly place on yourself. This is why you push yourself to exhaustion while accepting less than you deserve. It's why you doubt yourself when you spend money on something you actually want. It's why you stay quiet instead of asking for what you need. Unworthiness doesn't care how hard you work or how much you've proven yourself. It only cares about keeping you small, stuck, and second-guessing yourself.

This is why no amount of hustling or budgeting will ever close the wealth gap in your life. It does not close because you suddenly became smarter with money. It closes because you finally stand firm in the truth that you are worth holding it. Most people believe that money will completely change the way they see themselves. That belief falls apart in reality. This is why so many people save for years only to drain their account the moment a household repair or medical bill shows up. Their self-image never caught up to the money they built, so the wealth slipped away before they could hold it. The way forward is not punishing yourself with endless grind. The way forward is not cutting deeper with sacrifice. The way forward is building a new identity that matches the wealth you want to keep. You expand your worth first, and then your wealth expands to meet it without resistance.

Say this to yourself until you believe it fully that money stays because you are worth holding it. Money does not make you valuable. You make money valuable by deciding it is safe with you. You are not here to chase wealth like it is some prize sitting outside of you. You are the prize. Wealth shows up when you finally own that truth. Hold this belief tighter than any paycheck because everything else will follow once you do. The way you release unworthiness is by facing it directly. Call out the voice that says you are not enough and refuse to let it run the show. Replace it with the truth until your body accepts it as normal. Each time you practice this, unworthiness loosens its grip and your capacity to hold money grows stronger.

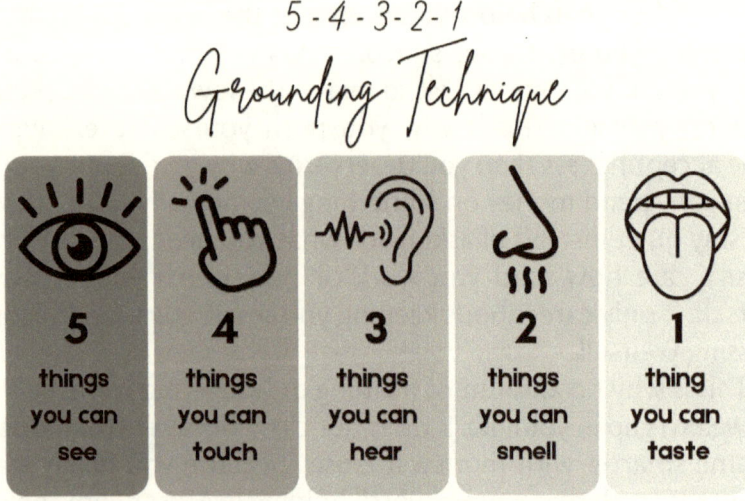

A simple grounding tool that uses your five senses to shift your focus from anxious thoughts to bringing you back to the present moment

Healing means you no longer punish yourself for the past. You build wealth from your worth, not your wounds.

Most people do not end up broke because they are clueless with numbers or careless with spending. They end up broke because they never cleared out the five emotional debts draining them behind the scenes.

Money is not only about what you earn. It is also about whether you have the strength to hold it. The more solid your self-worth becomes, the safer it feels to let cash stay. Patch these leaks and everything begins to shift because your cash no longer disappears as quickly as it comes in. You stop chasing every dollar like your survival depends on it. You stop begging for the next month to feel easier than the last. No exhausting new hustle is required. You do not need a strict budget that makes you miserable. You need a stronger version of yourself who finally trusts that they can hold wealth like an adult who knows they deserve it.

Pick one of these five emotional debts that hits you the hardest and keep it in your awareness. Notice when shame whispers and answer back with a louder truth. Notice when guilt pushes you to spend, I want you to pause long enough to hold back. Notice when fear tightens your chest, breathe until it releases. Notice when old hurt rises, remind yourself that the past cannot bankrupt your future. I want you to also notice when unworthiness shows up, and I want you to stand taller while telling yourself that money stays because you say so.

This is real healing, raw and honest. It comes after your journal pages and the morning routine that helps you feel grounded. Healing is practice, not performance, and it lives in the choices you repeat. You stop draining yourself for approval and stand firm on your value. You keep your money because you finally believe you can. Stay aware every day and choose the same truth again and again.

From this moment forward, your wealth stays because you do, and that single choice changes everything.

CHAPTER 38
Mind Your Money, Honey

NOBODY EVER SAID budgeting was sexy, and if someone did, they probably learned to get intimate with their money first. Managing money gets labeled scary long before anyone even notices the word budget. Even checking your bank balance can feel uncomfortable, almost like eating out alone for the first time. At first it feels awkward, but once you do it, the experience feels freeing. You order what you want, eat how you like, and there is zero judgment. That is the kind of freedom we need with our money too.

As kids, our brains were running on autopilot. Our subconscious was in control long before our conscious mind even showed up, and the conscious mind does not fully kick in until after about elementary school age. That means nearly everything we absorbed in those early years sank straight into our subconscious. The adults around us etched their money beliefs into our heads without ever needing to spell them out. We learned fast that talking about salaries, debt, or savings was off-limits. Money talk was labeled taboo, and it is long past time to break that silence and bring money into the open.

In most homes, you didn't ask what your parents made, and you rarely heard them talk about bills in a positive way. Talking about debt was completely off the table. Most kids never knew whether their family carried debt or not, and even if they did find out, they had no idea what it really meant. Adults stayed quiet about money, and when they finally mentioned it, the words were usually negative. That silence became a generational hand-me-down, passed along like a rule nobody questioned. Instead of clarity, it created confusion, avoidance, and shame. It was never personal, it was simply the norm. If we want to change our money story, we must start questioning who created those rules and why we continue to follow them.

That early conditioning runs deep. No wonder so many people avoid looking at their bank balance or tracking where their money goes. We were trained to ignore it, to hush it, and to treat money like something dangerous. But any relationship you neglect eventually falls apart. If you don't give your money care and respect, it will not stick around.

Think about how personal relationships crumble when they are ignored or treated poorly. Money responds the same way. Neglect it, disrespect it, and chaos eventually follows. That moment you shove loose change to the bottom of your purse or crumple a bill and shove it in your back pocket like trash? That tells a story. Would you ever treat a close friend that way, tossed in a corner and forgotten? Would you bury your partner under gum wrappers and old receipts and still expect love? Of course not. Yet many of us treat money exactly like that.

If you want money to stay, begin treating it like someone you respect. Smooth out the crumpled bills and place them neatly in your wallet. Give your change a proper home instead of tossing it into the black hole of your center console. The way you handle cash physically reveals how much you value it deep down. If you want more money, start by caring for what you already have. Respect sends a signal to the universe that you are ready for more. When you stuff change into your pockets or crumple up bills like garbage, you are not showing respect. Imagine being treated that way yourself—tossed aside and ignored. Real relationships would never survive that, and neither will your money. How often do you honestly sit down for a real date with your finances?

Sexy is the last word anyone would ever use for budgeting, but maybe it should be if you treated it like a date. When was the last time you actually went on a money date? If you're like most people, the answer is never. And no, a quick peek at your bank app doesn't count. Remember, ninety-two percent of our money isn't even physical cash. It's just numbers floating in the digital ether. That's why we need to get real, go deeper, and give those numbers the attention they deserve.

So why not turn it into a weekly ritual? A real money date where you don't just glance at what is coming and going but actually sit with your finances. Flirt with those numbers, celebrate every deposit like a win, and map out your spending with confidence. Make these dates a habit and watch how abundance shows up again and again. It's about making money magnetic, drawing it in, and giving it a reason to stay.

Get creative and make these money dates your own. They should feel like real dates, where you show up, make an effort, and pay attention. Maybe you write down your goals, speak your favorite mantras out loud, blast your playlist while you dance in the kitchen, or even draft a cheeky love letter to your bank account. However you do it, keep these dates intentional and fun. They are not stiff budget meetings. They are real dates. Light a candle, pour your drink of choice, and show your money the attention it deserves.

And yes, dress to impress, even for money. Put on your favorite outfit, swipe on lipstick, spritz your scent, and step into it like a celebration. Play music that lifts you up. Treat these dates like appointments you never cancel, because every one of them strengthens your connection. You're claiming your worth and when you treat money like it belongs with you, it does.

Crafting Your Cash Confessions

You've dressed up for your money, poured the drink, lit the candle, and started giving it the attention it deserves. Now it's time to take the conversation deeper. This is where you stop guessing how you feel about money and start writing it down. Think of this as your chance to confess what's really been running the show in your head and decide what you want to believe instead.

Money's Secret Meaning to You

Money is never just dollars and cents. It carries the weight of every story you grew up with, every memory tied to bills on the counter, and every win or loss you've ever felt around it. The meaning you attach to money shapes how it shows up in your life right now. Not the textbook version. Not what your parents drilled in. I'm talking about the truth that runs through your own head and heart. I want you to write it down, without filters and without second-guessing.

What's the very first thing that comes to mind when you think about money now?

Ritual Rendezvous

You've already seen how daily rituals shape your mornings and nights. Rituals ground you, steady you, and signal to your mind that it's time to shift. The same idea applies here, only now it's about your money. Rituals are how you show consistency, respect, and attention. This is where you take an honest look at the money practices you already have and decide which new ones you want to bring in. Think of it as upgrading the way you "date" your money—adding intention, care, and a little spark so the relationship grows stronger. That might mean setting aside ten quiet minutes with your coffee to peek at your accounts, putting a reminder in your phone every Friday to move a little into your savings, or turning your Sunday night into a standing "money date" with candles, playlists, and your notebook. You can also start updating your goals on sticky notes or speak your mantras while you track expenses. The point is that your rituals make money care a normal part of your life instead of something you avoid.

- *What's your current money ritual?*
- *What are your favorite money rituals?*
- *What new rituals or bold money date ideas are you curious to try next?*

The way you ritualize money is the way you prove you're ready for more.

Love Letter to Your Loot

Earlier in the book, you wrote a raw, honest letter to money. Maybe it felt heavy. Maybe it cracked something open. That exercise was about truth-telling. This one is different. Think of this one as the fun side of the conversation — the part where you let money know you're not afraid to flirt a little. You've already done the hard work. Now it's time to loosen up and add some fun.

- *Part 1: Your Love Letter to Money*
    - Grab your pen and let it flow. Write money a love letter like you're slipping a note across the desk in class, except this time it's about what you want more of in your life. Keep it playful, keep it light. Tell money what you like about it, and how you'd like things to feel between you. Let it sound flirty, playful, or fun, the way you would if you were teasing a crush.
- *Part 2: Money's Reply to You*
    - Now flip it. Imagine money scribbling a note back and sliding it your way. What would it say? How does it feel about the way you've treated it? Let the reply surprise you. Maybe it's grateful, maybe it's calling you out, maybe it's promising more if you keep showing up.

After writing your letter and imagining money's reply, notice the playful energy it brings. This isn't about digging up old wounds or carrying heavy truths. It's about building a lighter, more fun connection with your money. Let it feel like banter with a crush, not a therapy session. Keep that energy close, because the way you treat money with curiosity and play is the way it will keep showing up for you. And if part of you feels silly, embarrassed, or tempted to hide this page, don't. That's just old conditioning talking. You're not being graded here. You're reminding yourself that money doesn't have to be stiff or serious to be real.

The Final Healing

The heart and soul of this journey wasn't just about fixing your finances. It was about facing the lies, wounds, and habits that kept you broke, stuck, or surviving for far too long. You got honest about your relationship with money. You stopped avoiding your bank account and started treating money like a partner instead of a problem. You cleared out the emotional debts that had been draining you in silence and you began building something solid.

You learned how to mind your money every day, not just when payday comes. You built rituals that gave you trust in yourself and proof that money shows up when it feels cared for. Healing doesn't erase fear or old habits forever, but it does make you quicker to catch them before they run the show. This is not about perfection. It's about showing up, making progress, giving yourself permission, and stepping into your power.

Breathe this in: You are worthy. You are capable. You are ready to hold wealth and keep it.

This is what real money healing looks like. You did it, and you'll keep doing it. This is how you build wealth that lasts and step into the version of you who doesn't just hope for abundance but lives it.

Money doesn't heal by hiding what hurts. It heals when you finally face it with honesty and patience. Your past choices don't define you, and your old money story doesn't have the final word. What matters is how you show up now. You've already proven you can do the hard work, and this moment is about claiming the freedom that comes with it.

Healing your relationship with money has always been about more than fixing your finances. It has been about rewriting the story you tell yourself about your worth, your power, and your future. Along the way you faced the shame that once kept you silent, and you stopped ignoring your bank account. You began treating money like a best friend instead of a burden.

Healing was never neat or easy, but it proved itself powerful every time you chose to keep going. You looked inward and said, "I'm done carrying shame about money."

You chose to rewrite the script. You began seeing money as a relationship worth nurturing, and you set standards that matched the future you want. You let go of the old mistakes that once defined you and opened the door to something stronger. In the process you found yourself, not the broke or scared version, but the one who rises, levels up, and owns a 2.0 version of life.

Your identity is no longer tied to debt, scarcity, or chaos. Healing creates a ripple effect that stretches into wealth itself, because letting go of shame, fear, and old stories is what clears the ground to build the future you actually want. This isn't just about making peace with your past, it's also about moving forward into the wealth that you are meant to have. And the truth is, everyone has something to heal. Every single person needs some form of healing, and it's a pivotal step in wealth creation.

What does HEAL really mean? It means recognizing that wealth starts from the inside out. Healing shapes your future by changing the way you think, the way you feel, the way you act, and the way you lead. It means letting go of inherited shame and the ego that keeps you small, releasing the resentments that weigh you down, and dropping the stories that never belonged to you in the first place.

Healing isn't about fixing what's broken. It's about choosing to move forward with courage and confidence. It's the moment you stop circling the same old stories and start creating a life that actually reflects your strength, your vision, and the wealth you're here to hold.

Take a breath and own it.

You're done surviving your money story—you're building the life you were born to live.

HEAL was never about perfection. It was about permission.

Permission to unlearn.

Permission to feel good.

Permission to celebrate.

Permission to finally believe.

Permission to receive more without guilt.

Permission to outgrow the version of you that settled.

Permission to tell yourself, "Abundance is mine because I say so."

So, here's to the healed version of you, the one who honors

money, honors yourself, and honors this moment as the start of something wildly beautiful. And if this book cracked something open in you, you stepped closer to wealth, if it made you feel seen, inspired, fired up, or even just a little more you, then someone else needs it too. Don't keep the magic to yourself. Pass it forward with intention, recommend it, share it, or place it directly in someone else's hands. Let this book be the gift you give forward. Because when someone heals, another rises. You could be the reason someone else starts their journey.

This is how you claim your wealth story. This is where real wealth begins.

THE UNFOLDING

CHAPTER 39
Past, Present, Future

THE PAST–THE GHOSTS That Once Held You Back
LET'S TAKE A moment and go back. Back to the version of you who once believed wealth was for "other people." Back to the "you" who flinched when opening a bill, felt shame when the card declined, and whispered "someday" without ever really believing it.

Back to the "you" who grew up hearing things like:
"Money doesn't grow on trees."
"Rich people are greedy."
"Be grateful for what you have."
"You have to work hard to make money."

That version of you tried everything. You read the books, lit the candles, danced under the full moon, chanted affirmations, burned sage, and journaled until your hand cramped — and still… nothing stuck. You were searching, not broken. Frustrated, but not finished. You scrolled Pinterest and Instagram looking for signs, but still sat there asking, *Why not me?*

Your past self worked incredibly hard with the resources and beliefs they had about money, success, and value. You thought the answer was somewhere outside of yourself. That if you just read one more book, found one more coach, or stumbled into the right alignment on the right day, everything would click. What you didn't realize then was that you already carried everything you needed inside.

You weren't broken. You didn't need fixing. You needed to

remember. You needed truth. You needed permission. And this book — the one you're holding right now — has been your mirror, your time machine, and your awakening.

You were unaware that wealth operated on a frequency. That it isn't something you earn, chase, or fight for, but something to align with. You didn't understand the power of subconscious reprogramming. You didn't realize that money wounds weren't something to be ashamed of—they were common, and they were healable.

And yet, even without knowing all of that, you didn't stop. You kept searching, hoping, and believing in something more.

So, thank yourself.

Pause for a moment. Close your eyes.

Acknowledge the version of you that crawled through self-doubt, shame, lack, and fear. The one who still got up every day and tried again. Thank yourself for surviving, for dreaming, and for fighting even when you didn't know what the next step was.

You're the reason you're here now. While you may have lived through scarcity, fear, or confusion, you carried the spark. And that spark? It ignited everything that came next.

You are not here to be dismissed or shamed. You are here to be honored because you laid the foundation for your awakening.

The Present–The Shift Is Happening Now

Something clicked.

Somewhere in these pages, a line hit your soul. A story mirrored your own. A truth shattered a lie you've been carrying since childhood. And now—you see it. Something's shifted. There's a difference in how you feel, how you speak. Instead of letting old thoughts run on autopilot, you're noticing them and choosing differently in the moment. That awareness shifts everything.

This book wasn't about giving you a to-do list. It was about giving you your power back. Now you realize wealth isn't a one-size-fits-all approach. It's not about a paycheck or the balance in your bank account. It's about your daily choices, who you are, and what you decide wealth means on your own terms. Now you understand that wealth is part of your self-concept, and it's bigger than you or I. Wealth goes beyond material things, just like you've discovered in these pages. Wealth is the calm you feel when you trust yourself. Wealth is the freedom to make choices without fear. Wealth is the confidence to speak up, the clarity to say no, and the joy of saying yes. Wealth is time with the people you love, energy for the work that lights you up, and the belief that you were always meant for more. You don't chase it—you become the person who naturally attracts it.

In the present, you are no longer reacting. You are creating.

You are no longer begging. You are embodying.

You are no longer hoping. You are aligning.

You are no longer waiting. You are choosing.

And with that shift, even the voice inside your head sounds different now.

Your internal dialogue has shifted. You're catching the thoughts that used to run on autopilot and flipping them into something stronger.

"I'm broke" becomes "I'm building."

"I can't afford that" shifts into "How can I create that?"

"I'm not ready" turns into "I'm ready now."

This is the work of Thought Catching—the part of you that refuses to let old money lies run the show anymore. It's not just mindset; it's a practice, and it's proof that your present self is already different than your past. This is you, watching yourself in real time rewrite your money story, and that is powerful.

The wounds that once ran the show in silence are starting to heal. You've begun to question the rules you were raised with, and while that isn't easy, you're doing it anyway. The biggest shift? Realizing wealth was never just for the elite. It's your birthright. Wealth isn't something you wait to earn. It's something you step up and own.

The present is your turning point. You're no longer who you were, and not yet who you're becoming, this is the space in between.

Even in the middle of the process, before everything clicks perfectly into place, you're already living as the wealthier version of yourself. You're no longer chasing some distant identity, hoping one day you'll catch up. You're stepping into that identity now with every new thought, every shift in perspective, and every decision that says, "I choose differently this time." This is the becoming, and it's already happening.

So breathe. Take a moment to witness how far you've already come. This is no small shift—it's a full recalibration. You stand at the threshold, no longer a student of scarcity. You're a practitioner of alignment.

The Future — The Wealthy You Is Already Here

Close your eyes and picture the version of you who walks into any room without shrinking. Bank balances get checked with pride, not panic, and investing in yourself feels powerful instead of guilty. Calm and confidence radiate from within, and your energy pours from overflow, not exhaustion. There's no waiting for a seat at the table, because you build your own. You show up fully, claim your voice, and move with purpose. Your worth isn't questioned anymore — it's known. And instead of asking, "Can I afford this?" the real question becomes, "Why wouldn't I?" When the thought comes up, "Do I deserve this?" your answer is simple: "Of course I do."

This version of you isn't some far-off dream. You're not a fantasy or a paused life waiting for permission. You're here, right now, because of the choices you continue to make. Speaking in abundance keeps pulling you closer. When a limiting belief shows up, you flip it and step deeper into who you really are. You invest, expand, heal, trust, and believe, and every one of those choices amplifies your strength. You're not waiting for the universe to deliver anymore. You are the breakthrough.

Every version of yourself who has struggled, doubted, hesitated, or delayed still matters. Those parts got you here, and they deserve to be honored, but they are no longer in charge. You walk with clarity, steady and sure of yourself. You lead with power. Rejection is no longer your fear, you're too magnetic for that. Wealth doesn't shake you anymore. It holds you steady. You are no longer stuck in waiting mode. You are owning it now, and you can finally look at yourself, proud as a hell. Not because you are perfect, but because you chose again.

Wealth was never outside of you. It was never about grinding harder, waiting for permission, or proving yourself worthy. It was never about fixing every flaw. It has always been about stepping into the future version of you and choosing how you want to live.

You are no longer asking, "How long will it take?"

Now you ask, "How good can it get?"

You're not behind, and you're not late. Nothing about you is missing or small. You are ready, and your time is now. Wealth isn't waiting in the distance. It's already here. The shift has happened. There's no going back.

You are the past, healed.

The present, embodied.

And the future? It's already unfolding.

Now go live it.

CHAPTER 40
Letter From Your Future Self

THERE'S SOMETHING POWERFUL about documenting your journey and having something real to look back on. At the moment, growth can feel subtle or even invisible, but when you revisit your own words, you see the transformation you didn't even realize was happening. You see the proof that you've been changing all along. You see the version of you who once struggled to believe and the version who finally begins to rise. That's the kind of evidence no one can take away from you.

The letters I asked you to write in this book were never random or repetitive. They were designed to work together, a trilogy of moments on your journey. Each one captures a stage you've walked through: the past you released, the present you honored, and the future you're stepping into. Together, they hold the proof of your transformation and the story only you could write.

- Past (Chapter 6): a letter of apology to money, releasing the past, clearing old stories, and letting go of what once held you back.
- Present (Chapter 38): a playful love letter to money, honoring the healing process and acknowledging the growth you've claimed.
- Future (Chapter 40): a letter from your future self, calling what's next and stepping into the wealthy version of you who already exists.

Past, present, and now future, each one marking a stage of your transformation. This is the final letter in your trilogy.

Take a slow breath and put everything on the page. This is your reality right now, and it deserves to be written in full.

Now, fast forward. Picture the version of you who fully lives what you've been learning here. Visualize it so clearly you can feel it in every part of you. See the people who surround you, the life you've built, and the version of you who lives this reality every single day.

Write a letter as your future self, speaking directly to who you are today.

Describe what your daily life looks like and feels like in that future, from the way you wake up to how you go about your day. Talk about what you're doing and how you're living. You can also mention what you stopped doing and what you let go of in your life. Let your future self tell your now self what's going on, what feels exciting, and how it feels to be wealthy and live from that place every day. Share the lessons and decisions that carried you here, the ones that changed how you think, act, and decide. Be honest about the fears you've let go of and the strength that's taken their place. Ask yourself what your future self would thank you for doing right now. Let this letter be unfiltered and real, something you can return to whenever you need to remember the version of you who already made it. Be raw, honest, and generous, letting this letter serve as your guide for how you step forward.

When you finish, read it out loud. Let every word sink in and move through you. This isn't just another exercise. It's a promise to step into the version of you who already lives inside that vision. Your story is unfolding in the best way. Keep writing it and keep living it. The future is already yours, and you're ready to claim it.

CHAPTER 41
Final Message

THERE'S SOMETHING POWERFUL about holding a book in your hands, not a scroll, not a swipe, but real pages, filled with intention. Seasons change, and so will you. Revisit this book at least twice a year. Each time you rise, your wealth within will meet you at a new level. And just like I don't want you to close this book and forget about it, I'm not about to disappear on you either. Leaving a phone call and blaming bad cell service is like hopping off a Zoom call and blaming your Wi-Fi. We're not ghosting each other, right? Leaving a gathering without saying goodbye is taboo in my world. We can agree it's fun to say hello but who enjoys saying goodbye? Not those leaving, and not those left behind. Goodbyes drag out the end of the night. They turn into weird small talk that no one really wants. We throw out half-hearted promises to catch up, stall with empty chatter, then slowly drift off in different directions. Let's free ourselves from this meaningless, uncomfortable awkwardness.

Fortunately, the time has not come for us to say goodbye.

If you'd like to stay connected beyond these pages, **follow me on social media @iamchristinaostroski**

Keep this book close — highlight it, scribble in it, dog-ear it. Let it be your reset every time you grow. When you're ready, grab a fresh copy or gift it to someone who's ready to rise too.

With Love, Wealth, and Abundance,
Christina

THE NEXT SEQUENCE

You didn't just finish a book. You finished a version of yourself.

Sequence to Aligned Wealth wasn't about learning more. It was about *remembering* — your value, your voice, your vision, and your personal power.

It was about burning down the beliefs that kept you broke, small, and waiting for permission. And now, you're here. Different. You've shifted. You've felt what alignment actually is.

But let's be honest, this work doesn't end when the last page turns. It *begins*. Because what's the point of building a wealth-aligned identity if you're not going to *live like it*?

Living the W.E.A.L.T.H. Experience

Book 1 cracked the code to aligned wealth. The next sequence is the evolution of that embodiment.

This is the version of you who doesn't just talk the talk, you show up, lead, and move in full energetic alignment. It's the kind of work that moves people without saying a word. Shrinking or spiraling isn't an option. Performing is off the table and explanations aren't required. Your presence says it all. It's the energy others *feel* when you enter the room. This is where you become undeniable proof of the work you've done. And inside this next body of work, we go deeper into identity, energy, consistency, and embodiment. We bring the W.E.A.L.T.H. Method off the page and into every part of your life.

Some people will stop here and say, "That was a good book," and feel complete. And that's okay. But if you feel something stir, a knowing, a fire, a quiet voice that says, "There's more for me." If that's you, the next book is calling your name. The second sequence isn't about learning. It's about embodying what you already know, louder, clearer, bolder.

The Sequence to Aligned Wealth showed you who you are. The Next Sequence shows the world!

376

YOUR EXCLUSIVE WEALTH BONUSES

THIS IS JUST the beginning of what's possible.

If this book spoke to you, I'd love to hear about it. Sharing your thoughts in a review is one of the most powerful ways to help others find this work and start their own shift. Even a few lines can spark something in someone else who's ready for change. If you feel called, your words can keep this message moving and open the door for someone else's wealth journey.

You've done the work. Now make it easier to keep going.

As a thank-you for reading *The Sequence to Aligned Wealth*, I've created a printable PDF version of all the cheat sheets, tools, and exercises from the book. You can access them through my Instagram @iamchristinaostroski — just scan the QR code below.

These pages are designed to help you stay consistent, focused, and aligned with the wealth identity you are building.

Print them. Use them. Keep your momentum strong.

This is your next move.

Follow me on Instagram @iamchristinaostroski and tag me when you share your wins. Let's show the world what aligned wealth really looks like.

You're not alone on this path.

BIBLIOGRAPHY

Hill, N. (2016). *Think and grow rich*. Sound Wisdom. (Original work published 1937)

Jung, C. G. (1964). *Man and his symbols*. Doubleday.

Clear, J. (2018). *Atomic habits: An easy & proven way to build good habits & break bad ones*. Avery.

Dispenza, J. (2014). *You are the placebo: Making your mind matter*. Hay House.

Goddard, N. (2005). *The power of awareness*. Martino Publishing. (Original work published 1952)

Hendricks, G. (2009). *The big leap: Conquer your hidden fear and take life to the next level*. HarperOne.

CHRISTINA OSTROSKI

CHRISTINA OSTROSKI IS a respected leader in personal development and wealth mindset, as well as a proud mother of three. Her journey from facing the challenges of being a pregnant teen to becoming an acclaimed NLP Trainer, Master Mindset Life and Success Coach, Hypnotherapist, EFT Practitioner, and Astrologer is living proof that transformation is possible for anyone ready to rewrite their story.

Christina's life is anchored in love, loyalty, and an unshakeable belief that you can have both a fulfilling family life and true financial freedom. Her journey of overcoming hardship and rewriting her own money story fuels the raw, relatable insights she shares with students and readers around the world. Her approach to wealth and personal growth blends neuroscience, energetics, psychology, metaphysics, quantum physics, and ancient wisdom into practical, powerful teachings that cut past trends and buzzwords. She guides her clients to peel back layers of conditioning and embody their limitless, wealthy selves.

With over a decade in the personal development arena, Christina doesn't just teach, she transforms. She certifies and trains NLP practitioners, EFT practitioners, and life coaches, shaping them into confident, skilled leaders. Through her signature frameworks, she helps people break toxic money cycles and claim the wealth and self-worth they were born for. Christina's life and work stand as proof that with the right tools and deep inner work, transformation isn't just possible, it's inevitable. She shows it daily. You don't just chase wealth, you become it.

www.ingramcontent.com/pod-product-compliance
Lightning Source LLC
Chambersburg PA
CBHW060349080526
44583CB00012B/226